Other books by Charlene Spretnak

GREEN POLITICS: The Global Promise
(co-author with Fritjof Capra)

THE POLITICS OF WOMEN'S SPIRITUALITY:
Essays on the Rise of Spiritual Power
within the Feminist Movement (editor)

LOST GODDESSES OF EARLY GREECE:
A Collection of Pre-Hellenic Myths

THE SPIRITUAL
DIMENSION
OF GREEN POLITICS

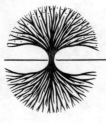

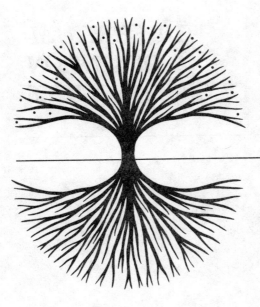

Bear & Company
Santa Fe, New Mexico

THE *SPIRITUAL*
DIMENSION
OF *GREEN*
POLITICS

Charlene Spretnak

ISBN: 0-939680-29-7

Library of Congress Card Number: 86-70255

Bear & Company, Inc.
P.O. Box 2860
Santa Fe, New Mexico 87504

Design: Mina Yamashita
Typography: Copygraphics, Santa Fe
Printed in the United States by BookCrafters, Inc.

for Lissa

CONTENTS

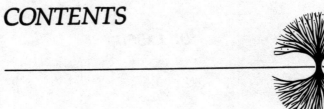

9

Preface

Around the time *Green Politics: The Global Promise* was published in spring 1984, the E.F. Schumacher Society of America invited me to prepare an address on that subject for their annual gathering in the fall. I was honored to join the company of the courageous visionaries who have delivered the Schumacher lectures in this country: Wendell Berry, Wes Jackson, Elise Boulding, George McRobie, Jane Jacobs, Kirkpatrick Sale, John McKnight, Frances Moore Lappé, and John Todd. *However,* I explained to the Society, if I were to spend a good deal of time on such a major presentation, which the Society publishes as a booklet, I would want to ruminate on the aspect of Green politics that interests me the most: the spiritual dimension. My response sent ripples of concern through some of the Schumacher Society board members, which I found gently amusing. They wanted a *regular* lecture on Green politics, not something that might be embarrassingly soupy. After some deliberations they generously extended the benefit of a doubt and approved my title, "Green Politics: The Spiritual Dimension."

In October I presented the lecture at an off-Yale site and was gratified by the response. (The gathering was relocated from the campus to a private school nearby because of the Yale clerical workers' strike.) I had many fruitful conversations with members of the audience, and we all benefited from the insights presented by the formal respondents: Thomas Berry, Elizabeth Dodson Gray, and Patricia Mische.

In the ensuing months, two unexpected developments demonstrated to me that the spiritual dimension of Green politics was not as idiosyncratic an interest as it had initially appeared. First, the Schumacher Society kindly informed me that they had received more orders for the text of this lecture than any other. Similarly, I received reports from many grassroots Green organizing meetings that the very title on the booklet attracted much interest at their book sales table.

Second, in lecturing to various groups I discovered widespread desire to incorporate spiritual values into the emergent postliberal, postsocialist, postconservative politics. This desire was most surprising among audiences who had purportedly come for reasons quite apart from spirituality, such as a gathering at a school of economics and a national meeting of legal aid attorneys. I always fulfilled my contractual obligations by presenting a "regular" lecture on Green politics and then mentioned only in the last part that my personal interest is in helping to develop the spiritual component of Green political philosophy. Invariably, faces in the audience lit up. It was usually the case that most — and sometimes all — of the questions during the discussion period were on this topic.

Clearly, *something* is happening across this land. Greens, of course, are not the first to notice the contemporary spiritual awakening. Some forms of that awakening — such as the ill will and distortions vehemently expressed by certain of the "pray TV" preachers in the name of Christianity — are frightening to many Americans. One reaction has been a call for strict separation of religious values from all political activity. Such a course is barren and unsatisfying to most of the American Greens I have met. I have witnessed, again and again, their courage and their dedication to shaping a new politics reflective of the spiritual wisdom in America's religious teachings *and respectful of the pluralism in our unique society.*

I am deeply grateful for the support and encouragement I have received in this work over the past two years. I hope this book will serve as a catalyst to stimulate discussions and further work in this area.

Charlene Spretnak
March 1986

A PILGRIM'S PROGRESS

Coming of age in the modern era marks a passage into emptiness. At puberty we put aside the ways of childhood, not only the toys and stuffed animals, but also our secret and magical sense of the world, our special relationship with the family pet, with the big tree in the backyard, with the old delivery man, and with our favorite grandparents. We had entered preschool shining forth with a very personal cosmology and a numinous sense of the world around us. This we had expressed in totemic fingerpaintings of smiling suns and lovable animals and later in stories and puppet shows our grade-school teachers encouraged us to create. All that we left behind as we moved anxiously into the adult world through gradual steps during adolescence. We began to pay some attention to the journals and magazines our parents subscribed to and to the news analysis programs they watched on television. We ceased to tune out their discussions with other grown-ups, and we even tried to listen to the weekly sermons in church — until they became too abstract and boring to hold us. Everywhere we sought clues to the adult worldview, which would replace the childish one we had proudly outgrown.

We discovered that the adult world was brimming over with things to do, both work and diversions. After going to a job or studying, people drove fast cars, went to the movies, cheered at sporting events, watched sit-coms on television, visited amusement parks, and shopped and shopped, and shopped. So endlessly varied and attractively marketed were the diversions that many of us moved unquestioningly into the modern world. Others of us gradually realized, with a low level of horror, that *there is no inner life in modern, technological society.* We retreated with disillusionment we could not articulate into private worlds of reading books or making art or, for some, futile acts of rebellion.

In my own life, I rationalized a way out: I would go to a church-oriented university because religion probably held the answer to counter the emptiness of modern society and I had simply missed it since my parents, although Catholic, had sent us to the public schools in our suburb, which were quite good. I matriculated as an optimistic pilgrim at a Jesuit school, St. Louis University. Any literary historian familiar with the biographies of numerous sensitive writers educated by the Jesuits could have predicted the outcome: I paid my money, received a good education, and lost my faith — in the Catholic Church in particular, and Christianity at large. I was not embittered, merely disappointed at what seemed to me to be a spiritual emptiness.*

I drifted for a couple of years as an agnostic skeptic, moving in and out of a Ph.D. program at a prestigious university that seemed to me devoid of meaning and arriving eventually in India in late 1969. There I searched for spiritual teachings that illuminated the human experience, but did not entail guru worship, ritual or other cultural baggage, or the subjugation of women. I found it in Buddhist Vipassana ("insight") meditation, which by the way, turns out to be the same kind of meditation practiced by E.F. Schumacher and advocated in his book *A Guide for the Perplexed (1977)*. Sometime later, when I was back in the United States, I became interested in feminist research into pre-Christian cultures in Europe, focusing in my own work on the pre-Hellenic mythology of Greece. I learned new meanings of ritual by participating in feminist spirituality groups where Nature and the mysteries of creation, our bodies, our feelings, and our transformative powers were honored.

Although my own practice has remained Vipassana meditation, I am also drawn to the wisdom tradition of the Christian mystics and "creation spirituality," which honors the natural world as the most profound expression of the Divine. To a lesser extent, I have studied

---

* Since then, spiritual counseling has been established on many Jesuit campuses.

Taoism and Native American spirituality, which turns out to be a bittersweet experience. To explore a philosophy of life as profoundly Nature-based as either of those paths is to realize how very far our society is from comprehending, let alone abiding by, the deepest levels of ecological wisdom. One encounters, for instance, the frustration of the Hopi man who had been asked too many times to explain how Hopi economics and culture related to their intimate reverence for Nature: "Almost everything we do is a religious act, from the time we get up to the time we go to sleep. How can the white man ever understand that?"[1]

THE PROMISE OF
GREEN POLITICS

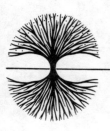

When I began learning of the Green Party in West Germany, I was intrigued by their slogan — "We are neither left nor right; we are in front" — and by their key principles of ecological wisdom, social responsibility, grassroots democracy, nonviolence, decentralization, and postpatriarchal consciousness. But I was most intrigued by the occasional mention in their publications of "the spiritual impoverishment of modern society" or "of an industrialized society." I thought, "Aha! They have found an antidote — *and* they have integrated it with the new politics!" This was my main motivation for pushing aside other projects in my life, convincing a holistic friend who is a native speaker of German, Fritjof Capra, to join me, writing a book proposal, studying reams of Green publications, and flying to West Germany, by myself, in June 1983.

My first group of interviews was with Green parliamentarians in the Bundestag. I asked questions on the entire range of Green politics, and then near the end I asked each one, "Is there a spiritual dimension to Green politics?" Nearly all of them answered in the affirmative, after which I asked, "How is it manifested? I don't notice much attention to it." At that point they would often look down or look out the window and finally explain that because the Nazis manipulated religion, especially a pre-Christian, Nature-based religion (the Nordic myths and "sacred" soil of Germany), it is practically *verboten* to bring religious impulses into German politics today. In addition, I was told that those German Greens who had come from a Marxist background squelched talk of spiritual values and the feelings of reverence for Nature, which had been prevalent in the Greens' first campaign, the European Parliament election of June 1979. In short, I learned on my research trip that the spiritual dimension of Green politics is unlikely to come out of West Germany, even though it provides motivation for many German Greens.*

While my spiritual quest drew a blank in West Germany, I did learn a great deal about Green politics, and I have since then learned still more through trying to establish Green politics in this country. The core concepts are *sustainability* and *interrelatedness*. In fact, one could say that human systems are sustainable to the extent that they

---

* Since my research trip in 1983, a group called Christians in the Greens has established itself in every West German state.

reflect the fact of interrelatedness: the dynamics of Nature arching and stretching through the cycles of her permutations; the dynamics of humans interacting, deftly or brutally, with the rest of Nature; the dynamics of the person interacting with a system and that system with others. That is why the Greens have such slogans as "No investment without a future!" Enterprises that deplete resources in needless quantities when alternatives are feasible are not sustainable over time; neither are businesses that breed alienation and resentment among workers because all matters of control and profit are far removed, whether in a highly centralized socialist government or a gargantuan corporation.

The Green principle of ecological wisdom always occupies the primary position because it means far more than mere environmentalism or saving what's left. The Greens have in mind deep ecology. Deep ecology encompasses the study of Nature's subtle web of interrelated processes and the application of that study to our interactions with Nature and among ourselves. Principles of deep ecology are that the well-being and flourishing of human and nonhuman life on earth have inherent value, that richness and diversity of life forms contribute to the realization of these values and are also values in themselves, and that humans have no right to reduce this richness and diversity except to satisfy vital needs.[2] Human systems may take from Nature lessons concerning interdependence, diversity, openness to change within a system, flexibility, and the ability to adapt to new events or conditions outside the system.

With that model, one can easily guess that Green politics eschews human systems — whether economic, political, or social — that are rigidly constructed around an ideal of tightly centralized control. Rather, Green politics advocates decentralizing much political and economic power so that decisions and regulations over money are placed at the smallest scale (that is, the level closest to home) that is efficient and practical.[3] In the area of economics, Green proposals are built on the ideas of E.F. Schumacher (who was often cited as a primary influence by the German Greens during my interviews) and others who advocate locally or regionally oriented enterprises that are employee-owned and operate with workplace democracy. As such, Green politics stands as a distinct alternative to socialism.

The Green alternative is also distinct from a radical decentralism that lacks global responsibility. While many of our mechanisms of governance are too large (that is, too far removed from the problems they address), some are not large enough. The latter are inadequate for such tasks as safeguarding the health of the oceans and the rest of the biosphere, regulating arms trafficking, and monitoring the multinationals. Appropriate scale is the challenge.

24 Although Green political movements are taking root in many parts of the world — and not only in industrialized

countries — several aspects of the Green vision for society are merely in an embryonic stage. Still, enough work has been done at this point that one can speak not only of Green ideas for sustainable economy and sustainable democracy but also for a sustainable world order, sustainable modes of health maintenance, and sustainable education which would teach conflict resolution. It is when we turn to the issue of spiritual matters that we are faced with a huge hole in Green politics[4]: *What is sustainable religion?*

BEYOND HUMANISM, MODERNITY, AND PATRIARCHY

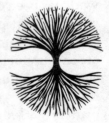

Any delineation of spiritual values within the vision of Green politics must reflect three essential elements of the cultural direction in which the movement is growing. First, Green politics rejects the anthropocentric orientation of humanism, a philosophy which posits that humans have the ability to confront and solve the many problems we face by applying human reason and by rearranging the natural world and the interactions of men and women so that human life will prosper.[5] We need only consider the proportions of the environmental crisis today to realize the dangerous self-deception contained in both religious and secular humanism. It is *hubris* to declare that humans are the central figures of life on Earth and that we are in control. In the long run, *Nature is in control.*

Commenting on the delusion of our anthropocentric self-aggrandizement, the biologist Lewis Thomas has written

Except for us, the life of the planet conducts itself as though it were an immense, coherent body of connected life, an intricate system, an organism. Our deepest folly is the notion that we are in charge of the place, that we own it and can somehow run it. We are a living part of Earth's life, owned and operated by the Earth, probably specialized for functions on its behalf that we have not yet glimpsed.[6]

In rejecting humanism, Green politics separates itself from much of the "New Age" movement and the belief that humans are the epitome of creation rather than being *part* of the far more glorious unfolding universe. Our goal is for human society to operate in a learning mode and to cultivate biocentric wisdom. Such wisdom entails a sophisticated understanding of how the natural world — including us — works.

I disagree with most critics of humanism when they declare that our problem has been too much reliance on "reason" and not enough on emotion. In fact, we have been employing merely the truncated version of reason used in mechanistic thinking to focus attention on only the most obvious "figures" in a situation while ignoring the subtle, intricate field around them. In the area of human systems, emotions are always part of the field. If we valued a comprehensive grasp of the context, or *gestalt*, of various situations, we civilized humans would not have to stumble along ignoring most of the contextual data, arriving at inadequate conclusions, and congratulating ourselves on our powers of "reason." In Germany I sometimes heard fears that any turn away from rationalist solutions is extremely dangerous because it could lead to the kind of mass manipulation the Nazis employed so successfully. The essential point is that holistic, or ecological, thinking is not a retreat from reason; it is an enlargement of it to more comprehensive and hence more efficient means of analysis.

Green politics goes beyond not only the anthropocentric assumptions of humanism but also the broader constellation of values that constitute modernity. Modern culture — as we all recognize since we live in the belly of the beast — is based on mechanistic analysis and control of human systems as well as Nature, rootless cosmopolitanism, nationalistic chauvinism, sterile secularism, and monoculture shaped by mass media. Some critics of modernity have noted that it consists of revolt against traditional values even to the extent of being "an unyielding rage against the official order."[7] An enthusiast of modernity has little use for the traditional institutions that further human bonding — the family, the church or synagogue, community groups, ethnic associations — championing instead an "individual-liberationist stance."[8]

The values of modernity inform both socialist and capitalist nation-states. It is not surprising that citizens' resistance networks in socialist countries often find a resonant home in the churches, that both liberal and conservative churches in capitalist countries are rethinking religion's contemporary role as an inconsequential observer who is to make accommodations to the modern world and not interfere with "progress."

Many critics of modernity, while unable to suggest a comprehensive alternative, conclude that the transformation of modern society is "going to have something to do with religion." Whatever the particulars of postmodern culture, it will not signify an uncritical return to the values of the medieval world that immediately preceded the Enlightenment or those of the Gilded Age preceding World War I and the aggressive burst of modernism that followed it. The pioneers of modernity were right to reject certain conventions and restrictions that were stultifying to the human spirit. But, with the impulses of a rebellious adolescent, they destroyed too much and embraced a radical disregard for limits, especially concerning the natural world. What we need now is the maturity to value freedom *and* tradition, the individual *and* the community, science *and* Nature, men *and* women.

The third cultural force that Green politics counters is patriarchal values. In a narrow sense these entail male domination and exploitation of women. But in a broader sense the term "patriarchal culture" in most feminist circles connotes not only injustice toward women but also the accompanying cultural traits: love of hierarchical structure and competition, love of dominance-or-submission modes of relating, alienation from Nature, suppression of empathy and other emotions, and haunting insecurity about all of those matters.[9] These traits usually show up in anyone, male or female, who opts to play by the rules of patriarchal culture.

In recent months I have been reading all the critiques of modernity I could find. Most of those that made it into print are by men, and I must note that "postmodern" seems to be edging out "postpatriarchal" as the blanket term for our evolving stage of transformation. I do not object to that actually; it will probably play better in Peoria. I believe those male authors are sincere in including and valuing the feminist critique of contemporary society — and I even came across a male Catholic theologian who declared that we live in a "hyper-masculinized modern culture."[10] Imagine my surprise. (I must also note, however, that these well-intentioned men never seem to notice, while rhapsodizing over the need to return the "feminine symbol" to our notion of deity, that no flesh-and-blood females have been invited to speak on their panels, at their conferences, or in their journals.)

It is not when postmodern critics examine the present or the future that feminist insights are missing but, rather, when they analyze history, that is, the historical roots of modern society. Nearly always they lay blame at the door of the Enlightenment, which bequeathed upon us the mechanistic worldview of Descartes, Bacon, and Newton. This, they maintain, was the beginning of modern perception, before which there was the era of classical or traditional religion (Christian, Jewish, Roman, and Greek), and, before that the tribal era. They are forgetting a little detail: the neolithic era! We did not leap from the tribal stage into classical Greek society. For several thousands of years our neolithic ancestors lived in agricultural settlements. The archaeology of such settlements in Old Europe has revealed sophisticated art and religious symbols reflecting reverence for Mother Earth, the elements, and animals; egalitarian graves; and *no fortifications or evidence of warfare* before the invasions of the barbarian Indo-European tribes from the Eurasian steppes.[11]

Picture yourself as a witness of that decisive moment in history, that is, as a resident of the peaceful, artful, Goddess-oriented culture in Old Europe. (Don't think "matriarchy"! It may have been, but no one knows, and that is not the point.) It is 4500 B.C. You are walking along a high ridge, looking out across the plains to the east. In the distance you see a massive wave of horsemen galloping toward your world on strange, powerful animals. (The European ancestor of the horse had become extinct.) They brought few women, a chieftan system, and only a primitive stamping technique to impress their two symbols, the sun and a pine tree. They moved in waves first into southeastern Europe, later down into Greece, across all of Europe, also into the Middle and Near East, North Africa, and India. They brought a sky god, a warrior cult, and patriarchal social order. *And that is where we live today*—in an Indo-

European culture, albeit one that is very technologically advanced.*

Once reverence for the mysteries of the life force was removed from Nature and placed in a remote judgmental sky god — first Zeus, then Yahweh — it was only a matter of time before the "Great Chain of Being" would place the sky god at the top of "natural order" and Nature at the bottom (trailing just behind white women, white children, people of color, and animals). True, that medieval schema was rather organically conceived, but was it really such a radical break for the superstars of the Age of Enlightenment to look at the bottom of the chain and declare that Nature was actually an inert mechanism much like a clockworks, fully suitable for firm and systematic management by man? There is absolutely no doubt that the Enlightenment altered the course of human culture a great deal, but regarding it as the only source of our contemporary crisis reveals a shallow sense of history. Gary Snyder, who is a deep ecologist and a historian of culture as well as a poet, has expressed the matter quite succinctly: "Our troubles began with the invention of male deities located off the planet."[12]

* I am not suggesting that the pre-Indo-European neolithic era was perfect, nor that we should attempt to return to it. However, their art and artifacts demonstrate a sophisticated understanding of our interrelatedness with Nature and her cycles. Their honoring of those contextual processes contains lessons for us in sustainability.

The spiritual dimension of Green politics, then, will have to be compatible with the cultural direction of Green thought: posthumanist, postmodern, and postpatriarchal. That direction will probably come to bear the inclusive label "postmodern" —*unless* that tag has already been ruined almost before we have begun. Ever alert for the word of the moment, designers and advertisers have seized upon it to the extent that I now receive circulars in the mail urging me to purchase postmodern furniture, postmodern clothing, postmodern jewelry, postmodern haircuts, and so forth. Not only has the term been trivialized but these products lack any harmony, grace, or organic beauty — being, in fact, terminally modern, punky, disjointed, and ugly. The term may indeed be lost.

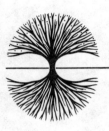

GREEN CRITERIA
FOR AN ANSWER

In exploring the spiritual dimension of Green politics, we can consider the questions from two directions. First, what is spiritual about Green politics itself? Second, what can Green principles contribute to the contemporary evolution of postmodern religion?

In addition to being true to the cultural direction of Green thinking, any aspect of the Green vision for society must be savvy about the facts of *realpolitik*, as well as Green principles and process. A primary consideration is that a delineation of the spiritual dimension of Green politics must honor the religious pluralism in our society. (There are 1200 kinds of "primary religious bodies" in the United States![13]) Second, it should resonate with people who are members of churches, synagogues, and temples (69% of the U.S. population above age 18[14]) and with unaffiliated people who hold spiritual beliefs. (*Ninety-four percent* of the U.S. population above age 18 believes in God "or a universal spirit."[15]) Third, it should resonate with people who are members of the Green political movement and with supportive nonmembers. (The latter constitute the essential base of support for Green parties in many countries. For example, Green Party membership in West Germany was only 30,000 during the 1983 Bundestag election, but two million people voted Green.) Fourth, it should inspire people to do their own thinking about the matter, rather than pushing a "package" at them. Last, it should integrate or be in harmony with the key principles of Green politics: ecological wisdom, social responsibility (personal, local, national, and global), grassroots democracy, nonviolence, decentralization of political and economic power, and postpatriarchal consciousness.

My own response to the need to define the spiritual dimension of Green politics has been shaped by my experiences during the past two years. Studying at close range a political party, in West Germany, and then co-founding a Green political organization* in this country has changed me. I now pay more attention to *what is* rather than concentrating solely on theories of what might be. *What is* in the area of religion is the Big Boys, Judaism and Christianity. We cannot hope to achieve broadbased social change by working only within circles of alternative religion. I am still attracted to the realm of ideas and visionary possibilities, but only in so far as they address getting to there *from here*. I have become interested in "spirituality at the precinct level" and in cutting across dividing lines in our pluralistic culture. To be successful, the expression of the spiritual dimension of

Green politics must present some rather complex ideas in very simple and commonsense terms *without watering down the power inherent in spiritual impulses.* (Frankly, I never expected my personal development to gravitate toward the mentality of a Chicago ward boss but, alas, here I am.)

---

* The major Green political organization in the U.S., the Committees of Correspondence (which was the name for grassroots political networks in the American Revolutionary Era and several times since then), is not a third party but, rather, a regionally based movement working in various areas to advance ecological populism and the Green values stated above. Our organization has been endorsed by many nationally known religious and community leaders who are committed to a postmodern vision for society that goes beyond what either the left or the right has to offer. For information please contact C.o.C. Clearinghouse, P.O. Box 30208, Kansas City, MO 64112.

I wish to emphasize that all proposals in this lecture are merely my own and are merely a beginning. They have not been presented to the Green organization and are not official positions of that group.

WHAT IS
SPIRITUALITY?

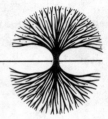

My own working definition of spirituality is that it is the focusing of human awareness on the subtle aspects of existence, a practice that reveals to us profound interconnectedness. A materialist explanation of life works somewhat well at the gross levels of perception, much as Newtonian physics can explain the behavior of matter in a certain middle range. At the subatomic and astrophysical levels, however, Newtonian explanations are inadequate. Similarly, our perceptions at the gross levels — that we are all separate from Nature and from each other — are revealed as illusion once we employ the subtle, suprarational reaches of mind, which can reveal the true nature of being: all is One, all forms of existence are comprised of one continuous dance of matter/energy arising and falling away, arising and falling away.

The experience of union with the One has been called God consciousness, cosmic consciousness, knowing the One mind, and so forth. It is the core experience common to the sages of all the great religions and has been expressed in the rapture of Christian saints as well as the simple words of a *haiku* poem. It is not a one-time realization but, rather, a level of understanding that deepens as one continues spiritual practice. To live with a deep awareness of the elemental Oneness of all creation is to partake of "God consciousness." Such experiential, rather than merely intellectual, awareness of the profound connectedness is what I hold to be the true meaning of being in "a state of grace." Awe at the intricate wonders of creation and celebration of the cosmic unfolding are the roots of worship.

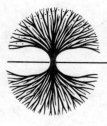

BACK TO BASICS

Green politics is about values in our daily lives, how we live and love and work and play. Core values are informed by deep thinking and existential explorations, which are spiritual perceptions. I would like to consider our core values by exploring three basic questions: Who are we? (or What is our nature?) How shall we relate to our context, the environment? How shall we relate to others?

1 *Who are we? What is our nature?* Moving from where we are now, we can draw some negative lessons from the modern answers to this pair of questions: we are not mechanistic cogs in the "machinery" of society, neither indistinguishable blobs in "the masses" nor isolated competitive units. We are not constitutionally alienated creatures who have a need to seek "freedom" from Nature and traditional modes of human bonding. The societal systems of a modern culture often inflict what the Greens call "structural violence" to the person

45

because of the dehumanizing assumptions and expectations. Apathy, numbness, and resentment are the results. Hence such an interpretation of our nature is not humane and is not sustainable over time.

We discover our true nature not by absorbing cultural projections but by cultivating self-awareness and self-knowledge. Schumacher filled several pages of *A Guide for the Perplexed* with injunctions from the great religions that one must pursue the inner journey. He asserted that the traditional function of religion has been to teach the basic truth that "at the human Level of Being, the *invisibilia* are of infinitely greater power and significance than the *visibilia*." It is because Western civilization has abandoned religion and lost that teaching, Schumacher felt, that our society has become incapable of "dealing with the real problems of life at the human Level of Being."[16] In order to seek "knowledge for wisdom," rather than settle for the much narrower "knowledge for manipulation," Schumacher personally chose the practice of Buddhist Vipassana ("insight") meditation, in which one meticulously observes the workings of one's own mind — especially the source of suffering and its eradication — and *experientially* grasps the profound truth of Oneness and eternal flux, even to the level of the most minute vibrations ever rippling in and around us.

However, Schumacher's personal choice, which is also my own, is not useful for us here, as it is extremely unlikely that most Americans will ever practice Buddhist

meditation.* (I know this from family reunions in Ohio!)
A more practical way for postmodern religion to counter
the emptiness of modern life would be to investigate,
elevate, and promote the teachings and practices *inherent
in every religious tradition* that further inner growth leading
to wisdom. With Christianity and Judaism that may
require some digging, as their "mystical" traditions have
been shunted off to the sidelines. In fact, so peripheral a
role do they play in the twentieth century that Freud
insisted the Judeo-Christian tradition "keeps people
stupid" because it hands them everything and denies,
even forbids, them the individual quest that results in
true growth and wisdom. Fortunately, three series of
books on the Western mystical teachings are now
available.[17]

I disagree with Freud that Western religion is devoid of
such possibilities, although one mostly finds
hierarchically dictated rituals (services) with minimal

---

*   I am not suggesting that we overlook the scores of
thousands of ethnic Buddhists who are recent
immigrants to the U.S. from Southeast Asia or the
many American-born Buddhist mediators. I mean only
that their numbers will probably always be
comparatively small.

Anyone interested in Vipassana ("insight") meditation
may contact the Vipassana Meditation Center, Box 24,
Shelburne Falls, MA 01370, for a schedule of courses in
North America.

personal involvement and some prescribed individual spiritual practices that are merely devotional in nature. These observances have a soothing effect and serve to block out the harshness of the modern world periodically — and as such they should certainly not be banned — but religion should be more than a playpen. I emphatically take issue with those critics of modern society who charge that liberal theology has become "too personal" or "too privatized." I do agree that modern religion has largely receded to an inconsequential sphere of influence, but at the level of the person, of the inner life, one would think that Western religion is spiritually bankrupt!

What would the life of *the person* be like with postmodern religion in a Green society? It must be emphasized that Greens do not wish to force social engineering on society. A Green culture would allow plenty of space for the 6% of Americans who do not believe in "a universal spirit" (Gallup's term) and for the larger percentage who have no interest in cultivating their spirituality. People who do wish to live a spiritually enriched life would be encouraged, first, to have a daily spiritual practice, which might be reading the Bible for a half-hour, or meditating, or performing various spiritual exercises of contemplation. The purpose of the practice would be to cultivate wisdom, loving kindness, compassion for all living things, sympathetic joy, and equanimity (a calm and balanced mind that does not react blindly to the words and deeds of others). Can you imagine going to work and encountering people all day long who were trying to apply the lessons and inspiration from their morning spiritual practice? In this vision most people would also meet once a month or even once a week with a small group of peers to discuss occurrences in their spiritual practice and ways to put spiritual goals such as compassion and loving kindness into action in their community. In addition, it would be commonplace for people to make a spiritual retreat once a year, to spend approximately a week mostly in silence and contemplation with other members of one's church, synagogue, or nonsectarian organization. Lectures, group discussions, and one-to-one consultations could provide spiritual guidance, but most of the time would be quiet space, away from daily responsibilities, time to nurture the inner life.

Spiritual experience would not be limited to the morning practice or weekly church service or group meeting. We would increase our awareness of "spiritual moments" in the most ordinary human experiences. I agree, for instance, with most critics of modern religion who surmise that postmodern religion will have "more to do with the body." Much could be gained by *paying attention* to our body wisdom rather than seeking transcendence "above" the body to realms of the sky god. Music, dance, and ritual are recognized ways to move one's consciousness beyond the mundane perceptions of the illusion that all beings are separate, mechanistic entities to the consciousness of Oneness. But we have not yet recognized the teachings I call "body parables," which are inherent in our sexuality. (I will give examples here from women's sexuality since that is my own experience, but I do not feel that body parables occur only in women.)

First, it is difficult for women living in patriarchal culture to acknowledge any positive aspects of menstruation since it is now called "the curse" rather than "the sacred blood," which was represented by red ochre rubbed on sacred statues of the Goddess from at least as far back as 25,000 B.C. until the time of the Indo-European invasions into Europe around 4500 B.C. The first day of menses, however, is experienced by many women as a consciousness of "soft boundaries" of the self and of openness. The sense that boundaries or separations between beings are only illusory is even stronger in the experiences of pregnancy, natural childbirth, nursing, and motherhood when the distinction between me and not me becomes "a little blurred to say the least," as a friend of mine has put it.[18] In modern psychology, of course, any sense of one's own boundaries or delineations being softened is interpreted as unhealthy. In fact, it is merely an experiential contact with the deeper truth of life on Earth.

What is perhaps the primary body parable occurs in the postorgasmic state. It is true that both partners during the act of sexual union experience moments of oneness between themselves. It is after climax, however, *if we focus awareness* instead of chattering or lighting up a cigarette, that women often experience a peaceful, expansive mindstate, an oceanic, free-floating sense of having no boundaries.* This mindstate is similar to a particular experience people strive for in meditation halls, and it reveals a teaching about the nature of being: boundaries, as modern physics has agreed, are arbitrary and relative. Oneness and interrelatedness is the deep reality.

This spiritual interpretation of the function of the orgasm, by the way, affords what I believe is the only answer to the question that has always baffled physiologists: "Just why does the female have a clitoris? It has no function in reproduction. It's just there for sexual pleasure!" Indeed — and orgasmic pleasure can be a gateway to experiencing the profound Oneness, or knowing grace. (I do not expect a papal encyclical to be forthcoming on this spiritual experience, as the church fathers generally deny the existence of the clitoris altogether, insisting that God gave us our genitals strictly for purposes of procreation. Women merely smile at that — and perhaps God herself is chuckling.)

---

*   Most males describe their postorgasmic state as a somewhat unpleasant time when they feel vulnerable and even fearful. In France, men call it *le petit mort* (the little death). Perhaps this response is merely a result of social conditioning in patriarchal culture. Perhaps in a postpatriarchal culture men would have fewer existential fears, would experience their postorgasmic state as positive, and would discover it to be a body parable. No doubt the context of a deeply bonded love relationship and the trust inherent in it, diminishes the fear for many men and does much to allow a positive perception.

2 *How shall we relate to our context, the environment?* In 1967 Lynn White, a professor of history at U.C.L.A., published in *Science* "The Historical Root of our Ecologic Crisis," a critical analysis of the attitudes Western religion has encouraged toward our environment. Since then ecologists often point to the injunctions in Genesis that humans should attempt to "subdue" the Earth and have "dominion" over all the creatures of the Earth as being bad advice with disastrous results. (Many of those critiques, however, have lacked a full sense of the Hebrew words.) Bill Devall, coauthor of *Deep Ecology* spoke for many activists when he declared in August 1984, "Unless major changes occur in churches, ecologists and all those working in ecology movements will feel very uncomfortable sitting in the pews of most American churches."

The disparity between Judeo-Christian religion and ecological wisdom is illustrated by the experience of a friend of mine who once lived in a seminary overlooking Lake Erie and says he spent two years contemplating the sufferings of Christ without ever noticing that Lake Erie was dying.[19] Even when Catholic clergy speak today of St. Francis of Assisi, whom Lynn White nominated as the patron saint of ecologists, they often take pains to insist that he was not some "nature mystic,"[20] which, of course, would taint him with "paganism."*

---

* "Pagan" is from the Latin word for "country people," *pagani*. It has nothing to do with Satan-worship.

Religion that sets itself in opposition to Nature and vehemently resists the resacralizing of the natural world on the grounds that it would be "pagan" to do so is not sustainable over time.

The cultural historian Thomas Berry has declared that we are entering a new era of human history, the Ecological Age.[21] How could our religion reflect ecological wisdom and aid the desperately needed transformation of culture?

First, I suggest that Judaism and Christianity should stop being ashamed of their "pagan" inheritance, *which is substantial*, and should proudly proclaim their many inherent ties to Nature. How many of us realize that the church sets Easter on the first Sunday after the first *full moon* after the *Vernal Equinox* and that most of the Jewish holy days are determined by a *lunar calendar*?[22] Numerous symbols, rituals, and names in Jewish and Christian holy days have roots directly in the Nature-revering Old Religion. The list is a long one and should be cause for self-congratulation and celebration among Christians and Jews.

Second, I hope the stewardship movement, which is gaining momentum in Christian and Jewish circles, will continue to deepen its analyses and its field of action. Those people are performing a valuable service by reinterpreting the overall biblical teachings about the natural world and finding ecological wisdom that balances or outweighs the "dominance" message. Virtually all spokespersons for the stewardship movement emphasize that Nature is to be honored as God's creation.[23]

In fact, that position is firmly rooted in the work of several noted theologians whose orientation is known as "creation spirituality." They emphasize the interrelatedness of all creation, the understanding that humans do not occupy the central position in the cosmic creation but have a responsible role to play, and the transformation of society in directions that will further the continuation of life. Hence peace is a central issue for creation theologians, as is justice. Nearly all of them give greater importance to the female dimension of creation than do other theologians. Among the Catholic, Protestant, and Jewish theologians of creation spirituality are Bernhard W. Anderson, Thomas Berry, Walter Bruggemann, Martin Buber, Marie-Dominique Chenu, Matthew Fox, Abraham Heschel, Jurgen Moltmann, Paul Santmire, Edward Schillebeeckx, Odil Hannes Steck, Pierre Teilhard de Chardin, and Samuel Terrien.[24]

The experience of knowing the Divine through communication with Nature has been a recurrent theme in art. Recently Alice Walker described a theologically sophisticated, elemental spiritual experience in her Pulitzer-Prize-winning novel *The Color Purple* when one black woman in rural Georgia explains to another that God "ain't a he or a she, but a It":

It ain't a picture show. It ain't something you can look at apart from anything else, including yourself. I believe God is everything, say Shug. Everything that is or ever was or ever will be. And when you can feel that, and be happy to feel that, you've found it. . . . My first step away from the old white man was trees. Then air. Then birds. Then other people. But one day when I was sitting quiet and feeling like a motherless child, which I was, it come to me: that feeling of being part of everything, not separate at all. I knew that if I cut a tree, my arm would bleed. And I laughed and I cried and I run all around the house. I knew just what it was. In fact, when it happen, you can't miss it. It sort of like you know what, she say, grinning and rubbing high up on my thigh.[25]

I am encouraged that a religion-based respect for Nature is showing up in numerous articles and books, especially books like *The Spirit of the Earth* (1984), in which John Hart urges study of and respect for Native American religious perspectives on nature *because that is the indigenous tradition of our land* and suggests compatibility between their religion and the Judeo-Christian tradition. Yet why is it that attention to loving and caring for Nature rarely makes it into the liturgy today?

I recently came across a newspaper article by Harold Gilliam in the *San Francisco Chronicle* describing a magnificent ecological service that spanned twenty-four hours, beginning at sunrise on the Autumnal Equinox, and took place in the gothic cathedral on Nob Hill in San Francisco, Grace Cathedral. At the sound of a bell and a conch shell, the Episcopal Bishop of California opened the service:

We are gathered here at sunrise to express our love and concern for the living waters of the Central Valley of California and for the burrowing owls, white-tailed kites, great blue herons, migratory waterfowl, willow trees, cord grass, water lilies, beaver, possum, striped bass, anchovies, and women, children, and men of the Great Family who derive their life and spiritual sustenance from these waters. Today we offer our concerns and prayers for the ascending health and spirit of these phenomena of life and their interwoven habitats and rights. . . . .

Poets, spiritual teachers, musicians, and ecologists all participated in the service, which included whale and wolf calls emanating from various corners of the cathedral's sound system, as well as the projection of Nature photography onto the walls and pillars. Gary Snyder and his family read his "Prayer for the Great Family," which is based on a Mohawk prayer.[26] The celebrants poured water from all the rivers of California into the baptismal font. They committed themselves to changing our society and our environment into "a truly Great Family," and they assigned to each U.S. Senator a totemic animal or plant from his or her region in order to accentuate the rights of our nonhuman Family members. I read the account with awe and then noticed with sadness that it was dated 17 October 1971. (No subsequent ecological services took place in that church because a few influential members of the congregation pronounced it paganism.) How many species have been lost since then, how many tons of topsoil washed away, how many aquifers polluted — while we have failed to include Nature in our religion?

56

Knowledge of Nature must precede respect and love for it. We could urge that ecological wisdom regarding God's creation be incorporated in Sunday school as well as in sermons and prayer.* We could suggest practices such as the planting of trees on certain holy days. We could mention in the church bulletin ecological issues that are crucial to our community.[27] There is no end to what we *could* do to focus spiritually based awareness and action on saving the Great Web of Life.

3   *How shall we relate to other people?* This last basic questions has two parts: distinction by gender and then by other groups.

Our lives are shaped to a great extent not by the differences between the sexes, but by the cultural response to those differences. There is no need to belabor the point that in patriarchal cultures the male is considered the norm and the female is considered "the Other." For our purposes here, however, it is relevant to note that Judeo-Christian religion has played a central role in constructing the subordinate role for women in Western culture. Suffice it to say that the eminent mythologist Joseph Campbell once remarked that in all his decades of studying religious texts worldwide he had

---

*   I will pass along my mother's technique for getting the priest's attention: she critiques his sermon on the back of the collection envelope before dropping it into the basket in church!

never encountered a more relentlessly misogynist book than the Old Testament. Numerous Christian saints and theologians have continued the tradition.

The results for traditional society of denying women education and opportunity have been an inestimable loss of talent, intelligence, and creativity. For women it has meant both structural and direct violence. Of the former, Virginia Woolf observed that women under patriarchy are uncomfortable with themselves because they know society holds them in low esteem. The structural violence of forced dependency sometimes provides the conditions for physical violence, that is, battering. Finally, patriarchal culture usurps control over a woman's body from the woman herself, often inflicting tortuous pain. It has been reported that in China today women are forced to undergo abortions even in the third trimester under the government's one-child-only policy. (The women who must undergo forced abortion are those who have incurred shame and the wrath of their husbands and in-laws by previously giving birth to a girl and later try desperately to carry a boy baby to term unnoticed by the government. Sometimes the women in that patriarchal culture simply drown themselves immediately after giving birth to a daughter.)

Some people accuse the Greens of being hypocritical in calling themselves a "party of life" and adopting a "pro-choice" stance on abortion. In spring 1984, the European Greens, a coalition of Green parties throughout Western

Europe endorsed, after much debate, a position *against* social and political sanctions that force birthing and *for* free choice. The quality of the debate in Green parties over abortion has more integrity than that currently being waged in American politics precisely because all aspects of the issue are considered. In our country half of the debate often seems to be missing: women's suffering. The issue is obviously complex, and there are people of good conscience on both sides. I offer my views merely as personal ones, not official positions of American Greens.

Church leaders of many varieties are demanding an end to all legal (that is, medically safe) abortion. I suspect they can maintain a position demanding the criminalization of abortion only because they have never witnessed a woman going through pregnancy, labor, and delivery — or else they believe the biblical injunction that woman is *supposed* to suffer. Sometimes birth is textbook simple, but usually it is not.* Some men say they remember their wife's screams for months. Many men say the birth experience made them "pro-choice" on the abortion issue because they would never want to force any woman to go through such an ordeal against her will.

---

* I am not speaking from embittered experience, as I had a medically uncomplicated pregnancy and a brief, nearly painless delivery using Lamaze techniques plus meditation skills of concentrating the mind. It was a joyful experience, but without those two advantages it would have been a very different story.

As one of the most popular right-wing Christian preachers, Pat Robertson, likes to tell his TV audience (16.3 million households per month), " We are offering up 1½ million babies per year upon the altar of sensuality and selfishness."[28] Is that what it's all about — millions of sex-crazed, hedonistic women? Where is the compassion for the lonely teenager from an unnurturing family situation who tried to find affection and love where she could? Where is the compassion for the innocent victims of rape, including incestual rape and the increasing frequency of the "date rape" and "acquaintance rape"? Where is the compassion for *any* woman who discovers that she is "in trouble"? The number of abortions needed in this country would plummet if the problemmatic conditions were addressed effectively: disintegrated families; widespread pornography depicting violence against women; culturally approved hyper-macho behavior on dates; what has been called "patriarchy's dirty little secret" (the shocking statistics on sexual abuse by male relatives); selfishness and lack of spiritual grounding on the part of men who emotionally coerce their girlfriends; and lack of self-confidence and spiritual grounding in their own being among young women.

There comes a time at the end of many lives when life is not viable without machinery, and most people say they would like the machinery turned off if it came to that. Similarly, there is a time at the beginning of life when a fertilized egg and then a fetus is not viable life *unless* the woman is willing to give over her body and accept the suffering. To force a woman either to give birth or to abort is violence against the person. Most men and women know this in their hearts. They also know that countless women do not have the financial and other resources for the twenty-year task of raising a child. That is why a Gallup poll in June 1983 found that only 19% of American Catholics and 16% of the total American population want abortion to be illegal in all circumstances.[29] The Gallup organization released a poll on 20 February 1986 showing that the American public is evenly divided (45% to 45%) on the 1973 U.S. Supreme Court ruling that a woman may go to a doctor to have an abortion during the first three months of pregnancy. Interestingly, women's views were found to be statistically the same as in 1983, but men's support for the court ruling had fallen by 11%. Male fears of women's controlling their own sexuality are deeply rooted in patriarchal culture; during the Renaissance, for example, peasant healers were burned as "witches" for providing women with contraception and abortion. So the debate we are embroiled in is a very old one, and the campaign to "Save the embryo; damn the woman" has been mounted many times before.

Men, too, suffer under patriarchal culture. Because woman is regarded as the denigrated "Other," men are pressured to react and continually prove themselves very *un*like the female. This dynamic results in what some men have called "the male machine." It has also skewed much of our behavioral and cognitive science since thousands of careers and volumes of commentary on "sex

61

differences" have been funded, but no recognized field of "sex similarities" exists.[30] That would be too unnerving.

The most serious effect of men under patriarchy needing to prove themselves *very different* from women is the function of military combat as an initiation into true manhood and full citizenship. This deeply rooted belief surfaced as an unexpected element in the struggle to pass the Equal Rights Amendment, for instance. Feminist lobbyists in state legislatures throughout the 1970s were repeatedly informed, "When you ladies are ready to fight in a *war,* we'll be ready to discuss equal rights!"[31] Such an orientation is not sustainable in the nuclear age.

What role could religion play in removing the cultural insistence on women as Other and men as God-like and hence inherently superior? How could religion further the Green principle of postpatriarchal consciousness? We know the answers because they are already being tried: women must have equal participation in ritual (as ministers, rabbis, and priests); language in sermons and translations must be inclusive; and the Godhead must be considered female as well as male. These solutions are not new, but neither are they very effective because so many people do not take either the need or the means seriously. Instead, they resent these efforts and feel silly and somewhat embarrassed with the notion of a female God. Being forced to say "God the Mother" once in a while is pointless if people have in mind Yahweh-with-a-skirt. We must first understand who She is: She is not in the sky; She is Earth. Here is Her manifestation in the oldest creation story in Western culture:

The Myth of Gaia

Free of birth or destruction, of time or space, of form or condition, is the Void. From the eternal Void, Gaia danced forth and rolled Herself into a spinning ball. She molded mountains along Her spine, valleys in the hollows of Her flesh. A rhythm of hills and stretching plains followed Her contours. From Her warm moisture She bore a flow of gentle rain that fed Her surface and brought life. Wriggling creatures spawned in tidal pools, while tiny green shoots pushed upward through Her pores. She filled oceans and ponds and set rivers flowing through deep furrows. Gaia watched Her plants and animals grow. In time She brought forth from Her womb six women and six men. . . .

Unceasingly the Earth-Mother manifested gifts on Her surface and accepted the dead into her body. In return She was revered by all mortals. Offerings to Gaia of honey and barley cake were left in a small hole in the earth before plants were gathered. Many of Her temples were built near deep chasms where yearly the mortals offered sweet cakes into her womb. From within the darkness of Her secrets, Gaia received their gifts.[32]

Having addressed the self, Nature and gender, we now come to the last half of the last basic question, *How shall we relate to groups and other individuals?* There are, of course, a multiplicity of groups in society at the levels of family, community, region, state, nation, and planet. The following are merely some general considerations.

We must first analyze how our own mode of living affects others in the Great Family: Does the nature of our existence impose suffering on others — or does it support and assist those who are less privileged than we? Here we can enjoy the convergence of spiritual growth and political responsibility in the spiritual practice of cultivating moment-to-moment awareness, being fully "awake" and focused on our actions — a simple-sounding yet demanding task. There is a story in Zen of a student who studied very hard to master certain religious texts and then went before his spiritual teacher to be questioned. The *roshi* asked simply, "On which side of the umbrella did you place your shoes?" The student was defeated; he had lost awareness (or "spaced out," as we might say).

We can begin our day by focusing mindfulness on our every act. Turning on the water in the bathroom. Where does it come from? Is our town recklessly pumping water from the receding water table instead of calling for conservation measures? Where does our wastewater go when it leaves the sink? What happens after it is treated? Later we are in the kitchen, making breakfast. Where does our coffee come from? A worker-owned cooperative in the Third World or an exploitative multi-national corporation? Obviously, it is exhausting to continue this practice very long unless one is adept. (It *is* difficult — so much so that a friend of mine has added an amendment to a popular spiritual saying: "Be here now — or now and then.") But everyone can practice *some* mindfulness.

If we analyze our own situation, we may discover that we are benefitting from the suffering of others — and that we ourselves are uncomfortable with the structural systems in which we work. When one thinks of religious people working for economic or social change, the "liberation theology" movement probably comes to mind because of its size in Latin America and its coverage in the press lately. In that movement grassroots Catholic groups (base communities) meet frequently to discuss the teachings in the Gospels and applications of Marxist analysis.

But there is another way: a religion-based movement for social change is beginning to flourish that is completely in keeping with Green principles of private ownership and cooperative economics, decentralization, grassroots democracy, nonviolence, social responsibility, global awareness — and the spiritual truth of Oneness. This type of call for economic and social change is gaining momentum in Catholic, Protestant, and Jewish communities. We see it, for example, in the statement issued by the Catholic Bishops of Appalachia, *This Land Is My Home: A Pastoral Letter on Powerlessness in Appalachia*, which calls for worker-owned businesses and community-based economics. We see it in *Strangers and Guests: Toward Community in the Heartland* by the Catholic bishops of the Heartland (Midwest) and in *The Land: God's Giving, Our Caring* by the American Lutheran

Church, a statement which was then echoed by the Presbyterian Church. Both of these statements address ecological use of the land, and *Strangers and Guests* calls for small-is-beautiful *land reform* as the only sustainable course for rural America. Developing the applications of such principles as "the land should be distributed equitably" and "the land's workers should be able to become the land's owners," the Heartland bishops discuss elimination of capital gains tax laws which favor "wealthy investors and speculators" and disfavor "small and low-income farm families," taxation of agricultural land "according to its productive value rather than its speculative value," "taxing land progressively at a higher rate according to increases in size and quality of holdings" (a proposal in the Jeffersonian tradition), and low-interest loans to aspiring farmers as well as tax incentives for farmers with large holdings to sell land to them.

We see Green-oriented economic and social change now promoted in the Jewish periodical *Menorah* and by the Protestant multi-denominational association, Joint Strategy and Action Committee. The lead article in a 1984 issue of the JSAC newsletter began:

> If you want to know what eco-justice is, read the Psalms. The dual theme of justice in the social order and integrity in the natural order is pervasive and prominent. The Book is, in large part, a celebration of interrelationships, the interaction, the mutuality, the organic oneness and wholeness of it all that is, that is to say, the Creator and the creation, human and nonhuman.

The Green-oriented Jewish and Protestant leaders seek to locate justice *and* ecological wisdom in the Old Testament. Green-oriented Catholics usually turn to the papal encyclicals, especially Pope Pius XI's 1931 encyclical *Quadragesimo anno [Forty Years After]*,* which established three cardinal principles: *personalism* (the goal of society is to develop and enrich the individual human person), *subsidiarity* (no organization should be bigger than necessary and nothing should be done by a large and higher social unit than can be done effectively by a lower and smaller unit), and *pluralism* (that a healthy society is characterized by a wide variety of intermediate groups freely flourishing between the individual and the state).[33] Sounds like a lot of Green party platforms I've read recently! Andrew Greeley argues in *No Bigger Than Necessary* that Catholic social theory is firmly rooted in the communitarian, decentralist tradition and that Catholics who drifted into Marxism in recent decades are simply unaware that their own tradition contains a better solution. Joe Holland, a Catholic activist with the Center of Concern in Washington, D.C., argues, however, that left-oriented Catholics have never embraced "scientific Marxism" and the model of a machine-like centralized government and economy. They are attracted, rather, by communitarian ideals and are uncomfortable

---

* *Quadragesimo anno* was a commemoration and expansion of Pope Leo XIII's 1891 encyclical *Rerum Novarum [Of the New Situation of the Working Class]*.

with the modernity of many socialist assumptions.[34] Hence, we may assume, and I believe Joe Holland would agree, that many of these lukewarm leftists in Catholic circles would readily become Green.

The possibilities for locating and working with Green-oriented activists in mainline religions have never been better. For example, a task force of the Presbyterian Church in Pennsylvania, Ohio, and West Virginia has been instrumental in introducing Rodale Press' Regeneration Project in economically depressed communities. The Project's goals are to stimulate local economic vitality and to improve the overall quality of life.[35]

Within our own Green political organizations, however, the question remains of how much religious content is proper in pluralistic meetings and publications. I myself am uncertain about how much overt spirituality the "market will bear" in Green conferences and statements, and I am often dissatisfied afterward because I and other Greens have held back too much on spirituality so as not to exclude anyone in the group. I am not sure what the solutions may be but I am certain I shall be influenced by learning recently of that Gallup statistic that *only 6%* of Americans do not believe in God "or a universal spirit." What a vocal minority! Perhaps I should simply avoid Manhattan and university towns. . . .

Surely, no Green, whatever his or her spiritual orientation, could object to our structuring our groups according to the deep ecology principles of diversity, interdependence, openness, and adaptability — as well as the spiritual principles of cultivating wisdom and compassion. These can be our guidelines as we evolve the everchanging forms of Green politics.

FOUR GOALS
FOR THE
GREEN-AT-HEART

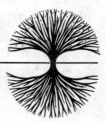

I believe the criteria I mentioned earlier for Green spirituality are satisfied by the four key points I have delineated. Sustainable religion in the Green vision for society entails the 1200 "primary religious bodies" in our country emphasizing four areas *that are already contained in their traditions*: spiritual development through inner growth, ecological wisdom, gender equality, and social responsibility. If we would simply *get serious* about these four areas, can you imagine the transformation of American religion that would result? The important feature is that all four of these Green-oriented goals are already in our religious traditions (although many aspects have been neutralized or hidden). We do not have to invent something new and try to get people to tack it onto their own ways. Rather, we need to encourage a shift, which will not be a small one or an easy one, toward sustainability and toward deeply meaningful religion that does not separate itself from Nature, from our bodies, and from women.

We should realize that the movement toward postmodern religion will continue with or without Green participation. My own hope, though, is that many American Greens will become involved because I believe that the deepest sources of Green principles are spiritual in nature and I believe we can make positive contributions to the process. I am concerned, for instance, that Harvey Cox's recent, and in many ways excellent, study of harbingers of postmodern religion, *Religion in the Secular City*, does not mention ecological wisdom as a necessary core component.

I am also concerned that religion-based activism in service of Green goals may be hindered by our differences. Deep ecologists and feminists may be thinking to themselves, "*Strangers and Guests*! The Heartland bishops chose *that* phrase from Leviticus* for their title and everyone thinks it's just fine?! They just don't get it! That's exactly what's wrong with patriarchal religion: it alienates us from the Earth!" But the deep ecologists and feminists should realize that the Jews and Christians are probably thinking about *them*, "They just don't get it! The Lord created Nature and that's why we should treat it well." And they should both be thinking, "*It doesn't matter* as long as we can work together to prevent ecocide and nuclear holocaust and to improve conditions for all our sisters and brothers in the Great

---

* "The land belongs to me, and to me you are strangers and guests." (Leviticus, 25:23).

Family." In times like these, to cling to our differences and ideological purity rather than mutual respect may be the most heinous of sins.

We have a model for inter-faith, religion-based social change activism in the Sarvodaya movement, which operates successful self-help projects in 8000 villages in Sri Lanka.[36] It combines the Gandhian model of a small-scale, community-based economy with spiritually informed ethics, mostly Buddhist but also Hindu, Moslem, and Christian. As I was finishing writing this lecture, the founder of Sarvodaya, Dr. A.T. Ariyaratne, passed through San Francisco and I attended a reception for him. Afterward I asked whether he felt that a spiritually based social change movement could flourish in a country with 1200 kinds of religious orientation. He first explained to me that Sarvodaya works with greater religious and ethnic diversity than I had thought. Then he smiled and said, "First you build a spiritual infrastructure for the community, based on everyone's having a personal practice. Then everyone will come to you."

I don't know whether "everyone" will ever come to Green politics, but I do believe that a "spiritual infrastructure" is essential for a successful transformation of our society in postmodern and Green directions. A spiritual grounding would not only answer a deep hunger in the modern experience, it would also be harmonious with various Green tendrils that have already begun to sprout: the

73

bioregional movement, which teaches us to "live in place," to know and appreciate the heritage and ecological character of our area; the evolving philosophy of deep ecology; the emergence of community-based ecological populism; the Green-oriented activism in mainline religion; the work of cultural/holistic feminists; the spiritual dimension appearing in the discussions of global responsibility[37] — and the worldwide network of Green parties and organizations. I do not mean to imply in a facile way that the transformation has already happened, or that the postmodern paradigm is in place, or that there are not serious holes, problems, and paradoxes. The scope of the task is enormous, it is true, but what else shall we do? Continue walking numbly toward high-tech ecocide and species suicide, propelling a system that in many respects seems wildly out of control? No. There is just cause to celebrate the frail but stubborn budding of a new vision — based on the oldest wisdom we contain. If we nurture that vision with the lifeblood of our ideas and our efforts, we — and our children — may be rewarded with a future worth living.

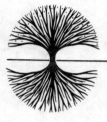

APPENDIX

TEN KEY VALUES
OF THE AMERICAN
GREEN MOVEMENT

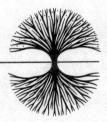

This list of values and questions for discussion were composed by a diverse group of people who are working to build a new politics, which has kinship with Green movements around the world. We feel the issues we have raised below are not being addressed adequately by the political left or right. We invite you to join with us in refining our values, sharpening our questions — and translating our perspective into practical and effective political actions. We are calling ourselves, for the interim, the Committees of Correspondence, which was the name for grassroots political networks in the American Revolutionary Era and several times since then. If you wish to receive information on activities in your area related to these values, please write to us: C.o.C. Clearinghouse, P.O. Box 30208, Kansas City, MO 64112.

1 ECOLOGICAL WISDOM   How can we operate human societies with the understanding that we are *part* of nature, not on top of it? How can we live within the ecological and resource limits of the planet, applying our technological knowledge to the challenge of an energy-efficient economy? How can we build a better relationship between cities and countryside? How can we guarantee the rights of nonhuman species? How can we promote sustainable agriculture and respect for self-regulating natural systems? How can we further biocentric wisdom in all spheres of life?

2 GRASSROOTS DEMOCRACY   How can we develop systems that allow and encourage us to control the decisions that affect our lives? How can we ensure that representatives will be fully accountable to the people who elect them? How can we develop planning mechanisms that would allow citizens to develop and implement their own preferences for policies and spending priorities? How can we encourage and assist the "mediating institutions" — family, neighborhood organization, church group, voluntary association, ethnic club — to recover some of the functions now performed by government? How can we relearn the best insights from American traditions of civic vitality, voluntary action, and community responsibility?

3 PERSONAL AND SOCIAL RESPONSIBILITY   How can we respond to human suffering in ways that promote dignity? How can we encourage people to commit themselves to lifestyles that promote their own health? How can we have a community-controlled education system that effectively teaches our children academic skills, ecological wisdom, social responsibility, and personal growth? How can we resolve interpersonal and intergroup conflicts without just turning them over to lawyers and judges? How can we take responsibility for reducing the crime rate in our neighborhoods? How can we encourage such values as simplicity and moderation?

4 NONVIOLENCE How can we, as a society, develop effective alternatives to our current patterns of violence, at all levels, from the family and the street to nations and the world? How can we eliminate nuclear weapons from the face of the Earth without being naive about the intentions of other governments? How can we most constructively use nonviolent methods to oppose practices and policies with which we disagree and in the process reduce the atmosphere of polarization and selfishness that is itself a source of violence?

5 DECENTRALIZATION How can we restore power and responsibility to individuals, institutions, communities, and regions? How can we encourage the flourishing of regionally-based culture rather than a dominant monoculture? How can we have a decentralized, democratic society with our political, economic, and social institutions locating power on the smallest scale (closest to home) that is efficient and practical? How can we redesign our institutions so that

fewer decisions and less regulation over money are granted as one moves from the community toward the national level? How can we reconcile the need for community and regional self-determination with the need for appropriate centralized regulation in certain matters?

6 COMMUNITY-BASED ECONOMICS   How can we redesign our work structures to encourage employee ownership and workplace democracy? How can we develop new economic activities and institutions that will allow us to use our new technologies in ways that are humane, freeing, ecological, and accountable and responsive to communities? How can we establish some form of basic economic security, open to all? How can we move beyond the narrow "job ethic" to new definitions of "work," "jobs," and "income" that reflect the changing economy? How can we restructure our patterns of income distribution to reflect the wealth created by those outside the formal, monetary economy: those who take responsibility for parenting, housekeeping, home gardens, community volunteer work, etc.? How can we restrict the size and concentrated power of corporations without discouraging superior efficiency or technological innovation?

7 POSTPATRIARCHAL VALUES   How can we replace the cultural ethics of dominance and control with more cooperative ways of interacting? How can we encourage people to care about persons outside their own group? How can we promote the building of respectful, positive, and responsible relationships across the lines of gender and other divisions? How can we encourage a rich, diverse political culture that respects feelings as well as rationalist approaches? How can we proceed with as much respect for the means as the end (the process as much as the products of our efforts)? How can we learn to respect the contemplative, inner part of life as much as the outer activities?

8 RESPECT FOR DIVERSITY How can we honor cultural, ethnic, racial, sexual, religious, and spiritual diversity within the context of individual responsibility toward all beings? How can we reclaim our country's finest shared ideals: the dignity of the individual, democratic participation, and liberty and justice for all?

9 GLOBAL RESPONSIBILITY How can we be of genuine assistance to grassroots groups in the Third World? What can we learn from such groups? How can we help other countries make the transition to self-sufficiency in food and other basic necessities? How can we cut our defense budget while maintaining an adequate defense? How can we promote these ten Green values in the reshaping of global order? How can we reshape world order without creating just another enormous nation-state?

81

10 FUTURE FOCUS   How can we induce people and institutions to think in terms of the long-range future, and not just in terms of their short-range selfish interest? How can we encourage people to develop their own visions of the future and move more effec-tively toward them? How can we judge whether new technologies are socially useful — and use those judgments to shape our society? How can we induce our government and other institutions to practice fiscal responsibility? How can we make the quality of life, rather than open-ended economic growth, the focus of future thinking?

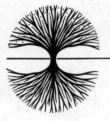

REFERENCES

1. *Hopi Voices*, ed. by Harold Courlander, Albuquerque: University of New Mexico Press, 1982, p. xxv.

2. Arne Naess and George Sessions, *Ecophilosophy*, Sierra College, Rocklin, California 95677, No. 4, May 1984, pp. 5-7. Also see *Deep Ecology* by Bill Devall and George Sessions (Layton, Utah: Peregrine Smith Press, 1984).

3. See *Human Scale* by Kirkpatrick Sale (New York: Putnam Books, 1982).

4. The Green Party in England (formerly the Ecology Party) has gone further than other Green parties by including a half page on "The Spirit" in *Politics for Life*, their 1983 Election Manifesto. While I applaud their effort, I find their discussion too vague to be satisfying.

   Similarly, Rudolf Bahro in West Germany has tried to convince his Green colleagues that a spiritual perspective is the "loadbearing base" of the fundamental Green work.

5. David Ehrenfeld, *The Arrogance of Humanism* (Oxford: Oxford University Press, 1978), p. 5.

6. LewisThomas, *"Human Responsibility," Phenomenon of Change* (New York: Cooper-Hewitt Museum, 1986), p. 1.

7. Andrew Greeley approvingly citing Daniel Bell approvingly quoting Irving Howe, *No Bigger than Necessary* (New York: New American Library, 1977), p. 154.

8. See Harry Boyte and Sara Evans, "Strategies in Search of America: Cultural Radicalism, Populism, and Democratic Culture," *Socialist Review,* no. 75/76, May-August 1984, pp. 73-100. Also see *Community is Possible: Repairing America's Roots* by Harry Boyte (New York: Harper and Row, 1984).

9. Numerous cultural feminists (a grouping distinct from materialist/socialist feminists and liberal feminists) have analyzed the ills of patriarchal culture. *Green Paradise Lost* by Elizabeth Dodson Gray (Wellesley, MA: Roundtable Press, 1979) is a cultural-feminist analysis that contains much biocentric spiritual wisdom.

10. Joe Holland, *The Spiritual Crisis of Modern Culture* (Washington, D.C.: Center of Concern, 1983), p. 13.

11. See *Goddesses and Gods of Old Europe, 6500-3500 B.C.* by Marija Gimbutas (London: Thames and Hudson; Berkeley: University of California Press, 1974).

12. Gary Snyder, "Anarchism, Buddhism, and Political Economy," lecture at Fort Mason Center, San Francisco, 27 February 1984.

13. *Encyclopedia of American Religion* by J. Gordon Melton (Wilmington, NC: McGrath Publishing Co., 1978).

14. Center for Religion Research, Gallup Organization, Princeton, NJ, information given via telephone to the author on 16 October 1984.

15. Center for Religion Research, Gallup Organization, Princeton, NJ, information given via telephone to the author on 16 October 1984.

16. E.F. Schumacher, *A Guide for the Perplexed* (New York: Harper and Row, 1977), p. 74.

17. Bear & Company publishes *Meditations With Hildegard of Bingen; Meditations With Mechtild of Magdeburg; Meditations With Meister Eckhart; Meditations With Dante Aligheri; Meditations With Teresa of Avila; Meditations With Julian of Norwich; Meditations With Native Americans — Lakota Spirituality; Meditations With the Hopi; Meditations With Animals — A Native American Bestiary;* and *Illuminations of Hildegard of Bingen.*

New Directions publishes the Wisdom Series, with such titles as *The Wisdom of the English Mystics, The Wisdom of the Jewish Mystics, The Wisdom of the Spanish Mystics,* and *The Wisdom of the Desert [Fathers].*

Paulist Press publishes a series called "The Classics of Western Spirituality: A Library of the Great Spiritual Masters." It features works by such sages as Julian of Norwich, Jacob Boehme, Nahman of Bratslav, Gregory of Nyssa, Bonaventure, Abraham Isaac Kook, Catherine of Genoa, and two volumes on Native American spirituality.

18. Nancy F.W. Passmore, "Consciousness Manifesto," *The Politics of Women's Spirituality,* ed. by Charlene Spretnak (New York: Anchor/Doubleday, 1982), p. 169.

19. Paul Ryan, "Relationships," *Talking Wood,* Pompton Lakes, NJ, vol. 1, no. 4, 1980.

20. One example, although by no means the only one, is *The Way of St. Francis* by Murray Bodo, O.F.M. (Garden City, NY: Doubleday, 1984).

21. Collections of Thomas Berry's papers, such as *The Riverdale Papers on the Earth Community*, are available from the Riverdale Center for Religious Research, 5801 Palisade Avenue, Riverdale, NY 10471. His work is also presented by the physicist Brian Swimme in *The Universe is a Green Dragon* (Santa Fe: Bear & Company, 1984).

22. Arthur Waskow, *Seasons of Our Joy: A Celebration of Modern Jewish Renewal* (New York: Bantam Books, 1982).

23. See, for example, *The Earth is the Lord's: Essays on Stewardship*, ed. by Mary Evelyn Jegen and Bruno V. Manno (New York: Paulist Press, 1978); *A Worldly Spirituality: The Call to Take Care of the Earth* by Wesley Granberg-Michaelson (New York: Harper and Row, 1984); *The Spirit of the Earth: A Theology of the Land* by John Hart (New York: Paulist Press, 1984); *Ecology and Religion: Toward a New Christian Theology of Nature* by John Carmody (New York: Paulist Press, 1983); and *Earth May Be Fair: Reflections on Ethics, Religion, and Ecology*, ed. by Ian G. Barbour (Englewood Cliffs, NJ: Prentice-Hall, 1972).

24. In addition to the scores of books by the creation theologians cited in the text, there is a relevant anthology, *Cry of the Environment: Rebuilding the Christian Creation Tradition*, ed. by Philip N. Joranson and Ken Butigan (Santa Fe: Bear & Company, 1984).

    A partial "family tree of creation-centered spirituality" may be found in *Original Blessing* by Matthew Fox (Santa Fe: Bear & Company, 1983).

25. Alice Walker, *The Color Purple* (New York: Harcourt Brace Jovanovich, 1982), p. 167.

26. "Prayer for the Great Family" may be found in Gary Snyder's Pulitzer-Prize-winning volume of poetry, *Turtle Island* (New Directions Books).

27. See Byron Kennard, "Mixing Religion and Politics," Ecopinion, *Audubon*, March 1984.

28. "Power, Glory -- and Politics," *Time*, 17 February 1986, p. 65.

29. Center for Religion Research, Gallup Organization, Princeton, NJ, information given via telephone to the author on 16 October 1984.

30. Ruth Bleier, *Science and Gender* (New York: Pergamon Press, 1984).

31. See "Naming the Cultural Forces that Push Us Toward War" by Charlene Spretnak, *Journal of Humanistic Psychology,* Summer 1983; also in *Nuclear Strategy and the Code of the Warrior* (Atlantic Books, 1985). Also see the chapters on "The Soldier" and "War" in *A Choice of Heroes* by Mark Gerzon (Boston: Houghton Mifflin, 1982).

32. Charlene Spretnak, *Lost Goddesses of Early Greece: A Collection of Pre-Hellenic Myths* (Boston: Beacon Press, 1981). Also see *The Divine Female: The Biblical Imagery of God as Female* by Virginia Ramey Mollenkott (New York: Crossroad, 1984) for some useful compromise positions on the Great Mother.

33. Andrew M. Greeley, *No Bigger Than Necessary* (New York: New American Library, 1977), p. 10.

34 Joe Holland, *The Postmodern Paradigm Implicit in the Church's Shift to the Left* (Washington, D.C.: Center of Concern, 1984).

35. Regeneration Project, Rodale Press, 33 East Minor St., Emmaus, PA 18049.

36. *Dharma and Development: Religion as Resource in the Sarvodaya Self-Help Movement* by Joanna Macy (West Hartford, CT: Kumarian Press, 1983).

37. See, for example, *New Genesis: Shaping a Global Spirituality* by Robert Muller (Garden City, NY: Image/Doubleday, 1984) and *Toward a Human World Order* by Gerald and Patricia Mische (New York: Paulist Press, 1977).

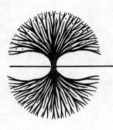

ACKNOWLEDGMENTS

I wish to thank the following friends and colleagues, who responded to my research queries with solid information and supportive good cheer: Jeff Bercuvitz, Thomas Berry, Harry Boyte, Mary Beth Edelson, Clare Fischer, Medard Gabel, Elizabeth and David Dodson Gray, David Haenke, Joe Holland, Helen Kenik Mainelli, Mike Miller, Nancy Morita, Magaly Rodriguez Mossman, Gary Snyder, and Arthur Waskow.

In the final stages I benefitted from the insights, encouragement, and critiques of Frederick Crews, Robert Hellrung and Cheryl Leeds, Paul Ryan, Mark Satin, and Brian Swimme.

I am grateful to Robert Swann and Susan Witt of the E.F. Schumacher Society of America for allowing this edition of my Schumacher lecture to be published so that the work might reach a larger audience.

My editor at Bear & Company, Barbara Clow, was efficient, wise, and warm. The book designer, Mina Yamashita, expressed and enhanced the text with her graceful aesthetics.

My literary agent, Frances Goldin, acted, as always, as my friend and advisor.

Most of all, I thank my daughter, Lissa, for her support and for her good company on our trip to New Haven when I delivered this lecture.

ABOUT THE AUTHOR

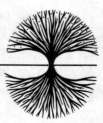

Charlene Spretnak holds degrees from St. Louis University and the University of California, Berkeley. She is coauthor of *Green Politics: The Global Promise*, which she wrote with Fritjof Capra. She is a co-founder of the Committees of Correspondence, the major Green political organization in the United States. She is also editor of *The Politics of Women's Spirituality: Essays on the Rise of Spiritual Power within the Feminist Movement* and author of *Lost Goddesses of Early Greece: A Collection of Pre-Hellenic Myths*. Her article "Naming the Cultural Forces that Push Us Toward War" (*Journal of Humanistic Psychology*, Summer 1983; also in *Nuclear Strategy and the Code of the Warrior*) is used in many peace studies programs.

Grassroots groups wishing to sell as a fundraising project either or both of the following books

Green Politics: The Global Promise
by Charlene Spretnak and Fritjof Capra

The Spiritual Dimension of Green Politics
by Charlene Spretnak

may write to: Sales Dept., Bear & Company, P.O. Drawer 2860, Santa Fe, NM 87504-2860 for information.

Homicide detective Jake Carrington takes murder personally . . .

The victim was bludgeoned, stripped, and left for dead. Shanna Wagner deserves justice—and there's no better cop than Lieutenant Jake Carrington to find her killer. The brutality of the crime reminds Jake of his sister's murder seventeen years ago, and the remorseless man responsible, now up for parole.

Then another woman is killed—and Jake goes dangerously close to the edge. He'll have to face his personal demons and focus his formidable skills if he hopes to stop a vicious murderer from striking again—and hold on to his career, and his life . . .

Visit us at www.kensingtonbooks.com

Books by Marian Lanouette

Jake Carrington Thrillers
All the Deadly Lies

Published by Kensington Publishing Corporation

All the Deadly Lies

A Jake Carrington Thriller

Marian Lanouette

LYRICAL PRESS
Kensington Publishing Corp.
www.kensingtonbooks.com

First Electronic Edition: February 2018
eISBN-13: 978-1-5161-0475-8
eISBN-10: 1-5161-0475-7

First Print Edition: February 2018
ISBN-13: 978-1-5161-0476-5
ISBN-10: 1-5161-0476-5

Printed in the United States of America

This book is dedicated to my husband Alan
for his continued love, support, and unshakable belief in my talent.

I couldn't have done this without you.

Chapter 1

"Sergeant, in my office, please." Captain Shamus McGuire stood at attention in his doorway, all six-feet-four inches of him. His steel-gray hair cut to military precision focused one's attention on his matching gray eyes.

Homicide Sergeant Jake Carrington of the Wilkesbury Police Department looked across his joined desk to his partner, and lifelong friend Louie Romanelli and shrugged. Louie threw him a questioning look as he adjusted his tie and started to rise from his chair.

"Just Jake, Louie," the captain said as he turned into his office.

Jake picked up their latest case file to update the captain and walked in to join McGuire.

"Take a seat, Jake." The captain pointed to one of the two institutional-gray ones in front of his desk. He took off his glasses and massaged his forehead.

Though Jake preferred to stand, he took the less beat-up seat on the right. The room was a monument to the man, all spit and polish. Sparse furnishing with a few awards and medals hung on the walls. Paperwork in precise piles, a picture of his family, the standard computer and phone were all he had on his desk. McGuire's appearance and stance spoke of his military background and warned his cops he took no crap from them. It wasn't like him to stall but that's exactly what he was doing at the moment. McGuire turned his smoky eyes on him. Jake went on alert. Something was up, something big.

"Captain?" Instincts had Jake bracing for what came next.

"Spaulding's coming up for parole again. And this time he's requesting a DNA test before he comes before the board." Jake's stomach curdled. McGuire continued, "He's also requesting the DNA samples from your sister's crime scene be tested against his sample."

"What bullshit, Shamus."

Jake jumped up, roamed the office. His mouth went dry. Deep down he was afraid the old samples somehow wouldn't match and would set Eva's killer free. This new development would split his attention. What could Spaulding gain from this maneuver? To catch a killer, you had to get inside his head. Did Spaulding assume the system would release him if he got a new trial?

He looked out the window and studied the downtown area as he ran every scenario through his mind. This was his town, though imperfect as it was. He and Eva had been born here of immigrant parents. Its one hundred thousand residents depended on him and those who had come before him to protect it.

Outside of his tour of military duty overseas he didn't venture far from it, a good city, though down on its luck since all the manufacturing jobs went overseas. Wilkesbury recently had the distinguished honor to be named one of the top five saddest rust belt cities. And it's the one that was farthest south of the belt. In its glory days, nothing could touch Wilkesbury. Most of the crime in the city came from the twenty percent of the Wilkesburians living under the national poverty level. The city had its mix of people, businesses, homeless, shoppers, and kids. More kids claimed the downtown area since UConn had put a branch right across the street from the station. Today some of the kids wore shorts to celebrate the hot weather. Last week it was in the forties. Today the temperatures hit the seventies. *New England, you gotta love it*, he thought.

Clearing his mind, he focused on The Palace Marquee. Next month Johnny Mathis would be here for two days. He thought it a monument to the citizens of Wilkesbury when private citizens and businesses raised the money to save the Palace. It had been closed for eighteen years. The last performer had been Tony Bennett in 1987. Bennett had opened the newly restored theater in 2004 and it was still going strong. Jake loved the old theater. It brought back good memories from his childhood. The grand old theater done in the tradition of the Met was a step back in time. Since it had been refurbished it drew some big-name performers and plays. *It's about time we got something decent in the downtown area,* he thought. Murders were down in recent years but overall crime continued. Eva's death was the reason he became a cop instead of going on to play pro ball after college.

Turning from the window, he walked back to stand in front of Shamus's desk. "I'm sorry, I didn't hear the last part," Jake said.

"The sperm gathered at the time of the autopsy was preserved, and with new technology he has the right to ask for the testing."

"When will it happen? I want to be there through the whole process from collection to testing to make sure there aren't any switch-ups." *What a way to start a Monday.*

"It hasn't been granted yet. His lawyer is working on the request," McGuire stated.

"When will it happen?" Jake rubbed his temples where a headache was forming.

"The board acts in their own time. I'd say toward the end of the month. I'm behind you, as is the entire department, Jake, to make sure Eva gets justice."

Jake paced the room. Seventeen years and it seemed like yesterday. "When they took him out after the trial, Spaulding whispered to me he'd done it and enjoyed every moment of it," Jake said. It was a moment in time he would never forget.

There were nights after the trial he dreamed up ways of killing Spaulding, making him suffer as much, if not more, than Eva had. Even today, when his moral code screamed there was no justification for taking a life, he understood deep down in his soul that, if given the chance, he'd remove George Spaulding from the face of this Earth and not look back. Captain McGuire's voice floated back into his head. Jake felt shame standing in front of Shamus with thoughts of murder in his head. If he did kill, what would separate him from the ones he hunted every day of his life?

"As a cop, you and I both understand the evidence is what convicts, along with a smart prosecutor. Spaulding's lawyer has petitioned the court. Even if the DNA isn't a match, it wouldn't get him an immediate release. There was other evidence putting him at the crime scene. And there was an eyewitness who saw him push Eva into his car. All it will get him is a new trial. If I remember this right, all of the evidence pointed to him. Have faith, Jake."

"Faith? Is that what I should tell Eva? Oh wait. I can't. Because she's dead!"

The captain ignored his outburst. "If he goes to trial I promise we'll reopen the case and work it along with our current files. But, you can't touch the file when we do."

"That's bullshit."

"No, it's not. If we want the chain of evidence to remain pure you can't touch it. I'll respect and appoint whoever you want to work it," McGuire said.

"Louie."

"It can't be him either." McGuire held up his hands before Jake could interrupt him. "He's too close to you."

"What's not to say any of the men in my department aren't too close to me?"

"Whoever you pick will have a state trooper working with him."

"You don't trust your own men?" Aggrieved, Jake threw up his hands. "Do you want answers?"

"Shamus, I already got my answer. I've no doubt Spaulding is guilty," Jake said.

"Then this is the best way to handle it. When we catch the killer, it will ensure a conviction," Shamus said.

Jake pushed a hand through his hair. The air thinned, cutting off his next breath. "I need to get out of here."

He rushed from McGuire's office. At his desk Jake grabbed his car keys and ignored Louie's questions. He didn't trust himself to speak. The pit of his stomach burned. What if the DNA didn't match Spaulding's? Damn, he wanted to punch something. No, not something. He wanted to punch out Spaulding.

I swear if they release him—I'll—I'll kill him.

"Jake, wait up." Louie Romanelli followed him out of the bullpen.

"Not now." Jake kept walking.

Louie caught up to him and grabbed his arm as he would a suspect and twirled him around. If he wanted to, Jake could've decked him. They were evenly matched in height and weight. Instead, he stood rigid. "Talk to me," Louie said.

"Give me a couple of hours to pull myself together. We'll meet at my house later if you can. In the meantime, work the Wagner case. I'd hate not to give the Wagners the answers they need." He didn't bother to mention the case was similar to Eva's that, he too needed the closure.

"Tell me what's wrong. Did McGuire fire you?" Louie's olive complexion whitened as he asked the question. His dark eyes searched Jake's face for an answer.

Leave it to Louie. For the first time in over a half hour, he laughed. "No, I'm not fired. Spaulding's up for parole again and has requested new testing."

He stared down his friend as Louie processed the information. If it wasn't for Louie and his family during the weeks and months that followed Eva's death, he wouldn't be standing here today.

How different we are, Jake thought. Louie, married for seventeen years to his grade-school sweetheart, now had three kids. He, on the other hand, liked being single. Side by side, though they matched each other in height, his skin tone paled next to Louie's dark Italian coloring.

"Shit."

"Go back to work. I'll talk to you later."

Jake walked away with his head down and his mind spinning out in every direction. No matter what Shamus said, he owed it to Eva to find the answers.

It's my fault she died.

* * * *

Louie checked the time. It was gonna be a tall order keeping Jake focused if Spaulding was released. McGuire beckoned him from his doorway as Louie reached for the Wagner file.

"Stay with Jake, he needs a friend right now."

"Cap, I'm meeting him at his house in a couple of hours. You want to fill me in?"

"Spaulding will come in front of the board sometime in late summer or early fall. The test results could make it sooner. It will depend on the lab's current and backlog caseloads," McGuire said.

"I got that from Jake. What aren't you telling me?" Louie asked.

"Spaulding's sure the results will clear him. He wants a new trial, an acquittal, this way he won't ever be tried again for the crime."

"It doesn't mean he'll get it." Louie ran a hand through his hair as he outlined the possibilities of Spaulding being set free.

"No, it doesn't. But a lot of prisoners have gone free with no DNA match, no matter what the other evidence against them was. Lawyers are now holding court in the press."

"If the case is reopened, who are you going to appoint to the case?"

"I'm not jumping the gun, but if it comes to it, Burke and Kraus."

* * * *

This time of day the bullpen came alive with activity. Criminals locked to chairs complained of their innocence or wrestled to free themselves. Some spit or let loose other bodily functions as revenge for getting caught. Victims cried, reliving their horror as they gave their accounts of events. Nervous witnesses sat waiting their turns to speak. In the midst of all the activities, Louie tried to concentrate on the Wagner file, but kept coming back to Jake and that horrible time in their lives.

Since they were ten, he and Jake had been as close as brothers. In fact, he was closer to Jake than to his own brother. Their lives had become a nightmare when Eva had been killed. Nothing he'd done had helped Jake deal with the tragedy. The only thing he had been able to do was be there for him. The helpless feeling overwhelmed him again. One event had changed many lives. What was he going to say to Jake? *Maybe I should ask Sophia to come with me? Nah, Jake would feel like we're ganging up on him.*

Louie picked up the Wagner file. A thick one with no answers, little evidence, and statements on how wonderful and perfect Shanna was. If they didn't catch a break soon, Shanna Wagner's case would go into the unsolved file. A shadow fell over his desk as he studied the file. Looking up, Louie bit back a curse. *Not her again.* The petite brunette with the sloe eyes stood with hand on hip, waiting on him to look up at her. *Chloe Wagner, the bane of Jake's existence,* Louie thought.

Thank God Jake didn't have to deal with her in his current state of mind. Louie looked around the bullpen as the noise level lowered to a hum. *There's no one nosier than a cop.* Chloe's frequent visits had become louder and more accusing since Jake had dropped her. Louie wondered if the woman had ever cared about her sister. *Oh well, deal with it.*

"How can I help you, Ms. Wagner?"

"I need answers. My parents need answers. When are we going to get them?"

"Your sister's case is being worked every day. But we need new evidence, something to lead us in a new direction. Everything we've investigated has led to dead ends."

"My family's torn apart. My mother checks up on me several times a day to make sure I'm okay. My father walks around in a fog, like he's lost. I'm positive they're heading toward a divorce. You say you can't do anything else? That's a load of crap. You expect your answer will make me go away? Well, it won't. I'll go over your head, Detective," she shouted. The other detectives in the bullpen came to attention and went on alert. Action or gossip, it didn't matter to the detectives as long as it got their adrenaline going.

"Take a seat, Ms. Wagner." Louie pointed to the single torn-up chair on the side of his desk.

Chloe Wagner didn't resemble her sister in looks, personality, or activities. Her five-foot-two-inch frame carried one hundred five pounds. Her almond-shaped eyes, along with her hair, were brown, offsetting a round face and full lips, and all of it wrapped in a bossy, possessive nature. Louie could see her appeal until she opened her mouth. Her personality would be a turnoff for any man, but a man like Jake, with commitment phobia—it had sent him running. He'd dumped her within a month, but for some reason, this one wouldn't let go. It would have been amusing if she wasn't hounding the entire department. Louie understood deep down that Chloe could ruin Jake's career. He never should've dated her while the investigation was going on, but Jake had ignored the rules. The decision seemed to be coming back to bite Jake on the ass ever since. Though they cleared her, Chloe was still a suspect.

Louie repeated himself. Maybe this time it would get through. "Ms. Wagner, we explained it all last week. We're working the file. Shanna is not forgotten." He picked up the file and held it out with Shanna's name facing Chloe. "We haven't given up."

"It's been over two months since she was found."

"We'll be interviewing everyone again. In the heat of the moment people sometimes forget the details. Once they calm down they remember more." He scribbled a number on his pad. A number he and Jake had given her every time she showed up there. "Here's the number to the station's switchboard if you have any further questions."

Chloe was a dog with a bone. "If I don't get answers soon, I'll be going over your heads!" she shouted. She didn't take the paper from his hand but lowered her voice. "Where's Jake?"

"He's out on another case. What else can I do for you?"

"Why's he not returning my phone calls?"

Her anger directed at Jake belonged to the killer. "I have no idea. You'll need to discuss it with him."

He stood, dismissing her as he started to walk her toward the door. "I would if he'd answer his freakin' phone," Chloe said in a huff.

"I don't get involved in his personal life, Ms. Wagner. I'll tell him you stopped by."

* * * *

Before he headed home, Jake walked around the downtown area hoping the distraction would clear his head. The weather for April suited him. It was said, if you didn't like the weather in New England, you only had to wait five minutes for it to change. *And that was no folktale*, he thought. The sixty-degree temperatures were a gift this time of year. Last week there was frost, this week heat. A mild breeze ruffled his auburn hair, the promise of summer in the air. *I was looking forward to summer and the outdoor activities until McGuire dropped his damn bomb.* He passed the new modern courthouse on Meadow Street. Smokers puffed away outside the building. The courthouse stood out against the nineteen-thirties architecture of the other municipal buildings lining the street. The size of the city suited him. One hundred thousand-plus residents made it a city, but kept the small-town attitudes and feelings alive.

His lanky stride ate up the sidewalk as he headed down Grand Street toward the federal building, which housed the main post office and other federal divisions. *Son of a gun, it isn't my day.* As he walked past city hall, Wilkesbury's idiot mayor, along with his entourage, stepped in front of him.

The Honorable John Velky sucked in his gut and puffed out his chest like he always did when he met up with him. Jake found it amusing most days. The mayor, with his styled brown hair and expensive suits, was a true politician. He kissed babies one moment and overtaxed their parents the next. Jake had never voted for him.

"You don't have anything better to do then stroll around town, Lieutenant?" Mayor Velky asked.

"Good morning, Mayor." It took all his control to be polite, as he tried to walk away. *Today isn't a good day to get in a pissing match with the mayor. It might cost me my career.*

Jake studied the quote over the doors of city hall as he tuned out the mayor. *Quid Aere Perennius.* The meaning was something you were taught in local schools. His father, as an immigrant and Wilkesbury cop, had him and Eva studying the history of Wilkesbury, "The Brass Capital of the World" in its heyday. Translated from Latin it meant, "What is More Lasting Than Brass?" He forced his attention back to the mayor.

"I'll be at the station this week in discussions with the commissioner," Mayor Velky said before walking away, leaving Jake baffled. He watched Velky jump into the back of the town car. *It takes all kinds*, he thought. His mind drifted back to Eva. A girl he would never see beyond her fifteen years, thanks to Spaulding.

* * * *

At home, Jake rummaged through his basement, searching for his father's records. *Why now?* He couldn't get the question out of his head. What did Spaulding and his lawyer hope to achieve with the new testing? Every couple of years he was subjected to this torment. And every couple of years he gathered his strength to face down the parole board with his gruesome evidence. The pictures of the crime scene, along with Eva's bruised and bloody body, gave them many reasons to deny Spaulding's request. His father had kept a copy of Eva's case file at home since he wasn't allowed to work it. The other detectives made sure he had every bit of evidence he needed. It was one of their own who'd been victimized. Nobody messed with a cop's family and got away with it. *Except maybe this time*, he thought as he rubbed his throbbing head. Had George Spaulding found a way to cheat the system? It couldn't be true after seventeen years that they had imprisoned the wrong man. If it was true, then who had killed his sister Eva? Jake couldn't wrap his mind around it.

No, it was George.

The fifth box he opened was dedicated to her case. On top, his father had marked it one of five. After hunting down the other boxes, he brought them upstairs and placed them in his office. The first box he opened sent him right back to hell and his first visit to the morgue. It was the year he had lost his innocence.

A buzzing rang out in his ears from the fluorescent lights overhead. The starkness of the corridor as their footsteps echoed in the silence created the crescendo of a day gone horribly wrong. The buzzing grew louder as they approached the door. The medical examiner, Doctor Ed Jerome, put his hand up to stop them.

Taking a deep breath, Doc Jerome said, "James, you've done this a hundred times, but this is different. I can make the identification for you."

"No, I need to do this, Ed," Captain James Carrington said.

"Okay. Why doesn't Jake wait out here?" Doctor Jerome offered, giving him an out.

He spoke up, his voice louder than intended. "I'm going in." He said it with such force it brooked no argument.

Ed pushed open the door.

On the table lay a body covered with a white sheet. Ed's assistants had set the victim up for viewing. There was no way to hide the odor of death, though they tried to camouflage it with disinfectant, air fresheners, and Clorox. "The house of death" is what the cops called it.

Jake inhaled as he looked to his father for support. His father, a tall man, who Jake favored in height only, squared his shoulders and nodded to the M.E.

"Show me," James demanded.

Doc Jerome pulled back the sheet to reveal a girl in her mid-teens, black and blue from head to toe, the violent trauma of death etched in her horrified expression. Fright forever pasted on her face.

"Was she raped?" James asked, while tears escaped his eyes.

"Yes," Doc Jerome said.

Neither man paid attention to Jake's weeping at their side. He couldn't stop as he viewed his younger sister. With a gentle caress, he touched her forehead, her cheek, then kissed her good-bye on the lips.

He turned away in grief, saw both his anger and his pain reflected in his father's face. His father's fists clenched, his shoulders racked with heavy sobs as he viewed the broken body of his daughter. Jake understood he looked with a father's eye, not a cop's.

"My baby," James cried.

Jake listened every night at dinner when his father spoke of his cases. It was something distant, stories that didn't touch his life. Until now.

The buzzing in his ears increased. Time and space slipped by, then someone held a glass of water to his lips. The stress of the situation had overtaken him—he'd collapsed on the floor.

"I'm sorry, Jake. I shouldn't have brought you here." James hugged him, crushing him to his chest.

"I'm fine, Dad. When you catch the bastard, I'm going to kill him for what he did to Eva. You need to know I'll do it."

It was the first time he'd ever cursed in front of his father.

It took every ounce of strength within him to pull himself out of the memory. A fist squeezed his heart. He couldn't do this alone. God, he needed a drink. No, he needed Louie.

After a couple of hours, Jake decided to go back to work. Until a new trial came to fruition, he'd continue to line up the info on the case if and when they needed the ammunition to get a second conviction on Spaulding. He'd have it ready. Tonight, he would lay out a strategy and organize the files as he would for any other case he worked.

* * * *

News traveled fast in a cop shop. Among curious glances thrown his way, or comments of support from his detectives in the bullpen, Jake ignored them all. He took a seat at his desk across from Louie. His friend eyeballed him but didn't comment, which Jake found out of character for him. The Wagner file he wanted to review wasn't in his desk drawer.

"You got the Wagner file?"

"Yes." Louie gathered the papers spread across his desk, placed them back in the file, closed it and handed the bulk of it to Jake.

As he took the file from Louie, Jake studied his partner and his messy desk. The finicky Louie didn't match up with how he maintained his area. His suits pressed, his pants creased to razor sharpness, along with his precisely knotted tie and styled black hair, were at odds with the mess on his desk.

He wondered how Louie worked with all the clutter. Jake kept a phone and computer on his desk. All his files were in the desk drawer, alphabetized for easy access. Louie had all his files on top, an in-and-out box, an empty coffee cup and this morning's wrapper from his breakfast sandwich. *A cluttered desk would clog up my mind*, Jake thought as he opened the file. Pushing Eva's case to the back burner, he tried to concentrate on Shanna's.

"Are you free tonight to throw a couple of things around?"

"Yep."

"We'll do it at my house after we get out of here. I'm going to suggest to McGuire that Burke and Kraus work Eva's case if Spaulding gets a new trial," Jake said.

"I agree."

"I'll need to tell him. And I don't care what he said. I need to be in on the briefing. I'll be right back."

Jake got up and walked into McGuire's office without knocking. "Shamus, give the case to Burke and Kraus. When the time comes, I'd like to be in on the initial meeting in case they have questions."

"I'll need them to come at it with fresh eyes, Jake, not with your preconceived notions."

"I'm not going to offer personal opinions. The file will speak for itself. No one is more familiar with it than me."

McGuire checked his calendar. "We might as well get ahead of this. Set it up in Conference Room One for three o'clock on Wednesday afternoon. I want to refamiliarize myself with the file and also give Burke and Kraus time to do the same. And Jake? I'm still in charge here." Jake took the mild slap on the wrist without comment.

After reserving the conference room, he left it up to the captain to speak with Burke and Kraus. All day he tried to keep his mind off Eva's case while he dug into Shanna Wagner's file and rearranged the contents to coincide with the timeline as they understood it.

"I'll let you catch up before I give you my thoughts on this." Louie scratched his head. "Chloe Wagner stopped in to see you."

"Shit." Jake blew out a breath.

"Yeah, she asked a few questions about her sister, but she seemed more concerned about you ignoring her calls."

He'd been an idiot to date her in the first place. Right from the beginning, he handled her wrong and now he was paying for it. Never before had he disregarded a regulation. *Ha, the one time I do and it's a catastrophe.* An indiscretion like this could cost him his career. He'd been flattered by the way she had pursued him. Her pretty girl-next-door looks fooled him. No matter where he turned, restaurants, bars, the grocery store, Chloe was there. Alarms should've sounded. What a fool he'd been. On the second date, she had insisted on bringing dinner to his house. Before he had a chance to open the cartons of takeout she was on him. He should've kicked her out then. Instead he took what she had to offer. Afterward when they lounged in bed, Chloe had started to talk of the future. She stressed how they both had dealt with death at an early age and understood it was important to live for today because there might not be a tomorrow. Before she had finished her sentence, he had her dressed and out the door. She had scared the living hell out of him. No way had he led her on about commitments and forever.

When she called the next day, he ended the relationship over the phone. In hindsight, maybe he should've done it after a third date, not the morning after, but the woman had shopped for a damn ring, for God's sake. After he broke it off, he decided to keep a journal of the times she had showed up at a place where he was dining or drinking. It went from flattering to creepy, fast. She seemed to have arrived at a place even before he made plans to be there. "Cripes, dating her was a mistake. What did you tell her?"

"I told her I don't get involved in your personal affairs."

"Oh please! I can't get you out of my personal life. There's something off with her. Did you feel it?"

"No," Louie said, wiping the grin off his face.

"Well I did, when I was with her. We should have taken a closer look at her sooner."

"You can't miss what's not there, Jake."

"I'm hoping we did. Otherwise we have nothing. Let's put everyone back on the suspect list and start over."

With fresh eyes, Jake studied the crime scene photos first. Once or twice he caught himself comparing them to Eva's wounds. It was difficult, but he forced himself to remain in the present. Such brutality in most cases meant the victim knew her killer. Somewhere along the line, Shanna had pissed off someone and paid the ultimate price. The question was who had she angered? *Rage,* Jake thought. The crime scene photos exhibited uncontrollable rage.

Everyone they had interviewed stated Shanna was well liked with no enemies. An ambitious woman, she was first in her class, a scholarship athlete like himself, and she had held down a job while attending college. Had she set off a competitor? Could her achievements be the foundation for jealousy? Eliminate her, eliminate the rivalry? Shanna had interned with an accounting firm who had offered her a job a year before she'd even graduated.

No steady relationships. Shanna had dated one person in the six-month period prior to her death. He was another accountant at the firm where she had interned. According to her family she hadn't dated often because she had been goal orientated. Maybe it was a guy she turned down and his ego couldn't handle it. But it seemed farfetched.

"Do you remember this Cavilla guy? The one she dated," Jake said.

"Yeah, he seemed a little old for her. Why?"

"The answers lie in the rage; this kind of violence suggests a scorned lover or wanna-be lover to me."

"We looked at him but nothing popped," Louie said.

"We did, but let's relook at his alibi."

"Got something?"

"No."

Jake dug around in the file until he unearthed the information on the boyfriend. Mark Cavilla, at five-nine, weighed about one hundred fifty pounds. He had black hair, black eyes, and a black temper to go with it.

"Your notes say his answers seemed rehearsed at the time. What else do you remember about him?"

"His statement seemed off and he had an attitude right from the beginning," Louie stated.

"He was alibied by the bartender at a bar less than two miles from the scene. I always believed the killer was a local guy since she was dumped in town even though she was supposed to be up at school in Storrs at the time of the killing. It's a long way to travel to dump a body unless you're familiar with the area and that particular construction site. They picked well. No one would be around a construction site at night. I want to re-interview the bartender before too much time goes by. Okay, what else...?" Jake's head snapped up.

A couple of his detectives were going at it. Amused, Jake listened in. He didn't do anything about them. These things tended to work themselves out if left alone.

"What was I going to say?"

"Christ, Carrington, can't you read without your lips moving? I'm trying to concentrate here," Burke yelled.

Al Burke had his moments. A detective in the department for over ten years, he'd seen it all. Fifteen years a cop and his face showed it. He wouldn't consider him attractive, with his hard eyes, the stomach the size of Jupiter, and a Rudolph-red nose from drinking. Jake figured Burke had a few more years on the job before it crushed him. The guy'd been divorced three times, and produced five children. A heavy drinker, he could turn on a dime, but his investigative skills were prime. He had no problems going through a door with Burke.

"Al, how'd you get the black eye?" Jake asked with a wide grin on his face. He knew, but he wanted Al to say it out loud.

"Shut up. Everyone, shut up," Burke said, walking toward the coffee machine.

"A ninety-year-old woman landed a punch when his guard was down," Kraus, Burke's partner, said.

"I'm warning you, Kraus. Shut up." Burke slammed down his coffee cup. "You guys don't know the half of it."

Laughing, Detective Gunther "Gunner" Kraus continued, "To his credit, Sarge, she was like a pit bull."

"I'll say mean." Burke took over the story as he yanked up his pants and tightened his belt. "Never mind like one, she was. I got away easy. You should have seen what she did to her poor husband. Carved him like a roast because he complained about her smoking. Her freakin' smoking? I thought those things were supposed to kill you. She's ninety freaking years old. What I saw today, she'll last another ten years, if a day. I feel sorry for her cellmate. Her poor sliced-up husband lived with the witch for seventy-five years. Me, I would have killed myself around year two."

"We can help. What's your choice of weapons, Al?" Louie threw in to bait him.

"Funny. I'm breaking my stitches on that one, Romanelli."

Movement to the side of Jake pulled him from the banter between his detectives. McGuire stood in his doorway with his arms folded over his chest as he listened in on the conversation.

"Jake, you got a minute?" Shamus asked.

"Sure, what's up?" Twice in one day, he hoped it was better news than this morning.

"We'll talk in my office." McGuire turned and walked in. Jake followed. "Shut the door."

"More bad news on Spaulding?"

"No. The board reviewed your request." *Lord Christ, the man has the best poker face I've ever seen.*

"What's their decision?" Jake braced himself for the news. The way this day was going, it couldn't be good.

"The chief and I feel you're not ready to sit at a desk handling administrative issues. We feel you and the citizens of Wilkesbury will be happier and better served with you on the streets with Louie," McGuire said.

With his stomach sinking to his knees, he asked, "Did the board review any other items on their agenda?"

McGuire stared him down for a second before he stuck out his hand. "Congratulations, Lieutenant! You've earned it, Jake. This division is yours, if you still want it."

"I do." He'd been apprehensive when he took the exam. If he passed he wasn't guaranteed homicide. The brass would put him where they felt he was needed. This was a gift.

"You're a credit to this department and the city. The ceremony will take place at the mayor's office on the twenty-fifth at noon. Congratulations again."

"Thank you, sir. I'm sure we'll go out for a couple of beers to celebrate. Join us?"

"I'd love to. Instead I'll be sitting in a hot, sweaty room, waiting for my child to dance, applauding like I'm at a Broadway show. Boys are much easier to raise than girls. Think of me when you lift your glass. I've never had a better officer on my team than you, Jake."

Those recitals could take hours. Louie once guilted him into one of Marisa's, and as her godfather, he'd had no choice but to say yes. Every year after that he made damn sure he had plans. He washed the horrific memory of it out of his head.

Ignoring Louie's finger tapping when he returned to his desk, Jake picked up the Wagner file and started to read.

"Okay, what gives? What did the captain want this time?"

"That's Lieutenant to you, Detective."

Louie jumped up. He pulled Jake into his arms for a hug instead of giving him a handshake. "Well this calls for a real celebration. Hey, Burke, Sergeant Carrington is now your Lieutenant. He's the head cheese of homicide. Hot damn!"

Louie threw a couple air punches. Jake hoped Louie's test results were positive this time around. It killed Louie when he'd failed the sergeant's test not once but twice. But maybe the third time around was the charm. He wondered why Louie's face didn't split in half with such a wide grin on it.

Cops swarmed Jake's desk from all divisions.

Louie tapped him on the shoulder. "Captain wants to see you again."

Jake broke away from the crowd. "Yeah, Cap?"

"The title comes with an office. Pick one out as soon as possible."

McGuire came around his desk with his briefcase in his hand. He patted Jake on the back, then turned off his office light and left.

How would this promotion affect the dynamics between him and Louie? *What a day. First the news about Spaulding and now he'd been promoted.* He couldn't figure out if he wanted to celebrate or punch someone out.

"This is great, because you're already coming to dinner. Oh, but weren't we going to review your files?"

"They can wait until tomorrow night, Louie. We cancel the celebration now, Burke would stone us."

"Okay, we celebrate and then have dinner with Sophia and the kids. I'll call her now. Have her make a great dessert." Louie's face gleamed.

"Thanks, Louie."

That night, when he got home, he'd try to get through the files on his own. The words his father had spoken to him on the day of his promotion to detective echoed in his head.

"With command comes great responsibility, son. Treat your officers the way you'd want to be treated." Then Captain James Carrington pinned the new gold shield onto Jake's dress uniform. Pride shone in his father's eyes as he saluted him. Days later his father died of a heart attack.

Jake felt his father had died of a broken heart.

With his father gone, Jake had one close relative this side of the ocean, his mother. The rest resided in Ireland, where his parents were from. She hated his job. He thought better of sharing his news with her.

Though unrelated, his mom felt his sister's death had resulted from her husband's job. Not logical. A spoiled kid had ruined their lives. Eva had turned him down. He had taken what he'd wanted anyway, punishing her for rejecting him.

Thoughts of his mother surged into his head and brought on the familiar guilt. Jake promised himself he'd visit her this week. Cripes, he hated walking into the nursing home. The odors assaulted his olfactory senses. He always held his breath until he reached his mother's room. The crying and begging from the residents as they reached out to him when he walked by tore at his heart. He tried not to rush by them. He hoped to God he never wound up there. In his opinion, a bullet to the head would be better.

His beautiful mother had brownish-red hair, cream-colored flawless skin, high cheekbones, and sad emerald eyes. She had forgotten how to live after Eva died. He got his height from his father, but his coloring from his mother. At five-six Maddie packed quite a punch when her temper flared. It wasn't something you wanted to be on the receiving end of. Now trapped in the past, his mother lay in bed all day, crying, telling stories about her Eva through her tears. Jake wondered why she hadn't run out of them.

We lost two people on the day Eva died. My mother blamed me. She blamed my father. She blamed the police, the school—and anyone else who popped into her head . . . Something snapped in her brain on the day Eva died. He didn't understand if she couldn't or wouldn't move forward. *A tight family unit, once happy—never the same after that day,* he thought. *We all loved each other, and were looking forward to the bright future ahead of us. Yes, I'll visit her tomorrow.*

Louie touched his arm, brought him back to the present. "Hey, you in there? Let's head out now." Louie grabbed his jacket off the back of his chair. "Oh, boss . . ."

"Funny, Louie. What?"

"First round's on me. I want everyone to know I'm playing up to the new boss. Got it?"

"Oh, Louie—rounds two, plus three and four, are also on you," Jake said shrugging into his jacket.

Maybe he'd take tonight off before he immersed himself in Eva's file. God, he'd need to get a boatload of courage before he ran through it all.

Chapter 2

Four hours later, he and Louie walked in Louie's front door, smashed to the gills, their arms wrapped around each other's shoulders as they laughed like loons. Sophia, Louie's beautiful wife, was not amused and told them in no uncertain terms. Jake tried to focus.

"Where have the two of you been?" she asked, flipping her long curly brown hair over her shoulder as she approached Louie with a wooden spoon in her hand. "You stink! What have you been drinking? Why have you been drinking?"

"Does she always talk in riddles?" Jake tilted his head down to focus on Sophia. Her brown eyes hadn't an ounce of tolerance in them.

"I never noticed. I can't get past the beauty," Louie slurred. "Isn't she voluptuous?"

Jake pleaded the fifth.

"Louie, I'm counting to three—I want answers. This is disgraceful. The children can't see you like this. And you, Jake, you should be ashamed of yourself, getting him drunk." She hit him on the arm. "You know he can't hold his liquor."

"Ouch! It wasn't me, he got me drunk. We went for a drink or two to celebrate with the other guys. We tried to leave an hour ago, but they wouldn't let us. Well, one drink led to another, and now we're here."

"Lucky me, here you are. Give me your keys, Jake. Who drove you home?"

Concentrate your anger on Louie. This is why I'm not married.

"I love you. You're sexy when you're mad," Louie said, losing his balance as he leaned in for a kiss.

Jake laughed and grabbed Louie, almost over balancing them both when Sophia rolled her eyes and pushed Louie away. At five-four Sophia's temper could pack a punch. "Jake, who drove the both of you home?" she asked again, guiding them into the kitchen. The table was set for two.

"I need your pasta, Sophia, before I can answer. I'm sure it was one of the uniforms." He scratched his head and swayed.

"Good. Sit down."

She dished out penne topped with sauce and cheese onto a plate with the wooden spoon in her hand.

"Sophia, go easy on him, please."

"Mind your own business and eat, Jake. You're staying here tonight."

"Won't Louie get upset? When did I start turning you on?" He put his hands up to avoid her slap.

"You idiot! You're on the couch, Louie's in the bed. Or maybe I should make him sleep on the couch with you."

Louie lifted his head from the table. "I'm home. When's dinner?" he asked, dropping his head down and banging it on the table.

Tomorrow he'll have quite the bump, Jake thought.

"Help me get him upstairs. He's gone."

"Sophia, we don't do this often."

"You're missing the point, Jake. I'm not used to the two of you like this. Drinking on empty stomachs wasn't smart. How could you be so stupid? And be quiet, the kids are doing their homework in their rooms. I don't want them to see him, or you, in this condition."

Louie wrapped his arm around Sophia's waist as they headed upstairs. "I love you, more than anything."

He's getting sloppy, Jake thought.

"Yes, Louie, I know."

"Want to make love?"

"You're a piece of work. Yes, but not tonight. You're going to bed, to sleep, walk."

"You sure? I'm excellent in the sack and you're—"

She cut him off with a hand over his mouth.

Jake couldn't help himself. He started laughing and almost lost his balance again. His head spun as he tried to straighten up.

"What are you laughing at? Be quiet." She punched his arm. "Idiots."

Jake kept his mouth shut. After helping to put Louie to bed, he went to the study, pulled the drapes shut and lay down. Once on the couch, he passed out without another thought.

* * * *

At dawn, gray shadows swirled around the room from the one curtain Jake had forgotten to pull closed last night. Disoriented, he rolled over in search of his watch and found it on his wrist. He tried to sit up, but crashed back down, covering his eyes as millions of tiny lights exploded in his head. Damn, his whole body ached from sleeping on the lumpy couch. He tried one more time to sit up without his head exploding—then jumped when two sets of brown eyes greeted him. Where the hell was he?

"How come you're here, Uncle Jake?" Marisa asked.

Muscles tightened then relaxed as his eyes searched the room and landed on the familiar. *I'm at Louie's. Christ, my head hurts.* It was a blessing the drapes were drawn on most of the windows, otherwise he'd go blind. As it was, the little bit of light filtering through them could kill a man.

"I had a late night with your father. Instead of going home, I slept here."

"It wouldn't have anything to do with you and Daddy drinking, would it?" she asked, twirling a strand of hair around her finger.

Why couldn't they leave him alone? The kids had left the door to the den open when they'd intruded on his sleep. He heard Sophia banging dishes around in the kitchen. Jake wondered if she banged them on purpose. With each clash, his head felt as though a snare drum was vibrating through his skull.

"I heard you guys come in last night. You were funny. But Mom didn't think so," she continued. "She's still kind of pissed off."

"Come on, Marisa. Leave him alone. Uncle Jake looks sick," Carmen said.

"Thanks, Carmen. I could use another hour. Why aren't you guys in school?"

Marisa answered. "Because it's six o'clock in the morning and school doesn't start for another two hours. We always come down for breakfast at this time." As with any thirteen-year-old, she changed the subject to herself. "Uncle Jake, you're coming to my birthday party, right?"

"When have I ever missed one?" He realized there'd be no more sleep here today.

"You missed the year that guy cut up all those college girls, remember?" Marisa looked at him.

"Marisa, work comes first. I'll be at your party, as long as work doesn't interfere. You're a cop's kid, you should understand that."

"Yeah, but I don't have to like it. My friend Gigi has a crush on you."

"She's twelve, isn't she?"

"Uh-uh, but for some reason, even though you're old, she likes you."

"See what kind of birthday gift I get you."

The minute he shook his head the room flipped upside down. What a mistake that was. He needed to move them along. "I've got to get going. Why don't you guys go into the kitchen? Get breakfast or whatever you do at six o'clock in the morning, I need to get up."

"Carmen, go to the kitchen, I want to talk to Uncle Jake," Marisa said, ignoring Carmen's protests. "Go now, Carmen, or I'll hurt you."

"Oh, all right, but I'm stronger than you are and you don't scare me. And I don't fight women," Carmen said before leaving the room.

"You should be nicer to him, Marisa. Someday he's going to be much bigger than you."

"I need to talk to you alone, Uncle Jake. You have to talk to my parents about me going to this party on Friday. It's an important party. Anyone who counts is going to be there. They'll listen to you. Please?" she said, her eyes pleading with him.

"Marisa, your father told me about the party. I agree with them on this. You're asking for trouble with no adult supervision. Plus, I'm not at the top of your mother's good list right now." He rubbed his aching forehead.

"So, your answer is no? I thought you loved me," she whined.

"I do, but I'm not talking to them about this. Maybe I should tell this kid's parents he's planning on having a wild party while they're away." He studied her.

"You can't, Uncle Jake. Promise me you won't. I wouldn't be able to show my face in school ever again. Please promise?" Marisa begged.

"I'll think about it, now scram."

Sophia walked into the room as Marisa rushed out.

"Aren't you the mean one first thing in the morning? How do you feel today?"

"Crowded."

* * * *

After turning down Sophia's offer of breakfast, Jake drove home to shower and changed before heading to the station. At the threshold of the bullpen, Jake looked around. No one was in any shape to work except the captain. He walked to his desk and started right in on the murder book for Shanna Wagner's case.

"Hey, Lieutenant, you left early last night," Burke shouted from across the room.

"Yep, I left for a special dinner engagement. Sophia served homemade pasta and sauce with fresh baked bread. Who could pass up such a succulent dinner?" Burke looked ill. "She also served homemade tiramisu. The best I've ever tasted, talk about pure nirvana. I had two helpings," he lied.

"God, don't talk food right now, it could get messy. Got any antacids?" Burke asked.

"Amateurs," Jake said, his head pounding like a bass guitar, as he immersed himself in the Wagner file.

The evidence was the evidence was the evidence. He had read this file on and off for the last few weeks. Nothing popped out saying, "Hey, you missed me." But there had to be something they'd missed along the way, some important fact. Yesterday his attention was divided in all directions. Today he'd concentrate on Shanna's murder. Not trusting his emotions or the similarities to Eva's case, Jake decided to start over with no distractions. He had fun last night, but he should have stayed home and worked Eva's file. He'd never forgive himself if Spaulding went free.

Each crime needed new eyes and no preconceived notions. He put everyone back on the suspect list, even the ones he and Louie had cleared. He picked up the crime scene photos and laid them out on his desk. Every insult, every trauma Shanna received was graphically displayed. Kids had discovered her body in the woods at the end of a cul-de-sac of a new housing development. None of the houses had been occupied at the time. The naked body had landed face up. Her clothes never turned up, nor did the item the killer had used to strangle her. The M.E. concluded the deep ligature marks around Shanna's neck was the cause of death. She'd been sexually assaulted—severe bruising in and around the genitals. Doctor Lang estimated the rape had been committed with a long, hard stick due to the severity of the bruising. No semen was found in or around the body. The killer must've used protection, if he did penetrate her. Rolled, not placed, Jake remembered. She'd been in the field about four days according to the M.E. There were no fibers under her nails. He figured the scratches on the torso and the face were caused when she was rolled down the short embankment. Trace didn't find any skin or hair other than the victim's. No fibers were found near the body. No jewelry left on the victim, a fact that had always bothered him. The killer had tried to make it look as if a robbery had gone bad. The perp had left Shanna with nothing.

He wrote down new questions. *Was it a crime of passion or jealousy or a robbery gone bad? Why take the jewelry? Was it an afterthought? Did he try to conceal her identity? Why, to delay identification, to humiliate, or both? One killer or two?* He and Louie always assumed one. *Why not dump her further into the field to make it more difficult to find her? Was the killer not strong enough to carry her far?* On his list of things to recheck first he listed pawn shops. He'd redistribute the pictures of the missing jewelry. Maybe by some miracle of God some of it had showed up and a careless clerk didn't report it. *Did the killer take the emerald ring and other items as a souvenir or for their value?*

The emerald ring, an heirloom passed down from grandmother to granddaughter for generations, Shanna never took it off, according to family members. Valued at fifty thousand dollars, the ring alone provided a motive. Every day, she had worn a gold cross with a diamond in the center, and a name bracelet her sister Chloe had given her for her birthday. Earrings she had varied with her outfits. Two of the three items would have made identification easy, even if they hadn't had fingerprints and dental records.

He made a note to ask Mrs. Wagner what, if anything, Chloe had received from her grandmother.

Next, he'd redo the timeline for her parents and sister at the time of the murder. Did Shanna and Chloe fight often? Two sisters, close in age, each unique. Their coloring differed, as did their personalities, friends, and interests. Did they hang out together? Did they share friends? Did they dip into the same dating pool?

Movement at the captain's door caught his eye. With a jerk of his head Shamus called him into his office.

"Tag Louie, there's a body in the trunk of a car at the Chevy dealer off exit 25," McGuire said, handing Jake a sheet of paper with few details. "Oh, and Jake, once you're settled into your office, you'll be assigning the cases."

"Louie won't be in great shape," Jake replied.

"No one in this squad is. How late did you guys stay out last night?"

"I'm not sure. Louie and I got driven home by a uniform. Sophia's pissed. She cooked dinner and we didn't show up. She made me stay on their couch."

McGuire chuckled. "Get him and secure the scene. Here's a list of missing persons. See who fits the description of the person in the trunk."

"Is it a man or a woman?" Jake asked. "I'll have Louie take the lead on this one, while I concentrate on the Wagner case."

"Your call. At this time, we don't have any more information. The salesman who found the body is on the lot throwing up. The manager didn't get much more out of him."

On the way back to his desk, he called Louie.

"How do you feel?"

"Like death warmed over. It's unfortunate but I'll live. I hope you're calling me about a case, because I have to get out of here. If Sophia bangs one more pan I swear..."

"We caught a new case, you're the lead on it. Meet me at the Chevy dealer off exit 25 and I'll fill you in. We should get there at about the same time. You gonna be okay? I don't need you sick when you get there."

"When have I ever been sick on a scene, Jake? Give me a break. What— you gonna bust my balls too?"

He hung up, ignoring Louie's complaint.

* * * *

Jake pulled into the car lot and parked by a group of guys standing around with their hands in their pockets. He drew back his jacket to expose his badge as he walked over to the group.

"Good afternoon, gentlemen, I'm Lieutenant Carrington." *It has such a nice ring,* he thought.

"Hey, Jake, over here." His head snapped up at the use of his first name. *Yep, just like a small town,* he thought. *And crap, Kevin Myers of all people.* He and Myers went through Hogan High School together. The guy lived in the past. Jake made a silent bet with himself that Myers would bring up the state championship game from high school. *Ah, my glory days, long gone and forgotten—so many other things put that trivial period of my life aside.* He should be thankful. The title and his part in winning it gave him a scholarship to UConn, where he played ball, but changed his major to Criminal Justice. Before graduation, he turned down the offer to play pro ball.

He focused his attention back to Myers. Not a violent guy, as he recalled, but people changed. Did Myers? "Kevin, you find the body?"

"No. Mike Murphy did. Hey guys, I want you to meet the man who put Wilkesbury on the map. Remember, Jake?"

"I remember, Kevin. Who did you say found the body?" Jake changed the subject before Myers took him down memory lane. It was another time, another life. One he didn't want to revisit, especially now.

Kevin motioned to a guy standing alone. Pale as a ghost, Murphy didn't approach him. Jake walked over to him, Myers on his tail. "Mike, this is Lieutenant Carrington."

"I don't have to go back over there, do I?" Murphy said, sweat dripping down his face.

"No, you don't. Tell me what you saw and if you touched anything."

"I...smelled something." Murphy ran through it for him. Jake stepped away a little when Murphy finished up. The poor man looked as if he'd lose his stomach contents again.

"Stay here. My partner, Detective Romanelli, will take your statement when he arrives." Jake pointed to the first row of cars where the other salesmen stood, and turned to Kevin. "Can you show me the car? Does it belong on the lot?" Jake asked.

"No, it's not one of ours, though it's parked between two of our cars in the last row."

"This is the first time someone noticed it?" Jake looked over at Kevin.

"I can't say. I didn't notice it. I'll ask the other salesmen if they did," Kevin offered.

"No, don't, Kevin. My partner or I'll ask them. Thanks for your help. This one?" Jake pointed, as he walked up to the car. No mistake. The stench of death never left you once you encountered it. It wasn't something you got used to either. Anyone who said they did, lied. The record-breaking heat for late April didn't help preserve the body or lighten the odor.

Myers nodded.

"Please go wait with the other salespeople. I'll get back to you in a little while." Jake dismissed him.

With the temperatures in the eighties, it would be hard to determine on scene how long the body had been in the trunk. Normal temps for Wilkesbury this time of year should be in the mid-sixties to low seventies. Point in case, last week it was in the forties. If this heat was a prelude to summer, it was going to be a scorcher.

He'd have to wait on the medical examiner for an estimation of TOD—time of death. Someone tapped Jake on the shoulder. Annoyed, he looked up to dismiss Myers again, but it was Louie standing there struggling.

"Man, this is not what I needed today," Louie said, rubbing the back of hand over his mouth, his skin the color of the Grinch.

"Want something to camouflage it?"

"No, it would make matters worse with that smell. Bad enough having to deal with the body." Louie pulled his handkerchief out of his pocket.

In unison, with a rhythm of working together for years, they went about their work. Louie took the pictures. Jake dusted the trunk for fingerprints. Louie bagged the items around the car. Jake bagged her hands, her feet, all the contents of the trunk, and marked the evidence bags. They worked together in a reverence born of experience, each absorbed in their individual tasks, until they hit a stopping point. There was nothing else for them to process until the M.E. did his thing. As he waited, Jake called in the license plate and the make of the car along with the VIN. If he was lucky, it would appear on a missing or stolen vehicle list and narrow down their timeline. The victim looked to be in her fifties with brown hair, and glassy brown eyes now defined by the death stare. It was hard to tell height and weight at this angle. Death stole the rest of a person's life and had leached the color from her skin. A hole in her forehead was mostly likely the cause of death. He leaned in closer to study the bullet wound. A brownish-orange tattooing marred the skin around the wound. The mark resulted when a weapon fired from a slight distance drove the gunpowder, both partially burned and unburned, into her skin. The shooter couldn't have been more than three feet away from the victim. Was it someone she had known? He'd have to wait for the M.E. for more information on the cause of death—COD. The M.E. would fingerprint her again once he got her in the morgue in Farmington.

All autopsies for the state, on suspicious deaths, were performed at the UConn Medical Center, the best facility in the country. He hoped they weren't loaded down. They did have a missing person report on a fifty-three-year-old woman, last seen a week ago Friday. They'd start their search locally, and if nothing turned up, they'd expand it to a statewide search and proceed from there.

Looking up, Jake watched the assistant M.E. approach him. "Hey, McKay."

Assistant Medical Examiner Tim McKay, MD, stood five-ten, and weighed in around a hundred and seventy, with a belly going to pot. At fifty-six, time had thinned McKay's wheat-colored hair, stripping his natural color out and leaving behind more salt than sand. The doc didn't seem to care about the change.

"I hear you're having a busy week, Jake. Second body, isn't it? And I also hear congratulations are in order, Lieutenant." McKay exaggerated the title.

"Thanks, Tim, I'm still getting used to it. Yes, the second one this week. But the first one was an open and shut suicide. This one's all yours. Once you transport her, I'll have the car taken in. I want the lab working on it while you work on her."

"Then I better get started," McKay said.

"Give a shout out if you find an exit wound."

Jake liked Tim McKay. Tim handled the victim in a methodical way along with a gentleness and respect as if she still lived. A survey of the scene while McKay worked told Jake it was a perfect place for a body dump. The area would've been deserted at night—no one would have paid any attention to a car in a car lot. Clever killer.

"I'll call you once the post is done. Give me a couple of hours. By then I should have my initial report ready," McKay said.

"Thanks, Doc. If you could run the fingerprints first for an ID, I'd appreciate it. I'll talk to you later." Jake headed back to the sales personnel to question them.

Louie had already divided them into two groups. There were too many people for Louie to interview alone, though Jake wanted to get back on Shanna's case. She'd have to wait a little longer. He took his group a few feet away from Louie's.

The five salespeople in his group were Michael Murphy, who found the body, Kevin Myers, Craig Nelson, Jimmy Jackson, and Michelle Williams. He started with Michelle Williams.

"Ms. Williams," Jake said. Crime scenes tended to get innocent people babbling. Williams was no exception. The petite brunette in her twenties displayed an abundance of energy.

"I don't see how I can help you," Michelle said.

"Relax, Ms. Williams, this won't take long. I'll ask you a couple of questions now. If I need more after I check out your answers, I'll contact you here for a follow-up interview. If you remember anything after I leave you can call me," Jake said.

"I never saw the car, or smelled anything. I've been on for about three hours. I had no reason to come out here today. I didn't have any customers," Michelle rambled. He tried to keep up with her. "I won't have to go back there, will I?" Michelle asked.

"No. When we identify the victim, one of us will bring a picture of her and show it around to see if anyone recognizes her. It's possible the car was there all week. Are you sure you never noticed it?"

"I'm sure." She wiped at her mouth with a shaky hand.

"You never went to where the car's been parked all week?" Jake asked.

"No."

"Okay, did you work yesterday?"

"Yes, from noon until closing," Michelle said.

"Did you come back here yesterday?"

"I didn't go any farther than the row with the red Impala. I've only had one customer this week." She pointed to a spot four rows before the vehicle with the body. "My customer chose a car and we went into the office to process his paperwork."

"Okay, I'll need your customer's name to verify."

"Can you wait till he signs the rest of his paperwork? This is the first sale I've had this month... I don't want to scare him off." Her brown eyes pleaded with him.

"When are you signing everything?" Jake asked.

Michelle let out a deep breath. "Tonight, at six o'clock."

"Okay, we'll question him tomorrow, please get me the information I asked for." Jake handed her his card and moved on.

He read the list Louie had given him. A rail of a man with a comb-over took his outstretched hand. "Kevin Jones?"

"Yep."

"Man of few words, Kevin?"

"Naw, you haven't asked anything yet that required an answer," Jones said with a shrug.

"When did you come on this morning?"

"Eight o'clock."

"Do you always come in at that time?" Jake scribbled in his notebook.

"Yes, I like to catch the service crowd while they wait for their cars to be fixed, they browse. I sell a lot of cars that way."

"Did you sell any today?" Jake asked.

"No," Kevin said as he looked at what Jake was writing in his notebook.

Jake tilted the book out of his view. "Did you have any reason to come back to the last row today or any other time this week?"

"No, I hadn't been out on the lot today until I heard Michael scream. His customer came running into the office asking for the manager. The rest of the week, I'm not sure. But if I smelled something, I would've investigated it."

"Did you work yesterday?" Jake asked.

"Nope, it was my day off. Six days on, one day off," Kevin finished, rubbing his chin.

"You don't look shaken, Kevin. Are you used to having dead bodies turn up?" Jake gauged his reaction.

"No. At this point, I haven't seen a dead body and I don't care to."

The rest of his interviews went much the same way. He re-interviewed Michael Murphy after he had calmed down but got nothing new from him.

At his car, he and Louie compared notes. Louie had interviewed Cathy Elder, Carl Hannon, Rob Greene, Gino Spino, and Byron Sommers. Jake looked over Louie's list. Louie's interviews mirrored his. Nothing stuck out.

"I need another shower. The air's like soup with this humidity," Louie said, wiping his brow. Jake noticed Louie's color wasn't as green as when he'd first arrived.

Back at the station, they headed into the locker room where they kept another set of clothes and towels and jumped into the showers. Jake made a mental note to replace the items. After his shower, he started the identification process on Jane Doe while Louie processed and tagged the contents from the car the lab boys left behind. Though he wanted to work Shanna's case, a fresh murder always took priority. The first forty-eight hours were critical. He'd need to jump back on the Wagner case when he was finished gathering information on the Adams woman. Luck was on his side—Chelsea's prints popped right up.

A social worker employed by the state, Chelsea Adams, worked in Wilkesbury, lived in Southington. Jake pulled her picture from her state ID. An attractive woman—brown hair, brown eyes, five-six, her weight at the time her picture was taken was a hundred thirty-five pounds. Her daughter had reported her missing last Friday, according to the printout.

The car she was found in was also reported missing last Friday. The late model, white Chevy Impala came back to an eighty-year-old woman. She'd left it running in her driveway while she took her groceries into the house. Mrs. Page said she'd planned on garaging it after she unpacked them.

The deceased had disappeared last Friday, April sixteenth, after having drinks with some coworkers. Her daughter Cara reported her missing on Saturday morning when she didn't show up at home. She tried her mother's cell phone, got no answer, and started to worry. Cara Adams's statement said she expected her mother to be home around ten o'clock Friday evening. She had stressed that her mother never stayed out any later. Cara had called the police station around midnight. The officer had followed procedure, explaining to Cara an adult had to be missing forty-eight hours before the department expended manpower searching unless there were extenuating circumstances.

* * * *

Cara Adams had listed her brother as a contact in the police report. Jake did a search for the work phone numbers for the kids. The notification couldn't wait until the end of the day in case the press got wind of it and released the victim's name first. It made a difficult job harder if the family heard it on the news. They'd start with the brother. Seth Adams, a paralegal with a downtown law firm, worked within a mile of the police station. Cara, an accountant, worked in Southington, ten miles outside of Wilkesbury.

Jake drove, while Louie processed information on his laptop. Seth worked in one of the old renovated mansions in Wilkesbury. The city had offered tax incentives to buyers as part of their revitalization project of the downtown area. The Jackson Healy Law Firm used the entire building for their practice. He and Louie entered a nicely appointed lobby done in neutral colors—beige walls, mauve sofa, accented with floral-upholstered chairs, and a deep burgundy rug.

The receptionist looked to be in her late twenties: blond hair, cut to look messy but sexy. Her snug blue suit showcased a spectacular body. At the same time, it emphasized her keen blue eyes as she studied them.

"Can I help you?"

"Yes. We'd like to speak to Seth Adams and somewhere private, if possible. He's not in any trouble, but it's important." Jake palmed his shield.

"Your name please?" she asked.

Louie took out his shield, laid it on the counter. "We don't have an appointment. My name's Detective Romanelli. This is my partner Lieutenant Carrington."

"I'll get him right away." She shot out of her chair and hurried down a long hallway. Jake's gaze followed her.

"A little young for you, isn't she?"

He ignored Louie's comment and took a seat while they waited for Seth to come out. Jake stared down the empty hallway, while Louie read a magazine. When Seth walked toward them, Jake sized him up. Five-eight, one-sixty, brown and brown, he noted in cop speak. The kid looked scared. Not guilty, scared, clearly afraid they were going to confirm what he had feared.

"Detectives…"

"Mr. Adams, is there a conference room we can use?" Louie asked.

The receptionist pointed to the one behind her. Seth led the way. They followed behind him and closed the door once they entered the room. *Do it quick*, Jake thought. Handle the shock and the emotions, which would follow later.

"Mr. Adams, your mother is Chelsea Adams?" Louie asked.

"Yes, did you find her? Is she okay? Where is she?" His voice was strained.

"Mr. Adams, I'm sorry to inform you. We found your mother this morning," Louie said.

"Alive?"

"No."

Seth grabbed the table. Jake thought for sure he'd pass out. The boy's face lost all color as he collapsed into a chair. "You're not mistaken? Did she have an accident?" Utter devastation filmed over his tear-filled eyes.

"We've identified her through her fingerprints. She was found this morning, in town. No, it wasn't an accident." Jake let it hang out there.

Seth stared at him for a long minute then started crying. Thank God Louie took over the job of comforting Seth.

"Seth, we're sorry for your loss. Can I get you a glass of water? Call someone for you?" Louie, a compassionate man, always dealt better with the survivor's grief.

"Did you tell my sister? Oh God, Cara." Seth lost it big time as sobs racked his body.

"No, we came here first. Do you want us to tell Cara, or do you want to?" Louie asked.

"Can we do it together?" Seth wrapped his arms around his waist. When he answered, it sounded like the voice of a little boy. He rocked and cried out again, "Mom."

Jake left Louie with Seth while he spoke with one of the partners he knew at the firm. He informed Attorney Ron Jacobson they'd be taking Seth home.

"Jake, please call me if he needs anything. They're a close-knit family. This will destroy them. His father on the other hand had left his mother last year for some twenty- or thirty-year-old, then up and moved to Florida," Ron Jacobson said.

"Thanks, Ron. We're going to need to question Seth and his sister. Do you want to be there?" Jake offered. Ron was a corporate attorney.

"Do you have to do it today?" Ron asked as he steepled his fingers in front of him.

"Yeah, we do."

"I'll meet you at their house in about an hour. Will you be able to pick up Cara and be there by then?"

"Yes, we'll see you there."

They escorted the dazed kid to Jake's car.

In the car, Louie asked again. "Seth, after we inform Cara, is there someone we can call to stay with both of you?"

"No, I don't want to talk to anyone right now," he said, staring out the window.

* * * *

Southington, a bedroom community to Hartford, was growing and expanding from a sleepy town to a full city friendly to businesses. It actively pursued all types of industries. It sat between Wilkesbury and Hartford. Jake pulled to the curb of the downtown office where Cara Adams worked. He left Seth in the car with Louie when he went into the doctor's offices. On the drive over, he'd called Cara's office and spoke with the receptionist. He learned Cara was an accountant in the billing department.

He walked into a small room crowded with patients. Jake discreetly held out his shield to the receptionist. He wanted to speak with Cara's boss first. The receptionist led him to Doctor Ira Charles's office and asked him to wait while she got the doctor. The doc didn't keep him waiting.

It's shocking," Dr. Charles said.

"She told you her mother was missing?" Jake asked.

"Of course, Cara's been upset all week. It's all she could talk about and who could blame her? Her mother disappeared without a trace... you found her?"

"We did. She's been murdered. Cara's brother's out in our car. What kind of doctor are you? Seth will need something to calm him down. We still have to inform Cara of her mother's death. Do you want to be there for support?"

"Yes. When we're done I'll see to her brother. He's also my patient."

He followed the doctor to an office across the hall from the reception area. Jake walked in first. A young woman who resembled their victim sat behind the desk with a phone to her ear. Cara's coloring matched her brother's—brown hair, big brown eyes, but slightly fuller lips. He'd have to wait until she stood to judge her height, though she appeared petite. She looked up when they came in, stopped in mid-sentence.

"Cara?" Jake said. He had clipped his badge to his belt in plain sight. She stared at his badge before she raised her terror-filled eyes to his.

"Yes, can I get you some coffee?" Stalling, Jake let her as he took the seat next to her.

"Cara, we don't need any coffee. We found your mother this morning. She's dead." Before she could interrupt, he continued. "We have your brother in the car outside. He's not in good shape. Why don't we take both of you home?"

She asked the same question her brother did. "Was it a car accident? No one noticed or helped? No one witnessed it?" Tears flooded her eyes, though they didn't fall. Jake watched her fight for control. Jake let her questions run out before he answered.

"No, she was murdered."

"Murdered!" She jumped up. "How? This can't be real. She has no enemies. Who would kill her?"

Jake held her hand, guided her back down into the chair. "I'm sorry for your loss, Cara. I'll answer the questions I can once we get both of you home. And I'll need to ask a few of my own."

"If you need anything...anything at all...call me. Do you want me to go with you?" Dr. Charles asked.

"No, I have to see to my brother. Is he okay?" This time the tears fell.

"He's upset," Jake said.

"Who could hurt her? She was a kind, gentle woman." Cara cried harder.

"We've started an investigation into her death." Jake picked up her purse and led her to his car. She jumped in the back seat and grabbed her brother, hugging him to her body.

* * * *

The four of them walked up a sidewalk lined with colorful tulips to the front door of the Adamses' house. The riot of color seemed a bit too cheerful for the occasion. Louie unlocked the front door with the keys Cara had supplied on the ride over. Cara led them into the modest, one-story house. The living room to the right of the foyer seemed like a good place to do the interview. Jake scanned the rooms as did Louie. Traditional furniture in bold navy with red accents, and an old solid wood table sat beside the sofa. Chairs were scattered around the room and doilies covered every tabletop. The hardwood floors visible under the oriental area rugs were polished to a glassy sheen. The living room connected with the dining area. He assumed the kitchen would be off the dining room. The dining area, decorated in peach and green fabrics, showcased a dark ornate table with matching hutch and buffet cabinet. The centerpiece of lilies surrounded by green leafy stems complemented the living room. A house well decorated. *A home*, Jake corrected as he waited for them to settle in.

He stood, as did Louie. The Adams kids sat on the sofa, their arms around each other, Seth's head on Cara's shoulder. He and Louie sat in the chairs facing them. Louie started the questioning.

"Can we call someone to come over?" Louie asked again.

"No, right now I don't want to talk to anyone," Cara said.

A loud musical chime filled the room. Jake got up, answered it and motioned Ronald Jacobson in and pointed out the living room. Once the lawyer sat down, the questions started on both sides.

"What happened to my mother? Did she suffer?" Cara asked.

"We don't have a lot of information yet. She was discovered this morning. Once the M.E. supplies the information we'll have more. Right now, I have to ask some difficult questions," Louie said.

"She wasn't raped, wasn't she?" Cara asked with apprehension.

They always ask, Jake thought, *as if death isn't enough of an insult on its own.* He fielded the question. "Cara, we don't have that information yet. The M.E. will determine her wounds during the autopsy." *Knowing won't help you to deal with it, believe me.*

"Okay," Cara answered for the both of them. She seemed the stronger of the two.

"Cara, where were you Friday night, between the hours of eleven PM and three AM?" Louie took over the questioning.

"Here, all night. I didn't go out. My boyfriend was working. I stayed home and watched television. I called the police at eleven PM because Mom didn't come home," Cara said. She ran her finger gently over the picture of her mother she picked up off the end table.

"Did you call from your cell phone or the house phone?" Louie asked.

"I called on the house phone. I'd never hurt my own mother."

"I understand, Cara, but this is standard procedure. Before we can move forward, we have to eliminate the both of you. We're also going to ask your father the same questions," Jake explained.

"The bastard's in Florida with a girl my brother's age. He left my mother last year around this time," Cara spat.

Such venom. Now if Jake had her father on the slab in the morgue, she might be his number one suspect. "Cara, who did she go out with on Friday night?" Jake asked. "I'll need her friends' names, addresses, and phone numbers, if you have them."

"She went out with her friend, Julie Cahns, and with Sara Hurdle from work. This week Mom said another girl from work was joining them. You'll have to ask her friends who that was. I'm not sure. I'll go get her address book." Cara stood to leave the room.

"Where did they go?" Louie asked. Years ago, Jake had found if he and Louie bounced the questions back and forth between them it kept suspects and witnesses off balance.

"They usually go to the golf course for dinner. If they're in the mood, they go into the lounge for drinks after."

"Which course?"

"Sorry…I can't remember. It's the one on the west side of town, the public one."

"Blakely Hills?" Jake questioned.

Cara left the room. Jake looked over at Seth. The kid looked devastated but managed to pull himself together, but he hadn't interrupted as they questioned his sister. "Seth, are you up to a few questions?" Louie asked.

"Yes, if it will help catch the person who did this to our mother." The kid's skin had gone transparent as happens with grief or shock. Black pouches had formed under his eyes. Despair aged the kid before his eyes.

"Where were you Friday night?" Louie asked.

"I went to dinner with my girlfriend, Olga. We ate at Cava's, in Southington. After dinner, we went back to her house. I spent the night, her parents weren't home..." Seth blushed.

"I'll need Olga's information," Louie said, as Cara returned to the room. She handed Jake her mother's address book.

Seth supplied the information for Olga. "Can I ask her to come over later?"

"Yes, but not right now. We need to speak with her before you do," Louie said.

"Is there anyone else who might've given your mother any trouble at work or in her personal life?" Jake asked.

"No, everyone liked her. She never harmed anyone or got into fights or arguments. She didn't date," Seth said, showing anger for the first time.

Jake preferred Seth's anger to the crying. The anger would help him deal with it.

"She hasn't dated since she divorced your father?" Louie clarified.

"She didn't divorce him, he divorced her. No, she didn't date. It shattered her when he came home and announced he was leaving her. It came right out of the blue."

"Do you keep in touch with him, Seth?" Louie asked.

"Yes, more than my sister does. She's angry. I mean full-blast angry with him. She won't even acknowledge his new wife. I dated the woman in high school."

It takes all kinds. Jake looked around at the lovely home, wondering why someone would decide to leave his family. He wrote in his notebook. *Trouble? Look into Chelsea's marriage.*

Seth continued, "Well, she thought she'd hit pay dirt with him. I fixed her. I got my mother the best divorce lawyer around. He stripped Dad with the alimony, including half his pensions and 401k's. If Lola wants any money, she'll have to work for it."

Jake saw it hit Seth again. His mother was gone. He wrapped his arms around his waist and rocked as he'd done back at his office.

All this time, Jacobson hadn't said anything. Jake turned to him. "Do you have any questions, counselor?"

"No, you've covered everything. When will you get the cause of death?"

"Not until the autopsy's finished," Louie answered.

"If you need to speak with them again, please give me a call."

"Will do. Cara, Seth, we'd like to have a look at your mother's room," Jake said.

"I don't want anyone pawing through her things. It's bad enough someone murdered her, now this?" Cara spewed.

Chapter 3

It killed Jake to watched Cara fight through his request. She looked at Jacobson. Ron reached over and patted her knee. "He has to, Cara, to help catch her murderer," Ron said.

"I need to lie down. I'm not watching you rifle through her things. She'd be mortified." Cara turned to leave the room, then spun back to Jake. "Make sure, Lieutenant, you catch the bastard who did this to our mother."

Seth chased after Cara, leaving them alone with Jacobson. "Are you staying, Ron?" Jake asked.

"Yes."

Jake stood outside the door of Chelsea's bedroom to get an impression of the woman while Louie went out to their car to grab the evidence kits and gloves. As soon as Louie came back they started their search. A neat woman with good quality clothes in muted colors, shoes, and furniture, nothing flashy for Chelsea. Not an overabundance of anything. It looked as if she lived within her means. All of Chelsea's jewelry was fourteen-karat gold. Everything in the room was precise, organized to an inch of its life. Clothes were color coordinated in both the closet and the drawers. He hadn't expected to get much and they didn't.

The top drawer held her functional underwear. Jake discovered the sexy lingerie in the second drawer. He couldn't tell if they were new or old. She took care of everything she owned. Her bathroom, free of clutter, was shined to a gloss. In her closet, her shoes were lined up under matching outfits. A high-end-looking fabric covered the bed without all the fuss of throw pillows. It told Jake a lot about Chelsea.

Chelsea Adams was a practical, confident, organized woman, who wasn't afraid to show her feminine side. But who was she showing it to?

He didn't get into details too much with the kids. They weren't up to it. After the search, they headed over to Chelsea's office.

* * * *

A social worker for the state, Chelsea had worked in an office on Thomaston Avenue in a long, gray concrete, unimaginative office building. The structure was divided in half. The unemployment office was situated on one side, social services occupied the other. Leaving the sunshine outside, he and Louie walked into the gray SS office. The receptionist didn't bother to look up. She pointed to a sign-in sheet as she continued to talk into the phone. On principle, Jake didn't sign in. He held his shield under her nose until she acknowledged him.

"What can I do for you, Officer?" she asked, after a couple of moments.

"That's Lieutenant. I need to speak with Mrs. Adams's supervisor." Instead of calling the supervisor, the woman got up, walked to the back of the room, and disappeared around a gray partition.

"You sure got used to 'Lieutenant' fast." Louie elbowed him.

"You bet," Jake said.

The rest of his comment was cut off by a small man of about five-four with a rounded pot belly in, of all things, a gray suit. He looked as if he'd swallowed a basketball. His gray hair kept to the color scheme, or lack of it, and he was sporting a comb-over. It always amused Jake what people did for vanity.

"Lieutenant, I'm Angelo Torres, Chelsea's supervisor. Please follow me to my office. It's a terrible tragedy. We heard a little while ago she'd been found."

He led the way through a maze of cubicles to an office the size of a postage stamp. The tight, small space told Jake Angelo's status in the department—a low-level manager.

"How did you hear?" Jake asked.

"Her daughter called here to speak with Sara, who then told all of us. Please have a seat," Angelo offered.

"Did Chelsea work for you, Mr. Torres?" Jake sat and jumped right in with his questions.

"Yes. I distribute the work load. I oversee everyone's files, including Chelsea's. If an employee has a problem or issue they can't resolve, it's handed over to me."

"Did Chelsea routinely have problems?" Louie asked.

"No, her clients respected her and she was fair to everyone, no bias. Never ran out of patience, like some do. She didn't make people feel uncomfortable or embarrassed for being here either. Chelsea had compassion for her clients. We'll miss her," Angelo concluded in a monotone voice.

"Did she ever have a client who wasn't satisfied? Or felt they deserved more than what was offered?" Louie asked.

"Once, about two years ago, a man who was denied benefits. He wouldn't leave her alone. In her best interest, we had her file a complaint with the police. After she filed, he didn't bother her anymore. His intimidation didn't work. Chelsea was a tough nut," Angelo said.

"Anything else? Any other information about Chelsea you might have that would help us catch whoever did this to her, Angelo?" Jake used his first name, hoping for some personal input on Chelsea, but got none.

"No, Chelsea didn't date anyone from the department. She did her job. I wish I had more workers like her. My life would be easier."

"Okay, thanks. We're going to need to interview her coworkers. Is there a place we can do the interviews in private? Here in your office or in a conference room?"

"Why don't I show you to the break room? I'll get you a list of employees who worked with Chelsea," Angelo said.

* * * *

He and Louie interviewed ten coworkers. All were shocked or sickened over Chelsea's death, but couldn't offer a reason why someone would hurt her. Her friends—the ones she went out to dinner with on April sixteenth—weren't at work. They left after being notified of her death, finding it too difficult to deal with their grief and their clients. Angelo gave Jake and Louie their home addresses and phone numbers. They started with the one closest to work. Jake wanted them interviewed as soon as possible.

First on the list was Sara Hurdle. She lived in the west end of town. Jake knocked on Hurdle's door. It opened only a couple of inches. A swollen green eye surrounded by red peered out at them through heavy security chains. "Ms. Hurdle, can we come in?" Jake asked as they identified themselves and offered their badges.

She pushed the door closed. He heard the rattle of chains as the door reopened. Though it was eighty something degrees outside, Sara stood there in a ratty, terry cloth bathrobe, bathed in grief. A grief he understood too well. The woman also looked scared.

"Some of my questions will be difficult but your answers will help Chelsea. May I call you Sara?" Beforehand, he and Louie had agreed he'd start the questioning.

"Yes, Sara's fine." She wiped at her eyes with a crumpled up tissue.

"We need to ask you about Friday night," Jake said still standing by the door.

"I've racked my brains for the last two hours trying to find answers. Nothing. I don't have any." Sara sobbed. "If we thought Chelsea was in any kind of trouble or someone was bothering her, we wouldn't have let her leave by herself." She wiped her tears. "I'm sorry."

"There's no reason for you to be sorry, Sara. Chelsea's death is a tragedy. Are those new locks on your door?" Jake asked, as they walked into the living room. Sara sat on the couch, Louie sat beside Sara on the burgundy sofa. Jake took a well-worn easy chair with a zig-zag print that dated back to the fifties.

"Yes, I changed them out last week when Chelsea went missing. It doesn't make any sense, but her disappearance scared me. I thought the new locks would help put me at ease."

"Why are you frightened, Sara?" Louie took over the questioning.

"This is something you read about in the newspapers, not something you expect to happen to you or anyone close to you. Deep down I knew something bad happened to her. Chelsea disappearing is out of character. When I say it out loud, it sounds stupid…"

"No, it doesn't. What we need to do is go through the whole night piece by piece. Are up to it?" Louie gentled his voice.

"I'll do anything I can to help. Chelsea was the best person in the whole world. We were friends as well as coworkers. I can't believe she's gone." Sara started sobbing again. Louie took her hand and patted it gently.

Jake's gaze roamed the room. Homey, but outdated. He wondered if she had continued living in the place where she was raised.

"Sara, I need you to pull yourself together. This is important. It will help Chelsea." Louie's voice held a firm gentleness, which seemed to bring the grieving woman around.

"I called her kids today. It was a difficult conversation. What can you say at a time like this? Everything seems trivial."

"I'm sure they appreciated the call. What time did you both leave work on Friday?" Louie asked.

"We left at four-thirty."

"What did you do when you left the office?" Jake listened, content to let Louie run the entire interview. Sara seemed more at ease with him.

"We went over to the Four Seasons for drinks before dinner. We'd decided last week to dine there." She stopped, gathered her thoughts. "We were seated around six o'clock. Chelsea's girlfriend joined us a little after six."

"I thought you always ate at the Hills?" Jake interrupted.

"Most times we did, but that night we decided to change it up."

"Who was the fourth woman who went to dinner with you?" Louie questioned.

"Jora Stein. She works with us."

"How long were you at the Four Seasons?"

"Dinner took about an hour. We sat in the restaurant another hour and talked to kill time. We didn't want to head out to the club too early. We were feeling no pain and enjoying each other's company. We had cocktails before we ate and then switched to wine with dinner. I had a nice buzz on."

"Was Chelsea also...flying?" Louie asked.

"No, she always paced herself. One drink lasted her the whole night. Our perpetual designated driver, we called her."

"What time did you leave the restaurant and head over to the club?" Louie prodded.

"Around eight-thirty because we got to the golf course about eight forty-five and the band hadn't started yet."

"What did you do when you got there?" Louie asked.

"Well, we sat at the bar and ordered some drinks. I could tell we were losing Chelsea."

"How do you mean, 'losing her'?" Louie questioned.

"Well, she was bored. Chelsea wasn't a clubber. She used to go out to dinner with us once a month when she was married but always headed right home afterward. After her divorce, she started to go out with us after we ate because Julie pushed her. Chelsea's a real homebody." Sara looked up, devastated. "I mean was a real homebody. Her bastard of an ex left her for a twenty-something bimbo."

"What time did Chelsea leave the bar?" Jake took over.

"She left around ten o'clock. She didn't even give the band a chance. Said she had a headache. We tried to talk her into staying. She wouldn't hear of it." Sara's tears started again. "It was the last time we saw her." Guilt washed over her face. Jake sympathized. You couldn't change the past though he wished and prayed like a little kid when Eva had died that he could. "We should have walked her to her car," Sara sobbed.

"Did you usually walk each other to your cars?" Jake asked.

"No, we didn't unless the bar was in a crappy neighborhood."

"Don't beat yourself up, Sara. Monday morning quarterbacking never accomplished anything. Did she mention whether she planned on meeting anyone after she left there?" Jake continued the questioning.

"No, not Chelsea. If she said she was going home, she went home."

"Was she talking or flirting with anyone at the bar who she blew off when she left?"

"No, Julie hooked up with some loser from high school. I don't know his name, Julie would. Chelsea would never ever hook up with someone."

"Here's my card if you remember anything else. We're sorry for your loss," Louie said.

Once outside of Sara's apartment, Jake said, "The woman appears to have floated through life without a blemish."

"Yeah, a quiet woman, one who's admired, and now she's dead. It's pointing to someone she knew. Somewhere on her way home, she met her death—a practical woman doesn't stop for a stranger."

"Agreed, let's reach out to the Neptune Police in Florida. We need to pin down her ex's whereabouts last Friday night."

"Next up is Jora Stein," Louie said, making notes next to Sara's name.

Stein's phone continued to ring until an answering machine picked up. Louie left a message and stressed the importance of a return call. They got the same response, and left a similar message when they tried to call the victim's friend, Julie Cahns.

* * * *

Jake returned to the station and placed a call to Neptune, Florida. A receptionist with a thick southern accent that was too southern for the area answered. He figured her for a transplant.

"This is Lieutenant Carrington, from the Wilkesbury, Connecticut, Police Department. May I speak with one of your detectives?"

"Hi, Lieutenant." She stretched out the second part of lieutenant, adding a few n's along the way.

"I didn't catch your name."

"Because I didn't throw it—it's Samantha, but most people call me Sammy." Sammy's infectious laugh lifted his spirits.

"Sammy, who would I speak with to get a follow-up on someone's whereabouts last Friday?"

"I'll give you to the chief. He can direct you to the right person."

"What's his name?"

"Beau Taylor. Hold please while I get him." Sammy put him on hold. He wasn't kept waiting long. "Well hello, Connecticut, what can I do for you?"

"Chief, I have a homicide here. If it's possible I need you to check on the whereabouts of the ex-husband," Jake asked.

"It's Beau, please, we're not formal here. I'd be happy to. Give me the pertinent info on him and the times and dates you want checked out. I'll do that today."

Jake supplied the information.

"Do you also want to know the whereabouts of the new wife?" Chief Taylor asked.

"Yes, I hear she wasn't happy with the alimony settlement."

Jake's radio crackled to life. "Any units in the vicinity of Highland Avenue and Chase Parkway respond to a two-one-one. Shots have been reported, along with hostages." The next code put the fear of God into every cop. It was a ten-one-o-eight.

"Chief, I have to go. I'll get you back later." Jake ended the call without waiting for an answer.

He grabbed his jacket. Louie was already up and running as he slipped into his jacket. Jake caught up to him. The bullpen also emptied as every available officer rushed to the scene. A ten-one-o-eight or one-o-eight meant officer down. No matter what department they belonged to, the wall of blue would be there to protect their own.

The drive to the bank located on Highland Avenue took Jake a little over ten minutes with traffic. Not everyone bothered to pull over at the sound of his sirens. Louie checked his gun while Jake navigated traffic. Armed bank robberies had increased across the nation along with the violence used by the suspects in desperate attempts to secure the cash.

"When was the last time you checked your gun, Jake?"

He appreciated Louie's concern though sometimes it baffled him when Louie asked an obvious question. He shrugged his shoulders. No matter what, Louie had his back. "This morning."

"Loaded?"

"Yes." Jake turned to Louie. "I load it every day. You?"

"Loaded."

They both knew some cops who didn't bother. Utter stupidity. Jake and Louie drove the rest of the way in silence, each putting his mind where it needed to be as they listened to the radio for updates.

* * * *

Chase Park, situated on five acres along the interstate, offered basketball courts, a sprinkler for kids in the summer, and a clubhouse for neighborhood meetings and gatherings. The lot looked as if it could accommodate up to fifty cars. Jake parked, and then he and Louie shrugged into their Kevlar vests. "Ready?" Jake asked.

"Ready."

Jake checked in with Lieutenant Nick Longo from Robbery who was in charge of the scene. Longo had blocked off Highland Avenue from both directions. He'd set up his control post behind a parked cruiser at the edge of the intersection. It looked like the whole force had turned out.

"Hey, Longo, what've you got?" Jake asked.

"Our intel tells us there are two gunmen, three tellers, one manager, and several customers, including a police officer. It's Tommy Sullivan," Longo replied.

"Oh shit! Tommy? Didn't his wife recently have a baby?" Louie said.

"Yep, two days ago. There were shots fired but we don't know if anyone's been hit. The ambulance is here and waiting. We've tried to contact the suspects, but they're not responding or giving any demands yet. I'm going to try again." Longo placed another call to the bank—it went unanswered.

Worse, Jake thought, *when they don't respond.* You couldn't get a bead on them.

Longo's division, tension etched in each officer's face, was equipped with long-range rifles. They were spread out around the building. The negotiator arrived.

Jake nodded to Jim Noones, an experienced negotiator, as he watched Noones slip on his vest. They both turned toward the bank to assess the situation. At five-nine, Noones had the stereotypical appearance of a jolly Irishman: a rounded belly, red nose, ruddy complexion, wheat-colored hair, and sky-blue eyes in a round, wide face. Always a joke on his lips, he went from casual to serious in less than a second when a situation called for it. Anyone who failed to take him seriously paid a dear price. Noones handled all his negotiations with a calm manner, trusting face, and a storyteller's smooth voice and timing.

"Hey, Jake, I hear congratulations are in order," Noones said as he tugged on the bottom of his vest.

"Thanks, Jim."

He turned to Longo. "How do you want to handle this?"

"Whichever way ends this fast and with no injuries, if possible," Longo said.

Noones grabbed the bullhorn and flipped the switch and started speaking to the suspects.

"This is Captain Noones of the Wilkesbury Police Department. I'd like to open communications with you. Please use the number on the display from your last call. It will come to my phone."

Jake waited beside Noones and Longo. The rest of the department scattered around the block, circling the bank. Taking in the whole scene without moving an inch, Jake tensed for action. He nodded to Louie to protect his flank. He spotted the reporters from Channels Eight, Three, and Sixty-One with their live cams. Helicopters hovered overhead, and would be offering a dramatic televised view of the incident. If the suspects were watching, they had the whole view as well, including law enforcement's tactical positions and the number of responding officers. The information age made these events even more difficult to manage, endangering countless lives.

"Have the schools been locked down?" Noones asked Longo.

"Yes, first thing."

"Good. My kid's at Kennedy," Noones said.

"Mine too," Longo responded.

"Mine are at Resurrection and Lord of the Cross, thank God," Louie said.

Jake caught movement at the door to the bank. "Here we go."

Noones lifted his bullhorn and waited.

The man used the bank manager as a shield as he brandished a gun and shouted. "Send over one unarmed officer. One. I'll give him a letter I've written with what we want. We don't need any heroes today. If our demands are met, everyone will go home healthy, understood?"

The suspect appeared to stand about six feet tall. He wore his black hair spiked on top, a red streak running down the center. When he turned, Jake saw a long, braided tail touching his shoulder blades. *So eighties.* He was dressed in all black and his wallet, secured with a chain, stuck out from his back pocket. Despite the day being warm, he also wore black gloves. His gun hand quivered—not a comforting sign. The gunman looked to be in his thirties, a solid hundred-eighty. He wore mirrored sunglasses; his bicep had a tattoo of a cross and skull. Jake memorized every detail for his report.

"Noones, who do you want to send over there?" Lieutenant Longo asked.

"I'll go," Jake spoke up.

"Any objections, Nick?"

"None," Lieutenant Longo said.

"No heroics," Louie said, as he leaned in and whispered in Jake's ear. "You got your ankle holster?" Most cops never used maximum force during their careers, though were trained to if a situation required it. Jake never needed to but Louie had.

"Don't worry, Mom, I'll be back before you know it." Jake tossed a smirk over his shoulder.

"We're sending over Detective Carrington. He's unarmed. In good faith, you release one of the hostages," Jim Noones said. By procedure Noones didn't use Jake's rank.

"Send the detective over," the gunman said, not agreeing to anything.

"Is anyone hurt?" Noones asked.

"We'll talk after you read the letter." The gunman never let loose his grip on the manager.

"He's coming over now," Noones replied.

The Kevlar vest created a furnace and had sweat pouring down Jake's back as he got closer to the gunman. The gunman's own sweat poured under his sunglasses. Jake wondered how the guy could see. The bank manager looked petrified. Jake held his hands up and away from his body as he approached. If things went wrong, his ankle holster—if he could get to it—would provide necessary protection.

"Okay, that's far enough. I'm going back into the bank with this woman here. When I reach the door, you can pick up the letter. But not before I reach the door. Understood?"

Jake looked into the frightened eyes of the manager. "Yes."

"Good." The suspect whispered something in the manager's ear then started backing up with her.

When gunman and hostage reached the door, Jake dropped to one knee to retrieve the note while keeping the bank robber in his line of sight. As he wrapped his fingers around it the gunman stepped inside and pushed the bank manager out onto the sidewalk. She fell to the ground. Jake ran forward to lift her up. He half carried, half dragged her back to the command post and safety.

The woman burst into tears when they reached Longo. Jake hoped no one could hear how fast and hard his heart pounded.

"I'm Lieutenant Longo," Nick said. "I have to ask you to pull yourself together right now. Anything you give us will help the others come out of this alive. What's your name?"

"Adeline Smith," she replied, swiping at her tears.

"Adeline, you need to be exact. How many people are in there? Is anyone hurt? How many gunmen are there? Where are they located?" Longo shot questions at her.

Jake's opinion of her went up as she composed herself.

"There are two tellers behind the counter. The assistant manager's at the counter with the second guy, at least he was when I came out. There are two gunmen, three customers…oh, and one was shot in the leg. He's a regular customer. Officer Tommy Sullivan. It isn't bad. We were able to stop the bleeding by applying some pressure to it." Jake appreciated how she tried to control her shaking.

"Adeline, you did great. Go with these detectives. We're going to keep you away from the press until this is over. Are you going be okay?" Nick asked.

"Yes, is everyone else going to be?"

"We hope so. These detectives will take your statement," Longo said.

Louie started to escort her to the ambulance. Adeline leaned over and thanked Jake for helping her.

"No problem. You sure you're good? The EMT is going to check you anyway, to be sure," Louie said

"I'll be fine. But I'm worried about the others. If I'd known they were going to let me go, I would've let someone else go out. He put a gun to my head… I thought I was a goner." She finished her statement, then leaned over and threw up.

Jake motioned for the EMT. Louie took the rest of her statement before he handed her off to a patrolman and then headed back to the command post.

"How is she?" Nick asked.

"She'll be fine. The gun to the head freaked her out," Louie said.

"That'll do it."

"What do they want?" Jake asked.

Louie added a question of his own. "Did they call Noones yet?"

"Yes. They want the usual," Nick Longo replied to both.

"It's not like they're going to get away with it," Jake said. Everyone's radios crackled to life.

It seemed the Channel Eight News chopper had picked up a hot pursuit on Route 8, heading from Wilkesbury to Bridgeport. The state police had tried to pull over a car on a routine check when it took off. They were now closing down entrance ramps, rerouting any cars not involved in the pursuit. *There is never a dull moment in this job.*

After seven long hours, the bank robbery suspects gave themselves up. Both gunmen incurred layoffs and had run out of money, with no job prospects in their futures. When questioned, they said they had run out of food to feed their families and after a night of drinking the idea came to them. It never shocked Jake how stupid most criminals were, but these two took the cake

The pursuit on Route 8 ended fast. It had nothing to do with the bank robbery as first reported.

On their way home, Louie reminded him again about the party for Marisa the following week. Tomorrow they'd handle the paperwork for this incident. Though a long day, he'd put in time on Eva's file tonight. He had to go into the meeting prepared. "What, do I look like I have no memory?" Jake asked. If Louie was setting him up again...he'd... *Never mind,* he thought, *it isn't worth it.*

"No, Marisa said to remind you. Gigi keeps asking if you're coming." Louie fluttered his eyelashes.

"Great. Can't you douse this before the party?"

"No, you can do it. It'll give you a lesson in parenting."

Jake shot him the snake eye. "For Marisa." Jake changed the subject. "Does Sophia want me to bring anything?"

"No, we're all set. Sophia hired the band and the bartender last week to lock them in. Good thing I've got a job."

"You're not fooling anyone. You get into this as much as Sophia."

"You're right, I love it."

Jake dropped Louie off at his house before he headed home.

* * * *

Outside of struggling with his emotions all week, Jake focused his concentration on the cases at hand. Otherwise it was a quiet week as they fell into the routine of murder—following up with witnesses, the M.E., and the lab. Like Shanna Wagner, Chelsea Adams was well-liked, minded her own business, and hadn't caused any ripples until her divorce. *Taking a husband to the cleaners could gain a person an enemy,* he mused.

A long, tedious day, had gotten longer when Jake stopped by the nursing home and visited his mother. She showed a few sparks when he walked into her room, but who knows? Long ago, she'd forgotten she had another child who needed her.

At home, he decided to continue to explore through Eva's files in small increments. Small doses were all he could handle in his melancholy mood. Each crime scene photo stabbed him in the heart. His father's neat print in the margins jumped off the pages. Jake bogged through his detectives' incident reports and evaluations to make sure no details were overlooked. Again, it hit him how similar Eva's and Shanna's cases were. The third box he opened hit hard. A sampling of Spaulding's stained shirt and jeans still held the coppery smell of blood. Eva's blood. His father's fellow officers had made sure he had all the evidence he'd need in the future if new evidence surfaced. Knuckling away a tear, he rummaged through the box. A sample of George Spaulding's brand of cigarettes, along with a smoked one, were stored in sealed envelopes. Jake decided to give one of the samples to Burke to have it tested against the recent samples of DNA collected from George. Though he thought he wanted Louie here, he found this first time through was better alone. It had been years since he'd subjected himself to the trauma. Maybe when he got to the fiftieth time through the file he'd be able to control his emotions.

* * * *

The next day, Jake woke to a typical rainy New England April day. The temps dropped to the low fifties. His concession to the weather was a heavier sports jacket. When he got into the station and sat at his desk, he put a call into Chief Beau Taylor.

Jake got him on the first try. "Chief, it's Jake Carrington from Wilkesbury, Connecticut."

"Please call me Beau. How did your situation turn out?"

"We got the guys. The officer who got shot is doing great. Thanks for asking."

"Good. I checked on Jeffrey Adams and his perky new bride Lola. I do need to tell you—she had quite the mouth on her. I thought I was talking to a trucker." Beau laughed. "She wasn't happy to see me."

"No?"

"No. She started off telling me she wasn't going talk to me without an attorney before I even explained why I was there. It got my eye a-twitching. Y'all understand my meaning, Connecticut?"

"I do, Chief. Who told her about the murder?"

"She said she got a call about the ex-wife's murder. She knew someone would come and start bothering them with questions. I pointed out Mrs. Adams wasn't happy about being dead, either."

Jake let out a laugh. "Sorry to interrupt, I would've loved to have been there."

"Oh yeah, a refreshing break in my routine. I told her to call her lawyer and we'd settle my questions at the police station. After a staring contest, the ex-husband said they'd be happy to answer any questions I have. Imagine that."

"I'm imagining. Did they give you anything?" Jake laughed. He could see the scene play out.

"Well, the ex-husband worked all weekend at his second job. He's an assistant manager at a small restaurant here in Neptune. His alibi checks out. Now his shy, delicate wife claimed to have spent the weekend with her girlfriend over in Miami while her husband worked. I called her girlfriend. She hemmed and hawed when I asked her to verify Lola's visit on the sixteenth. At first, she agreed, until I told her that if she lied, she would face charges, including prison time. Understanding the severity of the situation, she immediately corrected her previous statement. Said she hasn't seen Lola since her wedding. Connecticut, do you want me to verify flights on my end?"

"Thanks, Beau, I'll check them out from here. Can I get the girlfriend's information in Miami? I appreciate your time on this. If I run into any problems with the flights, I'll give you a call back."

"Anytime, Connecticut, I'll fax over my report and the info on the friend." Beau hung up.

"What's that all about, Jake?" Louie asked.

"Well, we might have to head down south," Jake said, pulling out the phone book.

"Awesome, I'll pack the sunscreen for you. What have you got?"

"What I got is a liar."

"Florida got good information for us?"

"Yep. The new, younger wife doesn't have an alibi for the weekend. The ex-husband does. He needs to work two jobs to support the new and improved model."

"The poor fellow, my heart bleeds," Louie snorted. "Where was the current wife?"

"Lola said she spent the weekend in Miami with her girlfriend. Girlfriend gets all nervous when it's explained to her that she could go to jail if she lies—she recants. She hasn't seen the current wife since her wedding last year."

"'Oh, what a tangled web we weave...when first we practice to deceive.' I love that quote by Walter Scott in 'Marmion,'" Louie said.

"You have a quote for everything."

"Hey, we can't go down south until after Marisa's party. She'd kill us. I'm already taking enough grief from her over the party we won't let her go to."

"Don't worry. If we have to go, it wouldn't be right away. We have other leads to pursue first."

"Good, 'cause I'd hate to miss how you're going to handle her friend Gigi who has, and I quote Marisa," Louie brought his hands together and fluttered his lashes. "'She has the world's biggest crush on Uncle Jake.'"

"I owe you one for this."

As promised, he walked into the conference room at three and updated Shamus, Burke, and Kraus on the evidence in Eva's case. He held back his personal feelings as McGuire had asked. Though it wasn't said, his men understood he'd be working the case too. While he was in the meeting Louie ran the airlines to see if Chelsea's ex-husband or his new wife were in town on the weekend of April sixteenth. After updating Burke and Kraus, Jake left the meeting and turned his attention back to the Adams case.

Chapter 4

At one on Saturday afternoon, Jake walked into Louie's house. The sounds of seven-year-olds running around, screaming at the top of their lungs, pierced his ear drums. He dodged a few as he passed the living room. Louie Jr., whom everyone called LJ to distinguish between father and son, sat with his friends, playing some video game and ribbing each other.

Jake caught LJ's eye and nodded as he worked his way to the kitchen.

"Hey, Uncle Jake, Dad's out back," LJ shouted.

The kitchen was organized chaos. Sophia, Louie's Italian beauty, was in the center of it, talking to a dark-haired woman in a low-cut red sundress and a short jacket. The unknown woman was five-nine in tall heels that showcased her long, shapely legs. She laughed at something Sophia said and the sound vibrated through him. Large gold hoop earrings dangled from her ears, a gold bracelet and an emerald ring sat on her right arm and hand, respectively. She wore nothing on her left. *Good detecting, Jake*, he thought.

Sophia moved around the kitchen while they spoke, each movement automatic. Food dishes containing different kinds of treats littered the counter. In his peripheral vision, he saw Sophia pull something out of the oven. It smelled wonderful, and kicked in his appetite, though he never took his eyes off the other woman who dipped a chip in some concoction before bringing it to her red lips. His eyes tracked each movement. As the chip disappeared between her lips he had to swallow hard.

They hadn't noticed him yet. He cleared his throat. "Hey, gorgeous, you've outdone yourself this time. Whatever it is, it smells great. Let me be the first to taste it." He leaned down to place a kiss on Sophia's cheek as he snuck a piece of meat off a tray. She whacked his hand with the spatula in her hand. "You lucked out with the weather today. Hot and sunny and I thought for sure we'd be rained out," Jake said as he chewed.

"Oh, I put my order in. It wouldn't dare rain on my picnic," Sophia said, pinning him with her chocolate-brown eyes, as she turned toward the woman at the counter. "Jake, glad you made it. This is my friend Mia Andrews."

Mia held out her hand. "It's nice to meet you. Sophia talks about you all the time."

He took her extended hand, surprised at the firm handshake and pleased with the soft skin, each sensation shooting through his body. Jake wished he'd dressed for the party. Instead he'd worn broken-in jeans with boots, a collared cotton shirt, the sleeves rolled halfway up his arms. He had a thing for belt buckles. Today he wore a silver American bald eagle.

"It's nice to meet you, Mia. I'll have to speak with Louie. He never mentioned you." He looked over at Sophia.

"Louie's out back, Jake. He's on grill duty. You should go help him," Sophia said.

"It looks like you need help in here. What do you need me to do?" He didn't want to leave the kitchen or Mia until he got to know her.

"She won't accept any help. Everyone's offered," Mia said.

"Oh, that's our girl. Come on, Sophia, what do you need?" Jake pushed.

"Nothing. Everything's done. We'll take them out when Louie finishes cooking. In fact, let me check with him to see how he's doing out there. I'll be right back." Sophia left them alone.

"Subtle, isn't she?" Mia said, flashing him a wide smile.

He swallowed hard as she locked her deep ocean blue eyes on his. He forced himself back to earth.

Marisa and her friend Gigi came running into the kitchen and saved him from making a fool of himself. He'd almost forgotten the reason for the party.

"Is that for me?" Marisa said, stretching out her hand.

He looked down at the wrapped pink box in his hands. "I don't know. It's for the prettiest fourteen-year-old girl who happens to have a birthday in a couple of days. Know anyone who fits that description?" Marisa threw her arms around him and gave him a hug as she planted a kiss on his cheek and tugged the package out of his hands.

"Thanks, Uncle Jake. What is it? It feels light." Marisa shook the box.

"I guess you have to open it to find out."

"I can't. Mom said I have to wait till after we eat to open my gifts," Marisa said, frustrated.

"We always break the rules. Your mother expects it of us. Go ahead. Open it." Jake encouraged her with a wink.

Marisa tore at the wrapping paper like a crazed dog searching for food. "You better hurry before your mother comes back in." Jake urged her on.

"You're a bad influence, Jake," Mia said.

"No, he's not." Marisa scorched Mia with a look.

Sophia came into the room. She looked from him to Marisa, then back at him.

"Jake!" she yelled. He started laughing.

"You're the best, Uncle Jake! Look Gigi, it's a gift card to the mall. How'd you know? Now I can get the outfit I've been wishing for. Thank you!" She threw her arms around him. Jake lifted her off the floor and swung her around before lowering her back down. "Mom, can we go to the mall tonight, after everyone leaves?"

"No, not today, we have company. We'll go tomorrow. Jake, this is way too much. You shouldn't have," Sophia said, looking over Marisa's shoulder at the gift card.

"What good is money if you don't spend it?" He wrapped an arm around Sophia's shoulder.

* * * *

Mia watched the exchange. She felt like an intruder, though it gave her some insight into Jake Carrington. When Sophia had suggested she meet him, she'd agreed with reluctance and skepticism. Cops were bad news. They lived hard. They played hard. Sophia and Louie must be the exception to the rule. Sophia had pushed until Mia had agreed to come to the party. Now, she was glad she did.

She liked the way he looked. Handsome in a rugged sort of way, and boy could he fill out a pair of jeans. His unusual hair color—a dark auburn, emphasized his vivid green eyes. She bet women fell at his feet. He was over six feet tall. She didn't have to worry about towering over him. His muscles bulged against his shirt when he lifted Marisa off the floor. No, he wasn't what she'd been expecting. It was a nice plus that he was good with children, or at least with Sophia's children. It was clear he was a member of this family.

"How do you know Sophia?" Jake asked Mia, pulling her back into the conversation.

"Oh, we work out together."

"Well, it shows…" As an afterthought, he added, "On both of you."

"Real smooth." Sophia patted him on the shoulder. "Jake, aren't you going outside to say hi to everyone?" Sophia asked.

* * * *

With some reluctance, he excused himself and found Louie right where Sophia said he would be, on grill duty. With a beer in one hand, a spatula in the other, Louie wore one of those cook aprons. It read, *Don't bite the cook. Chef humor,* Jake figured, though he didn't get it. Louie's shorts showed off his knobby knees. On his head, he wore a Yankees baseball cap. *In this crowd of cops and wives alike, after a few drinks, that hat could get fists flying,* he thought. Yankees or Red Sox? He loved the Yankees, win, lose or draw.

"Aren't you the height of fashion?" Jake greeted him.

"Oh yeah." Louie held out his apron, took a bow. Looking around Jake, he raised his eyebrows.

"What?"

"Where is she?"

"Who?"

"You know who." Louie flipped over a couple of burgers, and then forked some hot dogs onto a plate.

"Is this another one of Sophia's setups?" Jake tried to pull off a frown.

"Don't know what you're talking about."

"You two are like a tag team." Jake rubbed his chin. This time maybe Sophia had gotten it right.

"Well, this one isn't bad. Not bad at all. If I were single…"

"Well, you're not, hands off. But you're right, this one isn't bad. And she's got a personality."

"Well, I'll be damned, you're interested." Louie grinned.

"We'll see. I spent all of five minutes with her." Though, at the moment, he couldn't keep his mind or eyes off her. Time would tell. "In fact, I think I'll go back to the kitchen and see what Sophia wants me to bring out."

When Jake stepped back into the kitchen, he noticed the shift in conversation. The kind that meant the speakers were talking about the person who had just entered the room. Good or bad?

"Am I intruding?"

"No, we were deciding what dishes should go out first," Sophia said smoothly.

Oh, she's good, he thought. "Need help?"

"Why don't the two of you take out the salads?" Sophia pointed.

"Can do." Jake saluted her.

Marisa ran back into the kitchen with her friend. "Uncle Jake, this is my friend, Gigi. I forgot to introduce her before." Marisa smiled. Gigi lowered her eyes in a shy gesture.

He held out his hand. "Hi, Gigi, it's nice to meet you." He took her hand and shook it.

"Hi, Mister Carrington." Gigi blushed.

"Let's drop the mister. You can call me Jake." Gigi's face lit up.

"You know she has a crush on you," Marisa whispered in his ear.

"There are no secrets here, Marisa. It's rude to whisper when other people are around," Sophia scolded.

"Well, isn't that the time to whisper? When would you do it, when you're alone?" Marisa asked.

Laughing, Jake said, "She's got you there, Sophia." He winked at Marisa. Gigi stared up at him.

"Jake, you can be punished right along with Marisa," Sophia said. "Now take the salads out."

Mia grabbed a bowl. Jake handed Gigi and Marisa plates to take out. He picked up a meat platter. "You were great with Gigi, Jake. A girl's first crush can be devastating if not handled correctly," Mia said.

"Yeah, Marisa warned me last week. Can I get you a drink?" Jake asked after they set down the food.

"Yes, I'll have a vodka and tonic with lemon."

"Okay, I'll be right back."

A party at the Romanellis' always reminded Jake of a wedding. Incredible food, strong drinks, good music, a professional bartender, and a live band. He threw a couple of dollars into the tip jar and continued his study of the place as he waited for his drinks. Louie's backyard was set up for entertaining. Chairs and tables were arranged in groups. Off to the side, lounge chairs clustered around the pool that Louie had yet to open this season. Louie never opened it before Memorial Day, no matter what the weather. Outside the gated pool he'd arranged tables, chairs, and lawn games. The older Italians were already playing bocce. A big brick grill, equipped with a refrigerator and a side cabinet, which stored the plastic outdoor dishes, was steaming with meats on all burners.

"This is some event," Mia said when he came back with the drinks.

"Yeah, I can't wait to see how they top these birthday parties when one of the kids gets married," Jake joked.

"Can they top it?"

"Sophia always says, 'These are my children and they deserve the best. Plus, I'm Italian. I'm allowed, even expected, to entertain this way.'" Jake mimicked her voice, pleased when he got a laugh out of Mia. "Louie loves these events as much as Sophia does."

"It shows. They're a great couple, aren't they?"

"Yep. Besides loving each other, they enjoy each other's company." Jake looked at them when he said it. "You know I'm a cop, what do you do?"

"I'm a psychologist and part-time writer."

"Anything I would've read of yours?"

"Not unless you read *Cosmo.*"

* * * *

Sophia joined Louie at the grill. He grabbed her by the waist and gave her a kiss.

"They look like they're getting along," Sophia said to Louie under her breath, trying to go for casual as they glanced over at Jake and Mia.

"Yeah, we have a winner," Louie whispered in Sophia's ear while he nibbled on it.

"Hey, stop it. You said no whispering, Mom. It's rude in front of people." Marisa had snuck up behind them.

"Why do my words always come back to bite me?" Sophia asked. "This is one of those times, Marisa, when you do as I say, not as I do."

"I can't wait to be old." Marisa rolled her eyes and walked away.

"Wow. She got her point across and insulted me, all in one sentence. Our little girl's growing up, hon." Sophia changed the subject. "Look at them. They took the table farthest away from everyone. Why don't we sit with them and see how it's going?"

"No, they're doing fine on their own. He hasn't taken his eyes off her. Best of all, she's conversing, not staring or ogling him like he's some work of art. This one's smart. She'll be a keeper," Louie said, wiggling his brows.

"A keeper—you consider women prizes?"

"You're my prize. The best I've ever won. To this day, don't know how I accomplished it, but thank God you're blind." Louie kissed her.

"Cut it out, we have guests. And, Louie, I'm the biggest winner of all," Sophia said as she wrapped her arm around his waist.

* * * *

Across the yard, Jake turned to see what had caught Mia's attention. *Ah, Sophia and Louie.*

"I want a relationship like theirs when I grow up."

"You're not grown up yet, Jake?" Mia raised an eyebrow.

"Crap! Oh, sorry. I was just joking," he said stumbling over his words. "What they have, you can't practice for. It happens once in a lifetime if you're lucky."

"I've seen it happen to a lot of couples but I haven't been lucky there."

"There are a lot of empty shells out there you have to dig through before you find the pearl."

"You're right. What do you like, Jake?" Mia asked as she scooped a spoonful of peppers, sausages and onions into her mouth. Her hum of delight sent his imagination over the edge.

"I like a lot of things. Are you talking indoors, outdoors, recreation, work, clothes...?"

"Right, I forgot I'm talking to a cop. I need to be exact."

"Can I get you another drink or some food?"

"No thanks. I like to be in control. If I eat another thing, I'll burst. How can they both stay so thin with Sophia cooking like this?"

"It's always been a mystery to me. Want to dance?"

She seemed surprised he asked. The dance floor had not another soul on it.

"Sure," she said.

Jake surprised himself by asking. Dancing wasn't his thing. But he wanted—no, needed—to see how she'd fit in his arms. The band played "The Way You Look Tonight." He loved Sinatra. Later, he'd have to request the Chris De Burgh song, "Lady in Red." It said the same thing, ended the same way. And he'd never forget the way Mia looked tonight. He loved the red dress and was glad for the unusually high temperature today when she removed the jacket. No doubt about it, she got his blood boiling. Monopolizing Mia, Jake kept the socialization with the rest of the partiers to a minimum. He lost all sense of time as they danced. It shocked him when Sophia cut in to dance with him and Louie waltzed away with Mia.

He glanced around. *Hell. Everyone else has gone home.* He checked his watch as he danced with Sophia. Eleven PM was way past his hosts' bedtime. "Are we keeping you up?"

"No, what gives? I never got my dance from you tonight! Normally, I have to beg you." Sophia questioned with a sparkle in her eyes. Jake danced her around the makeshift floor.

"It was smart not telling me you were trying to fix me up again," Jake said in her ear.

"Well, we didn't want to scare you away. Looks like the two of you are hitting it off?"

"Time will tell, but, yeah, she's great. Thanks." Jake worked his way back to Mia. He exchanged partners with Louie, who had signaled the band to play one last song.

"Do you guys want help cleaning up?" Mia asked when the song was done.

"Oh no, you two take off and enjoy yourselves. We got this," Sophia said.

Louie mumbled, "Why'd you turn them down? We could use the help. I want to get you upstairs. How about we clean up tomorrow?"

"No, it won't take long and this way tomorrow we can stay in bed late—finish what we start tonight." She gave him the eyes.

He laughed. "All right. Bye, guys don't do anything I wouldn't do," Louie said.

Jake watched Louie start to clean up. "Bye, Louie," they said in unison.

Sophia walked them to their cars. "You both drive real careful. I don't want to hear you got pulled over or anything."

"We'll be fine, Sophia. Thanks for everything. I had a wonderful time," Mia said and hugged her.

"Anytime, Mia. Good night, Jake," Sophia said and kissed Jake on the cheek. She turned around and walked back inside. Jake watched her close the front door.

"You have a real affection for her, don't you?"

"I do. Sophia's a sister to me in every way but blood," Jake said.

Jake helped Mia into her car.

He cleared his throat. "Would you like to go for a drink?"

"It's getting late, Jake, maybe some other time."

"Drive carefully. If someone pulls you over, give me a call." Disappointed, he closed her door then walked to his car.

Chapter 5

He heard Mia start her car. Turning back for one last look, he watched her window lower.

"Jake?"

"Yes?"

"I could do one drink. Where would you like to go?"

"Why don't you follow me? I live around the corner. We can drop your car off there and take one car." He was thrilled she'd changed her mind. He wondered if he'd be able to find a place where he wouldn't know anyone. Tonight, he wanted Mia all to himself.

"Lead the way."

Jake pulled into his driveway on the left. Mia pulled in alongside him on the right. He walked over to her car and opened the door.

"We'll take my car, okay?" He stared down into her eyes as he offered a hand to help her out. She hesitated, conflict playing over her face. "What's wrong?"

"Do you...?"

Her pale skin turned a deep shade of red when she blushed—he liked it. "What?"

"Do you want to have the drink here?"

My lucky day. He hit his key remote, and opened the garage door in lieu of a response. "Do you want to put your car in the garage?"

"Taking a lot for granted, Jake?" Mia tilted her head up, challenging him.

"No. It offers protection for you and the car." He rubbed his hands up and down her arms.

"Always a cop, huh?"

"I can't be anything else. I hope it's not a problem?"

"No, it's not a problem, or I wouldn't be here."

Jake blew out his breath. "Good."

At the top of the stairs, between the garage and the living room, Jake reached around Mia to hit the button to lower the outside garage door before closing the connecting door to the house. He'd swear to it, that was his single intention. Instead, he took her in his arms and kissed her. She wrapped her arms around him, resting her hands on his lower back. A long, sweet kiss, he took it deeper when she kissed him back, engaging lips, tongue, and teeth as her soft, full lips caressed his mouth, promising more. God, he wanted to swallow her whole. Her sky-blue eyes darkened with passion as he was forced to pull back or he'd take this further than they should go tonight. Because once he started he wasn't stopping She gripped him by the front of his shirt and pulled him back to her. Mia gave him a mind-numbing, flame-driven kiss filled with promise. His vision blurred. They stood there, lost in time.

"Why don't we sit in the living room, get comfortable?" Breaking the embrace, Jake tried for some measure of control. He took her by the hand and led her to the sofa but she didn't sit.

"Sounds good," Mia said.

"Umm, what will you have to drink?"

"Do you have vodka or wine?"

"I have both." He concentrated hard on her answer because his body continued to respond to her other signals.

"The wine's good. Do you have white?"

"Yes, Pouilly-Fumé?" Jake looked over at her and felt himself stir once again.

"My favorite," Mia answered as she wandered around his living room.

* * * *

Jake's house, like the man, surprised her. She walked into a warm, cozy room done in different shades of blues with hints of green, beige, and mauve. The stone fireplace's imported material was the room's main focus. *Italy,* she thought, as her eyes roamed from floor to ceiling, appreciating the craftsmanship. A marble mantel in the same blue and mauve tones broke the otherwise unrelieved stone. The floor, a highly polished hardwood, poked out along the perimeter of the room, the center covered by a beige, oriental area rug with hints of blue, green, and rose. Mia liked that Jake didn't stint on quality.

Not your typical bachelor pad—neither masculine, nor feminine—it offered a person comfort. The large picture window was covered with quilted blue and green shades and a mauve valance, bringing the room together, along with the warm beige walls. *He had a good decorator,* she thought.

Mia ran her hand over the fabric on the back of the sofa. *Silk brocade,* she mused. The navy sofa sported green and beige pillows. The fabric he'd chosen for the two chairs and ottoman combined all the colors of the room. A sixty-five-inch HD TV graced the wall, proof that a man did, indeed, live here. Lamps in shades of beige and mauve sat on the marble end tables in the exact color of the hearth. The coffee table had a matching marble top. Mia took the glass of wine Jake handed her as he walked into the room and sat next to her on the couch. He draped an arm around her shoulder. Their two bodies could heat a house in New England for the winter. Mia sipped her wine though it wouldn't ease her craving.

"Your living room's beautiful. Did you have a decorator?"

"No, I picked out what I liked. If I got stuck, I asked Sophia for help. She argued about my color scheme, telling me it wouldn't work, but I like it."

"I like it too. It's relaxing."

She let Jake take the glass from her hand and place it on the table. When he took her in his arms she let him kiss her. Same reaction, not that she'd expected any different. Heat traveled through her, around her.

If he kept kissing her this way, she'd forget her own name. Her whole body had come alive with the kiss by the door. At the party—the instant they had made eye contact—he did it for her physically. Now if he could only do it for her mentally. The power of the kiss punched right through her, melting the Antarctic iceberg she'd hidden her emotions behind since her broken engagement. She needed to take control. But she struggled— they were mature adults, her mind reasoned against her body's passion, what would be the harm? How far should she go tonight? Would this be a physical relationship? What kind of reaction would she get if she jumped him? Did she want to stop? It had never been a question before. His voice brought her around.

"Mia, I could lift you up right now and take you to bed. Nothing would make me happier. I understand this is going to sound stupid or like a play but…I want to explore what's going on with us. We've got some kind of connection. It's intense, maybe a little scary too. What do you think?"

Speechless, she looked at him. It had to be a play. Did he make the connection with her name, her family? She'd been fighting off men's advances for years. Some wanted her money. Others wanted the prestige her name and wealth could supply. She did a fast assessment of Jake and liked what she saw. Besides, his jeweled-colored eyes, and chiseled face, and strong muscular frame almost had her begging to get laid, but more, conversation wasn't forced with him. *It's been way too long.* "I should go home. It's the smart thing to do," she said, pushing herself off the sofa. "I can't figure out if your words are smooth or genuine."

"Genuine." He grabbed her right hand and pulled her back down beside him. "You drank a lot today and it's close to one o'clock. Why don't you stay in the spare bedroom?" He grinned down at her. "You can trust me. I'm a cop. Besides, you might get snagged in a DUI trap."

"I'll be fine. I spaced out my drinks today. Before I leave you can tell me where the state troopers set up." Mia wiggled her brow to break the tension.

"No, I can't, they don't inform us of their schedule anymore then we do with ours. Stay. We'll have breakfast together." He gave her one of his flirty smiles. "And we'll spend the day together tomorrow if you don't have anything else to do."

She didn't think long on it. "All right, as long as you understand it'll be your fault if I climb into bed with you tonight." She threw a hand over her mouth. It wasn't like her to not be in control. Maybe she did have a little too much to drink. "You have me turned around." Mia pushed her hair behind her ear.

"Glad to know you're as undone by me as I am by you. Come on." He pulled her up and walked her down the hall to the spare room. He opened the door. She stepped inside and looked around.

"Nice."

The bed took up most of the space. The windows were treated in the same material as the spread, a yellow fabric with blue flowers. A blue area rug covered the floor, exposing two feet of bare hardwood all around. The night stands sat on either side of the bed, along with a tall dresser and a wide mirror which gave the room an airy feeling. As a psychologist, she tucked away the uniformed, uncluttered rooms throughout the house to analyze another day.

Thrilled when Jake pulled her back into his arms, she put everything into the kiss. "Pleasant dreams," he said.

"Oh, don't worry I'm sure they will be. Good night."

"Good night."

Mia closed the door and leaned against it.

* * * *

The next morning, Jake, after tossing and turning all night long with Mia in the next room, got up earlier than usual. He opened the back door to let in the mild spring breeze and inhaled. A hint of rain wafted in with the fresh scent of early blooms. He poured coffee into his large mug and decided to watch the sunrise on the back deck. A knock on the front door had him heading the other way. Jake rushed across the kitchen to answer it. He didn't want the visitor to disturb Mia's sleep. When he pulled the door open, Louie stood on the other side of it, frowning. There went his sunrise, Jake thought.

"Damn, you blew another perfect opportunity, Jake." Without a thought to who might be there, Louie walked into a room talking. "We set you up with a perfectly good woman—what'd you do, toss her back? What gives?"

"You know, Louie, I like you, though you can be crude at times. Whatever goes on with Mia and me is our business, got it?"

"I got it. You two seemed to be hitting it off last night. You even looked like…you know. When you left together, well…" Louie shrugged his shoulders, letting the rest of it hang out there.

"What will be, will be, Louie. Don't interfere. I'm fixing us breakfast. Do you want some?" Jake said and waited Louie out.

"What, she's here? You said—"

Jake interrupted him. "I said nothing. I asked if you wanted to join us. I hear her moving around in there. Would you like to knock on the spare bedroom door and see if she's ready to eat?" Jake turned away to hide his grin.

"The spare bedroom? What are you, Sir freakin' Lancelot?"

"The woman's a lady, Louie. I'm going to treat her like one. Don't screw this up for me."

"Me? Screw up what?" Louie knocked on the door to the spare bedroom as he mumbled.

* * * *

Mia sucked in the laughter bubbling in her throat. The last thing she wanted was for Louie to know she'd been eavesdropping. Jake and Louie acted like an old married couple. She'd heard law enforcement partnerships had a deep bond over time. These two personified it. Louie knocked again.

"Yes?"

"Umm…good morning. It's Louie."

She opened the door. "Good morning. I enjoyed myself yesterday. Thanks again for the invite." She wore the robe she'd found on the back of the door. She'd thought about dressing in last night's clothes but decided Jake should see the way she looked in the morning.

Louie stepped aside to let her out. She walked to the kitchen. When Jake turned, not all the heat came from the stove.

"Good morning," Jake said locking eyes with her.

"What smells so delicious?" He wore a pair of beat-up jeans. No shirt or shoes. Lordy, she wanted to jump him right then and there. It had been a long night.

"I made blueberry pancakes and western omelets. I didn't know if you preferred eggs or a more traditional Sunday breakfast?"

My God, he looks shy. The rapid pulse in his neck allowed her to see what she felt.

Louie cleared his throat. "Sophia's going to kill me. She sent me out for the paper over an hour ago, I better head home."

Neither paid any attention to Louie. "Did you say something?" Jake said, turning toward him.

"I said I'm leaving. Enjoy your breakfast."

* * * *

Mia sat down at the table, while Jake waited on her. Neither of them tasted the food he cooked, absorbed in each other, the world stood apart from them. They talked. They laughed. With his thumb, he wiped away a bit of syrup from her top lip. Before he could pull his hand away she took his thumb into her mouth and sucked it clean.

Mia pushed away from the table and started to clear the dishes. He took the plates out of her hands and placed them back on the table. He lowered his mouth to hers. She kissed him, dishes forgotten. Silky hands glided over his face before fisting in his hair. He broke the kiss as he searched her eyes. Mia tilted her head to the side to offer him her neck.

Jake gripped the lapels of the robe she wore and pulled them apart. All the air in his lungs escaped as he fought to breathe. He memorized every inch of her naked body. He never wanted to forget what she looked like, right there, right now.

"You're stunning." He trailed kisses down her throat, to her breasts, before exploring with his hands.

Her throaty moan encouraged him on. Straightening, he picked her up in his arms and carried her down the hallway as he worked his way toward his bedroom. Midway down the hall he stopped.

"Now would be the time to say stop," he whispered. *God, please don't let her stop.*

"I don't want to... I know we should," she whispered, short of breath, while she nuzzled his ear.

"Well...if we're not going to continue, I need a shower. An arctic shower," he said hoarsely, putting her down. He leaned her against the wall. His body pressed against hers as he caressed her breasts.

"We'll both need a cold shower, if you keep doing that," she moaned. "I have no willpower left."

* * * *

He said all the right things, she thought, glad for the time she spent in the gym. She felt like a teenager as he felt her up. The sensation sent tiny waves of heat through her bloodstream and shut down her brain. Her entire body was an inferno—if she didn't put a stop to it now, they might do something they'd regret later. Not that she believed for a second she'd regret it. Another couple of minutes and she wouldn't be able to stop. He pressed even closer into her, letting her know he wanted her. She wanted him—boy, did she want him. With all her strength, she pushed him away. And reminded herself she'd only met him yesterday.

"Jake." She didn't know what else to say. She did. But she didn't voice her thoughts. Instead she removed his hands from her breasts, held them together in her hands and kissed them. "Do you have plans for today?"

Mia watched him try to catch his breath, refocus.

"No, would you like to do something?" He quickly added, "But not here, or you know what we'll be doing."

"Oh yeah, I thought a nice hike would do us both good. Work off some of this excess energy we seem to have."

"Sounds like a plan. Let's take a shower." He grabbed her, threw her over his shoulder and walked into the bathroom. With her wiggling to get free, he turned on the water.

"Wait, put me down, Jake. I can't take a shower with you. It would be too intimate, too dangerous."

"I like danger."

"Jake, it would be torturous."

"I love torture." He grinned.

* * * *

It was excruciating as Jake soaped her up, sliding his hands all over her. Every nerve ending in her body burned like melted steel. He massaged her flesh, tormented her to the point she could no longer put two words together—need filled her. He must have read her mind. He finished up by washing her hair, a sensuous experience like no other. His hands slid through her strands. *Keep this up and I'm all yours*, she thought. His hands sent a warm feeling all the way down to her toes. She could think of nothing else but his hands as he continued to lather her up. In turn she teased him, rubbing him until he moaned for her. Egging him on, she took the kiss deeper. *Reason be damned.*

It was obvious he wanted her. She couldn't last much longer. Mia admired his control, pondering the moment they would take each other. Deep down she felt it would be the best sex of her life.

"We better get out of the shower and put some clothes on. Otherwise, I'll have to hang a flag of surrender on myself and swallow my pride. Maybe even my dignity," he said, his voice cracking with each word he spoke.

She laughed as he meant her to. "I can't wait to capture your flag."

"You're killing me! Out, get out now," he demanded, turning the water to freezing cold. She jumped out of the shower, screaming and laughing.

* * * *

They stopped at her condo for a change of clothes before heading to Sharon, Connecticut, for the day. The hour drive was worth it. And the weather cooperated. In the high seventies, it was about ten degrees over the normal temperature for this time of year. *It might even hit the low eighties*, the weatherman had teased. *Ah, the first weekend in May.* He picked Kent Falls State Park for the picnic. It offered coves for quiet, romantic picnics and a beautiful waterfall. They talked as they hiked, flirting with each other, until they found the perfect spot to lay out the blanket. Jake set up lunch while Mia poured the wine. They talked the afternoon away. He found Mia to be a good listener.

For the first time, he spoke of his childhood, his sister's death, its effect on him and his parents. He spoke of his mother's illness and his father's death. She listened without interrupting, unless she wanted him to clarify a point, or to ask a question. She didn't talk to talk. She listened, as if it would be horrible to miss something he said. And she laughed easily. It made him want to make her laugh more to hear the sound of it again. He hadn't had a carefree day like this in... He couldn't remember. He closed his eyes as he brought back the image of her in the shower. The memory so real, so vivid, he could see the water beading on her bare skin, rolling down between her breasts, down her stomach...

"What are you smiling about?" Mia asked.

"Number one, what a great laugh you have. Number two, thoughts of you in the shower with nothing on but your smile." He leaned over and kissed her.

"Mmm, just a smile?"

"Oh yeah."

He stretched out on his back on the blanket, putting his hands behind his head, and remembered every single curve and freckle on her naked body.

"I learned something about you today. You're a pervert," she said, bending down to kiss him back.

"Your point?"

"No point."

Chapter 6

For the first time in twelve years Jake walked into the bullpen at the stroke of nine. Jake's normal time was seven-thirty. Louie sat at his desk, facing the squad room door as he sipped from a cup of coffee.

"How nice, you decided to join us today, Lieutenant," he said over the rim of the cup.

"Oh, shove it, Louie."

"Aren't we grouchy today? If you'd listened to your hormones, you'd be in a better mood."

Jake stared him down. He didn't flinch. "Lieutenant, let me get you a cup of coffee."

"Louie, back off." Jake turned and left the squad room as the other cops stared after him. Louie followed him into an empty office.

"Hey, what gives?" he asked.

"Between us, Louie. No gossip."

"Okay."

"I watched Mia pull out of the garage this morning. I turned to close the garage door and when I turned back, do you know what I saw?" Jake's face turned red. Louie was afraid he'd blow a gasket.

"No, what?" Louie asked.

"Chloe Wagner pulled out from down the street. She started to follow Mia. I jumped in my car and cut her off before she could find out where Mia lived. When I confronted her, she said she was on her way to work. She had the balls to ask about Mia, by name. How the hell did she know her name?"

"Don't know, maybe she's stalking you? But who the hell stalks a cop?" Louie pulled at his nose.

"There's something off about her. I want to review every last piece of evidence today in Shanna Wagner's file. See if we missed anything. We need to close this one and get rid of Chloe. After we finish the interviews on the Adams case let's go through Shanna's together."

"I'll make the time."

Jake nodded.

"So, Mia spent the night again?" Louie slipped in.

"Get your mind out of the gutter. It's not what you think."

"Hey, what do I think?" Louie scowled all the way back to his desk.

Jake ignored him. As they stepped back into the squad room, the captain called Jake into his office.

"Take a seat." McGuire pointed to a chair.

"What's up, Captain?"

"I'm getting pressure from the other shifts. Their lieutenants want to settle in. Pick out your office. You have first choice because of your seniority and ranking."

"Okay, I'll do it now. Are they all set up or do they need to be outfitted for phones and computers?" Jake thought the corner office at the other end of the bullpen would offer privacy and a nice view of the downtown area. He liked this old shop town, even with all the empty factories. Some enterprising people were now trying to convert them into interesting businesses while grabbing the tax breaks being offered by the city.

"It's turn-key, go ahead and pick one out."

Jake started out of the captain's office.

"Is something bothering you, besides Spaulding?" McGuire asked.

"I'm distracted with my cases—my sister's, Wagner, and Adams." Guilt speared him. Mia had filled his whole weekend. He hadn't even thought about Eva.

At some point, I'll need to discuss Chloe with the captain, but not before I calm down.

"Do you have anything new on the Wagner or Adams cases?" McGuire asked.

"No, I took the weekend off. We'll be doing the follow-ups this morning."

"I'll let you get to it then."

He nodded, turned, and walked back to his desk.

"What did McGuire want?"

"I'm supposed to pick an office. You're not going to go ballistic on me, are you?" Jake smiled to lighten the blow.

Louie stared at him for the beat of five. "No, I'm not going to go crazy. It goes with the rank. But I can't help wishing it was me."

"You're not going to miss me?"

"No. I've been looking forward to this day for years. I thought I'd be the one in the office."

Louie always psyched himself out when it came to taking tests. It never failed—he worried his way to a low score. He'd done the same thing throughout high school. A brilliant detective, Louie had taken the sergeant's exam for the third time two weeks ago, around the same time Jake had taken the lieutenant's exam. He offered up a little prayer in hopes that Louie passed this time around.

"Next week you'll get to pick the office right next to mine. When you do, we won't be partners any longer. They'll give each of us someone to train, God help us."

"Yeah, like that would happen."

"If you want it, it'll happen," Jake said. "Let's do the follow-up with the two friends who went out with Chelsea Adams. You left messages on Friday for them. Did either of them respond? Have we heard back from the lab yet on the car?"

"Slow down, Jake, I'm on top of everything. I haven't gotten any lab results yet. I'll check my voicemail before I call the lab again. The M.E.'s report should be in later today." Louie rubbed his chin.

"Let's book an interview room for tonight around six o'clock. I'm pulling Chloe in after work. I want her to understand we're not kidding around. Let's start messing with her head," Jake said, catching Louie's expression. "What?"

"Are you doing this because she got under your skin, or because of the case?"

"She can't be following me—or Mia—around. I want to make it clear to her that stalking is a criminal offense. But more, what we need is to solve the case for Shanna."

"We're trying. It's not like we're not working it," Louie said.

"Remember a few months ago when we were leaning toward the guy she worked with, even though he had an alibi? Let's take another look at him. Review every statement in the file to see if we can pick up the trail again. The last time I saw Chloe, she made a point of mentioning how he kept in touch with her. It's weird. Shanna broke it off with him a month or two before her death," Jake said.

"I'll book the room."

"Damn, it was stupid to date her in the first place. I don't know what got into me. At some point, I'm going to have to let the captain in on it."

"Document it, Jake. You never know when someone's going to snap," Louie said.

"Let's leave it for now. We'll record the interview tonight. That will make it official."

"If you say so." Louie shrugged. He backed down. It wasn't his life. Jake would handle Chloe his own way.

After checking his voicemail, Louie noted calls from both Julie Cahns and Jora Stein, recorded their numbers on his pad, and then booked an interview room for six o'clock. He returned Julie Cahns's call first.

"Julie Cahns, please." A man answered the phone.

"Who's calling?"

"It's Detective Romanelli from the Wilkesbury Police Department."

"Oh, yes. This is about poor Chelsea, isn't it?"

"Yes. You are…?"

"Julie's brother, Dwayne."

"Okay. Did you know Chelsea?"

"Yes."

"Is Julie there?" Louie asked again. He put Dwayne's name on the list to interview at a later time.

"I'll get her."

Louie waited several minutes before Julie picked up.

"Hello."

"This is Detective Romanelli."

"Detective, I'm sorry I didn't get back to you sooner. I was away this weekend."

"How are you doing?" Louie noted the stress in her voice.

"Not good. I've known Chelsea since we were in high school. I can't put my head around it—I just can't believe she's gone." Julie cried, making her words difficult to understand. "I'm sorry. I'm having a hard time holding it together."

"Please try, we need to go through the night you all went out to dinner." Louie asked.

"Okay."

A half hour later, Louie ended the call. He'd gathered more information into Chelsea's life, both as a friend and as a mother, but he got nothing new from Julie concerning their last night together. Her story matched Sara's. Glad to be off the phone, he rubbed his ear to ease the pressure.

"Next one's yours," he told Jake.

"She talked for a long time."

"Chelsea's her best friend. You could feel her grief."

"What's the name of the next one?"

"Let me see—Jora Stein. She worked with Chelsea."

"Is this her work number or her home number?"

"Work," Louie answered.

* * * *

Jake got nothing new from Jora either. Nothing exciting happened to any one of them except for Chelsea's disappearance. No one else but Jora had interacted with anyone outside of their small group, and she had left right after Chelsea. Jora said the guy was an epitome of an asshole. She had never let it get past the stage of talking with him at the bar. Chelsea had left due to boredom, around ten o'clock.

According to Jora, Chelsea never complained about anyone bothering her—not socially, professionally, or personally. A quiet woman, a homebody who went to work then home, Chelsea didn't care to date. The divorce had left her bitter. Once a week, she'd go out with her friends for a quick meal.

Jake played the conversation over in his mind, frustrated with the lack of leads. Murder was rarely a random act—was this one of those times it was? In his cases throughout the years, with few exceptions, survivors had stated the victim had no enemies. But he always found at least one, if not more. A person didn't go through life without at least a smudge. He chided himself. It was too early yet in the investigation to classify it. A lot more work needed to be done before he'd give up. Tomorrow they'd dig deeper into the lives of her kids, the ex-husband, the new wife, and her friends.

Jake turned to Louie. "Did you hear back from the airlines yet? If not, do a follow-up call. See if we can't at least tie that up." Jake went down his list and checked off everything they'd accomplished today.

"Hmm! You're leaning toward the new model for this. Did she have enough time to fly in, kill Chelsea, and then out fly out again?"

"That's where my gut's leading me. I want to know why she lied. Could be innocent enough, if she didn't want to say where she had gone in front of her husband."

"Do you want to take a ride? The bartender over at the golf course returned my call. I'm heading over there now. It's close to lunchtime. We can grab something to eat there."

Jake's personal cell phone rang before he could respond. He took it out of his pocket to check the display and smiled.

"Let me guess—Mia?"

Jake nodded, turning away from Louie.

"I'm in Wilkesbury today. Do you want to meet for lunch?" Mia asked.

"I'd love to. Let me rearrange a few things and I'll call you right back," Jake said, as he ran down the list of to-dos in his mind. Everything could wait a half hour or more.

"Great," she said, before hanging up.

"Change of plans."

"I heard." Louie beamed like a proud papa. "Remember, Sophia and I fixed you up."

"I'll remember when things don't work out," Jake teased. He loved busting Louie's chops.

"Nice, Jake. See, it's doomed before it starts if you feel that way. I'll take lunch at the golf course alone. You do what you have to do."

Jake tolerated Louie's lectures most times. He appreciated it when Louie walked away, giving him some privacy. He punched in Mia's number.

"Where do you want to meet?" Mia asked.

"How about Café Pablo, right off the highway? Do you know where it is?"

"Yes, it's perfect because I'm in the east end of town today. When do you want to meet?"

"Now is good?"

"I'll need at least fifteen minutes to write up my meeting notes then I'll see you there," Mia said.

"Take your time. Depending on traffic, it'll take me ten or fifteen minutes to get there"

The day didn't start out well, but seeing Mia would turn it around. Should he tell her about Chloe? Did she see her this morning? Should he wait—see if it happened again?

"Let me remind you lunch is a half hour, buddy," Louie said, with a twinkle in his eye. "So, no nooners."

Jake wiggled his brow. "You're jealous. I'll be back when I'm back." He grabbed his jacket, tossed Louie a grin over his shoulder as he headed to his car for the drive across town.

* * * *

Before Jake reached his car, Louie had Sophia on the phone. "You'll never guess who's having lunch with whom," Louie said when Sophia answered.

"Oh Louie, you're such a child. Back off and don't screw this up for him."

"Geez, Sophia, you're the second person to accuse me of that today," Louie said.

"Well, you have a knack. So, it's working out. It took us what, ten years to get it right?"

"Yep. Also, I wanted to let you know that I might be working late. I'll let you know for sure after lunch."

"Okay."

"I have to run, bye." Louie hung up, turning his mind back to the business of murder. He bounced between cases. Could Jake be right about Chloe being involved in her sister's murder? Louie hoped not. Having dated her during the investigation could put a black mark on Jake's spotless record.

Chapter 7

Mia arrived at the restaurant before Jake and took the booth by the dessert display counter. It gave her a bull's-eye view of the front door. Located in a strip mall, Café Pablo used to be part of Frankie's, a famous local hot dog place. The manager had bought it from Frankie's owner. Café Pablo had flower pots outside with big, bright blooms announcing spring. The Frankie's side served fast food with ambience. A hodgepodge of memorabilia covered the walls, taking the diner back to another time and place. The owner, Tommy, greeted each guest as they arrived. Café Pablo's Italian flavor offered a relaxing atmosphere with scrumptious desserts. No matter which side you chose, you couldn't help but enjoy the food.

Mia caught a glimpse of Jake through the front window as he approached the restaurant. His graceful movements reminded her of a cat ready to spring. He wore a sport coat with jeans and a button-down shirt. He smiled when he spotted her and walked over to the booth. It surprised her when he leaned down and kissed her. She was glad public displays of affection didn't bother him. It put another plus in the yes column for dating him.

"Hi," he said, taking the seat across from her.

"I like your greetings. Another second, we'd have had to leave."

"Hmm, you're saying you're easy?" His eyes crinkled at the corners when he smiled over the menu at her. It was a simple gesture that quickened her pulse.

"It seems I am with you." Mia took his hand across the table.

"Good, I like that." Jake rubbed his fingers over her emerald ring.

"I can't explain why, but you put me at ease."

"I hope so, after this weekend." His green eyes sparkled with laughter.

Both stopped talking as the waiter approached their table and took their order.

And before Mia knew it, time ran out. After paying the bill, Jake walked her to her car. There, he took her in his arms and kissed her again. A car pulled alongside of them. Jake's adrenaline kicked in when he heard the window go down. He spun around, pushing Mia behind him and drew his weapon. He started to relax when he spotted one of his detectives at the wheel. Disgusted, he holstered his weapon.

"Is this what you do on company time, Lieutenant?" Kraus said.

"Funny, Kraus. Get the hell out of here."

"Nope, not until I get an introduction. You kept her all to yourself at the party."

"Mia, this jerk's Detective Gunther Kraus. He's also known to his friends as Gunner. Smart women stay clear of him."

"Nice, Jake. It's a pleasure to meet you, Mia. He's the shady one, so watch yourself." Kraus drove away without another word.

"Asshole," Jake muttered.

"Be nice." Mia laughed.

"I gotta go. I'll talk to you later?"

"I look forward to it. See ya."

Mia climbed into her car, ready to start the engine, when Jake leaned in the window to give her another kiss. A minute later, he watched her drive away. Not once did he broach the subject of Chloe. Was he wrong not to?

As he turned back to his department issued junker, he spotted a red vehicle at the other end of the parking lot. He'd swear it was Chloe's. He jumped into his car, turned it around and sped through the lot. By the time he reached the spot where he had seen it, it was gone. *Should I call Mia and warn her? Damned if I do. Damned if I don't. When I'm sure, I'll tell her.*

He decided to call Louie. "What's up?" he asked. "Taking the afternoon off?"

"No. Are we all set for tonight's interview?"

"Yes, why?"

Jake explained. An idea struck him. Maybe he could pull a warrant to check out the parking lot surveillance. He'd have to finagle it a bit to fit his cases but...

"I'm stopping at the dealership to show Chelsea's picture around. I'll be back in a half hour. Did you get anything on the airlines?"

"Yep, the new Mrs. Adams took a flight to Bermuda not Miami on the sixteenth," Louie said triumphantly.

"Is she having an affair?"

"I have no evidence pointing in that direction. I'm still waiting on information pertaining to her return-flight. They don't have her leaving on Sunday, but they're still researching."

"Let's throw it around when I get back. What happened with the bartender?" Louie had piqued his curiosity.

"His story is the same as her friends. He's familiar with them from coming in each week. He confirmed Chelsea was the quiet one. After one drink she'd split, like clockwork."

"Yeah, it wouldn't be hard to follow her with her routine, or to get her alone," Jake said, as he twirled it around inside his head.

"I'll see you when you get back. Are we working tonight? I need to let Sophia know."

"I want to. I haven't put hands on the Wagner case yet today. Do you want to do it at your house or mine? If we have time, I want to put a dent in my father's files too."

It was eating at him. He hadn't spent as much time as he should've on getting Eva justice. Since his meeting with Shamus, nothing new had been said about Spaulding, except Jake had gotten his required notice from the parole board that Spaulding was coming up in front of them again. Each time, he'd gone before them with pictures of Eva's bruised and bloodied body to make sure Spaulding never left prison. Would the evidence work to keep him behind bars this time?

Mia wasn't an excuse to shuck his responsibilities. His father would be ashamed of him. It bothered him that Burke hadn't pestered him with any questions yet. Did he even look at the file? Maybe tomorrow he'd take Al out to lunch and pick his brain.

"Your place is quieter. You figure we'll be about two hours?" Louie questioned.

"Yes, we should make some headway." Seven to nine—it would still be early enough to see Mia.

"Not seeing Mia tonight?" Louie asked, as though he read Jake's mind.

"I don't know. We didn't make plans."

* * * *

Jake showed Chelsea's picture to the salespeople at the dealership. No one recognized her. The manager, Kevin Myers, checked the company records for him. He wanted to know if any one of the Adamses had ever bought a car from them. He also checked for Lola Adams.

While he waited for Kevin, he walked around the showroom looking at cars. No less than four salespeople approached him, trying to sell him one.

There were no hits on the dealership's records for Chelsea Adams or her ex and his wife. Jake headed back to the station, frustrated. Somewhere, somehow, someone had to have encountered Chelsea on the night of her disappearance. Maybe he should reach out to the media—ask the public if anyone had seen someone on the car lot on the sixteenth.

Chapter 8

At six o'clock on the dot, Chloe sashayed into the station and asked to speak with Jake. A uniform escorted her to Interview Room Three. Jake made her wait while he observed her through the two-way mirror. Chloe went up to the mirror with a tube of lipstick in her hand. She applied it, smacked her lips together, then placed the tube of color back into her purse and fluffed her hair. She took a seat, only to tilt her head back to the glass. Chloe threw a kiss over her shoulder as she stuck the middle finger on her right hand in the air at the same time. Her arrogance pissed him off. As cool as the evening weather—well, he'd see about changing that. Chloe stood, strolled over to the water cooler, and helped herself to a glass of water. After a few minutes, she began to pace the room before she tired, and sat again.

"You should let Al and I work her." Louie narrowed his eyes as he watched her through the glass.

"I'm good. There's a policewoman in the room. Plus, you'll be there, the session is being recorded and Al will also record from behind the mirror. I still haven't figured out her game but I'm going to put a stop to it right now. Let's hope we put the fear of God in her."

Jake loved when the person in the interview exhibited restlessness. It worked in his favor. Five minutes later he and Louie walked in and nodded to the officer on duty. Chloe remained seated.

"Thanks for coming down, Chloe," Louie said, as he started the interview.

"Detective," Chloe said to Louie, never taking her eyes off Jake.

"Chloe, we don't want to keep you, let's get started," Jake spoke. He read the Miranda rights, informing Chloe that it was for her own protection.

"What's this about?"

"Let's start with you following—better yet, let's use today's term for it—stalking me and my guest."

"I don't know what you mean, Lieutenant."

"Chloe, I pulled you over today less than a quarter mile from my house. You were sitting in wait outside my home. I gave you a written warning not to follow my guests. Correct? To refresh your memory, all this happened at around eight o'clock this morning."

"I took your road on my way to work. I received a call on my cell phone. I pulled over to answer the phone. Is that a crime?"

"Can I have your phone?" Jake reached out for it.

She pulled the phone close to her chest. "If you're looking for the call, I deleted it. I didn't know it would be important. From now on, Jake, I'll give you a call—ask your permission before I delete anything you think is pertinent."

"We have ways of bringing back deleted calls," Jake said.

"Well then, get a warrant."

Ignoring her comments, he continued. "You live in the east end of Wilkesbury. You work in Southington, which is located closer to the east end of town, yet you drove to the west end of Wilkesbury to get to work? There's no logic in your reasoning, Chloe. Once again, why were you outside my house this morning?"

"Jake, you're out of line here. I already explained it to you this morning when you pulled me over. If there's a problem, you should make a formal complaint." Chloe held her hands out with a shrug.

Jake felt the heat climb up his face, the flush of anger burning his skin. He was aware that it showed. Stupid—that's what he was to have had dated her. He had jeopardized his career for this…this…tart.

Louie also noticed it and stepped in. "Chloe, you can consider this interview to be the formal complaint filed against you. Jake's captain has been made aware of your actions and dating history with Jake. That was two dates, correct?"

Her eyes flashed when he detailed the number of dates. He kept hammering the number home. "You were the aggressor, pursuing him until he accepted a date from you. You followed him, coordinating your times to show up at restaurants, bars, and the theater, wherever he was headed on a given night, correct?" Louie didn't wait for her answer. "I have the detective's description of each date. But before you answer, let me say Jake ended the relationship, making it quite clear after the second date that he didn't want to pursue it any further. Correct?"

To her credit, she held herself in check.

"Detective Romanelli, I'm aware of Lieutenant Carrington's feelings on the matter. He acted like a typical male. He took what he wanted and then left. Afterward, the few times I've contacted Lieutenant Carrington have pertained to my sister's murder case. I needed an update. Since neither one of you bothered to keep me or my parents informed, I wanted to know if you'd caught her killer yet. Have you caught my sister's killer?"

"Let me address the first part of your answer. Was a physical relationship freely offered?"

"Yes," Chloe said in a hushed voice.

"Please speak up for the record, Miss Wagner."

"Yes, damn it."

"Thank you," Louie said, and then continued. "For the middle part of your statement, you know from our conversation a few days ago that I don't know why he didn't return your calls. In fact, I told you to give him a call and ask him directly?" Louie asked, pushing the issue.

"Yes."

"Okay, for the last part of your question, you also know from the same discussion that we haven't caught your sister's killer. We need new information, a new direction, if you will, to lead us to the killer. Everything we've investigated has led to dead ends."

Her eyes scorched, burning with passion and hatred as she responded. "I did inquire why he hasn't returned my calls. Is that a crime?" she snarled, looking over at Jake.

"No, it's not a crime, though it is a crime to stalk someone. Lieutenant Carrington has kept records of every time he's run into you while out on his personal time. In fact, they are too numerous to be considered a coincidence. He also recorded the number of times you've contacted him on his personal cell, along with the messages you've left for him. None of them refer to your sister's case."

"I don't know what to tell you, Detective." Chloe shrugged.

"Chloe, tonight's interview is your formal notification that a complaint has been filed against you for stalking. As of now, you will not sit outside of the lieutenant's home. If you wish to inquire about your sister's case, you will contact the main number of this precinct and go through the switchboard. You can ask to be directed to either me or the lieutenant, but you may not contact us directly. Understood?" Louie finished.

"Understood. What do you have to say about this, Jake?"

Louie had to give it to her, the woman had balls. "Ms. Wagner, the lieutenant has nothing further to say on this matter. You're free to go."

She got up, undulated her hips as she left the room without a backward glance.

"Well, we couldn't ask for more fun, could we?" Jake said, without mirth.

"Boy, she's ballsy, no doubt about it. Burke, you can come in now."

"You've got a live one there, Jake," Burke said as he came through the door.

"I do, but let's hope it's over. I don't know if the other times I ran into her were coincidence, but I doubt it. Thanks, guys." He dreaded the thought of telling McGuire. It would be a censure against his record. But the time had come to cover his and the department's asses.

He tapped on McGuire's door. "Cap, can I come in?"

"What's up?"

He filled McGuire in. When he finished, Jake took a deep breath.

"You stepped out of line when you dated her. If it happens again, you'll lose your stripes. I have no choice, this will go into your permanent record. The interview also shows she's been told to stay away from you in case this goes any further. But let me remind you, you should've reported this sooner. You put the department in the crosshairs unnecessarily."

"It won't happen again," Jake said, standing at attention.

"No, it won't. You're supposed to be setting the standards for your department, not breaking them," McGuire said.

Chapter 9

Nerves jumping, Mia adjusted her short leather jacket and knocked on Jake's front door. *I hope he likes unexpected surprises. Too pushy*, she thought, turning toward the street. Her mind jumbled, she swung back, shifted the bottle of wine from her right hand to her left, and raised her hand to knock again. The door opened. She stopped mid-knock before she hit Jake in the face.

"Mia?"

"A whim… I should've called before dropping by," she said, embarrassed.

"No, I like whims." He smiled. Taking her in his arms, he gave her a kiss.

"Jake, what's up? Who's there?" Louie yelled from the kitchen.

Louie came running into the room with his gun drawn when Jake didn't answer. Startled, Mia tried pulling back. Jake pulled her in closer. They were still half in, half out the door.

"Damn it, answer a man when he asks you a question."

"Put the gun down, Louie. It's Mia."

"I can see that for my damn self who the hell it is. You guys are gonna get killed, if you don't respond the next time. I should've shot the both of you to teach you a lesson." Louie's voice wavered as he slammed his gun back in his holster. She watched him whirl and head back into the kitchen and thought his reaction a bit extreme.

* * * *

"Mia, come on into the kitchen. Here let me take that." Jake took the wine from her and placed it on the counter. "We need to talk."

"Ominous words." Mia looked from Jake to Louie, retreating back.

"Do you want a drink?" Jake asked.

"Coffee's good."

"I'll make a fresh pot," Jake said, placing the wine on the counter.

"No, I'll make the fresh pot. Tell me what's wrong." Mia hung her handbag off the chair and slipped her black leather jacket over it.

"I don't want to mess this up, what's going on between us." Taking a deep breath, he continued, "If Chloe Wagner ruins this…"

"Who?"

"Here goes." He gave her all the details. He finished up by saying, "I've kind of ignored her actions—that is, until she came after you this morning." He stopped, drank some coffee. It was weak. Civilians didn't know how to brew a decent cup.

"Something didn't add up with her from the beginning—she's off." He pointed to his head. "It got me questioning myself. I also questioned the direction of the investigation. I've no proof at this time that she might be involved in her sister's death but her actions have us looking closer at her."

"Is she dangerous and should I be worried?"

"To be honest, I would be. What she's capable of is anyone's guess. Why did she follow you in the first place? It bothers me both as a man and a cop. I don't think she'd hurt you, but it would be wise to err on the side of caution." He pursed his lips.

"I understand. I'm a big girl who's been on her own for a long time and I don't need a babysitter. I can protect myself. I'm not going to let her ruin whatever this is," Mia finished, pointing her index finger at Jake and back at herself. She sat down with her own coffee, sipped, and watched him over the rim as she analyzed everything he said.

"I can help analyze the case for you. My background will offer you insights into your killer," Mia said.

"I can't let you see the file, Mia, they're for authorized personnel only. It's still an open investigation." *I'm in this freaking situation because I broke the rules. Damn it!*

"I understand, though sometimes a new set of eyes can pick up something you missed."

Maybe down the road he'd let her look at Eva's, but not this one. "I agree, except I can't allow it. The department could be sued, not to mention it could be considered tampering with evidence by letting a civilian handle the investigator's file before it's closed and tried. It's not public record yet."

She nodded. "I understand."

"Do you want to hang around? We're going to be at least another hour. If you didn't eat, we could have a late supper."

"Dinner sounds good. I'll wait in the living room." Mia grabbed her coffee, walked into the living room with it, and settled in on his sofa. She pulled a book from her purse and started reading it.

Louie looked over at him.

"What?"

"Nothing, let's get back to this. The stack here is all the statements from the other detectives and in this pile on the right is ours. I figured we'd look over the other detectives' notes first, because we've got our memorized."

"Let's get it done. I'll take half, you take the other half. We'll get through it faster."

Jake opened the first file. Within fifteen minutes of reviewing Detective Kraus's interview with Shanna's best friend, something popped.

"Louie, didn't we also interview Meryl Drake?"

"I think we did." Louie went through his notes. "Yeah, we did a follow-up with her four days later. Kraus interviewed her first. Why?"

"When Kraus interviewed her, Meryl focused on the ring Shanna's grandmother gave her. But she skimmed over the ring in our interview. She made a point of telling Kraus Shanna never took the ring off. In fact, she verified Shanna wore it the last time Meryl saw her. According to the transcript from Kraus's interview, it would've been on the night Shanna disappeared. Don't our notes say she didn't see Shanna for a whole week before the disappearance, because they were both cramming for exams?" Jake pulled out his interview notes on Meryl and read them.

"What do yours say?" Jake scratched his head.

"I have to dig out my interview notes, it's not on top." Louie wet his index finger and flipped through the pile of papers at the speed of light. "Ah, here it is."

"Let's review mine first. I'll read her statement aloud. You make notes against yours where mine are different. Then we'll do the same thing with Kraus."

"Got yourself a little tingle there?" Louie said.

"Yeah, it's not much, but the statements don't add up. It's not embellishment, they don't match."

"Now you're leaning toward her friend?" Louie scratched his chin.

"No, but there has to be a reason her story changed. Let's see why with a follow-up interview. You know, pull a string, see what unravels," Jake said.

"Okay, start reading."

"I'm also gonna play the tape. This way, we can get their rhythm."

Jake scanned the statement—started reading it as he played the tape version. He listened as Kraus recorded the standard info and Miranda rights. He liked Kraus's and Brown's rhythm as they lead Meryl through their questions. Jake stopped the tape when Meryl mentioned the emerald ring before Kraus was able to. He hit rewind, replayed it and made notes.

Drake: Most of the time. We were friends our whole lives, but we didn't agree on everything, especially her sister. Chloe was mean to her. Shanna would never fight with her, though Chloe tried to fight with her all the time. She'd take Shanna's clothes, her jewelry, whatever she wanted at the moment, without asking.

Brown: They didn't get along?

Drake: Chloe doesn't get along with a lot of people. She's a self-involved bitch.

Brown: Who's older?

Drake: Chloe.

Brown: Give details why they didn't get along, Meryl. Did they fight over boyfriends, clothes, money?

Drake: Shanna excelled at everything she did. Her grades were the best. She had the best boyfriends—when she wanted one. Her parents doted on her. She's friendly, outgoing, she always volunteered to help if help was needed. I don't know. She was great. Chloe is the opposite, always jealous of her parents' attention toward Shanna. Plus, Chloe thought she should have been given the emerald ring because she was older than Shanna.

Jake noted the way Meryl switched from present to the past when referring to Shanna. A normal reaction when a person hadn't fully accepted the death. He continued to listen until Kraus asked her if she saw Shanna the week of her disappearance.

Kraus: Did you see Shanna the week she disappeared?

Drake: I saw her Friday night.

Jake flagged his notes.

Kraus: What did you guys do? Where did you go? It's important. I need you to describe your night in detail. Who did you talk to, especially Shanna?

Drake: We hung out in her room at the dorm. A couple of the girls from her floor came over around nine o'clock, asked if we wanted to join them for pizza and beer. We did, and a couple of guys from her school dropped by our table to chat, though they didn't stay long. Her cell phone rang the whole time the guys talked to us. She would check who was calling, then she'd look disgusted, and press the ignore button.

Kraus: Who kept calling her?

Drake: I don't know. She never said.

"What do you think, Louie?" Jake asked, when the tape concluded.

"I don't know. Why'd she lie to us? Because you're right, when we interviewed her, according to my notes, she claimed she didn't see Shanna on the night of her disappearance. She couldn't have forgotten what she said four days earlier. I'll set up a formal interview with her. Maybe this environment will shake something out of her." Louie made a notation on his pad.

"Let's pull Shanna's cell records tomorrow. For some reason, they're not in the file. I don't remember any repeat or excessive calls the day she disappeared. It's almost nine o'clock, why don't we pick this up again tomorrow. I've got a couple of stops in the morning before I'll be in. I want to go by the lab and have them explain the drugs they found in Adams's system. They're not prescription meds. You got kid duty tomorrow, don't you?" Jake asked.

His day wasn't done. After Mia left tonight he'd need to put in some time on Eva's files. Last night, a couple of things he had dug out had poked at him.

"Yeah, I have a conference with Marisa's teacher. I'll be in by nine though."

"I'll see you tomorrow." Jake held up Louie's jacket, walked him to the door, and all but pushed him out.

"Hey, I don't have to leave right away. Not gonna offer me a beer?" Louie said, shrugging into his jacket.

"No, I'm not. I've known you long enough to be rude." Jake lowered his voice. "Don't bust my chops. Say good night."

"Oh, all right. Good night, Mia," he said in the voice of a chastised child as he walked out.

"You didn't have to ask him to leave. I'm the one intruding here."

"I don't think you're intruding." Jake sat down next to her on the couch. "What would you like to eat?"

"I hadn't thought about it. Do you have anything in mind?" Mia asked.

"What I have in mind doesn't involve food. Well, then again..."

Mia laughed. "I'm starving."

"Let's go get some burgers. I can guarantee they won't be as good as what I had in mind."

"I'm sure. I want to talk about this morning."

He'd scared her with the warning, but what else could he do? "I understand. We'll do it over dinner."

He pulled her off the couch, wondering if this would be their last date.

Chapter 10

They never made it to dinner. On the way, Jake's radio crackled to life. The dispatcher reported a ten-forty in progress. The code for a shooting in progress, cautioned the responding officers to proceed with care. Dispatch phoned moments later, informing him of the shooting. As senior officer on call, he had no choice but to take it.

Jake was happy he and Mia had taken separate cars. He put on his lights and siren and pulled Mia over to explain. He phoned Louie and arranged to meet him there.

It was nine-fifteen when Jake arrived at the scene. He parked and observed the building and the neighborhood while he waited for Louie. Eleven Wiggins Street sat at the beginning of one of the worse neighborhoods in the city. The six-family brick apartment complex towered over the one- and two-family homes on either side of it. One window in the apartment complex had curtains, the rest were covered with sheets or shades.

It remained one of the most dangerous neighborhoods in the city despite the administration's campaign promises to clean up the streets. Once elections were over, both the candidates and the residents went back to business as usual. The area housed the local drug dealers and prostitutes, along with the city's poor and downtrodden.

A few minutes later, Louie pulled up and got out of his car. He wore jeans, his off-duty attire. The first officer on site, Connelly, told them a neighbor called in the 9-1-1 with no other information. Dispatch told them to see the woman in apartment 3C, at eleven Wiggins Street—they weren't sure if the shooter was still on the premises.

As they entered the lobby, their senses were assaulted with a combination of scents. The most prevalent was the distinct odor of pot, along with takeout Chinese, pizza, and unidentifiable home cooking. The familiar scent of decay hung in the air. Jake guessed a dead mouse or some other small animal must be lodged in the walls. He wondered why these places always smelled of urine.

Taking the stairs, he and Louie avoided the elevator and stopped to listen at each floor before heading up to the third floor. As they opened the hallway door on three the odors were stronger. Everyone had left their garbage outside their doors for tomorrow's trash collection.

Louie thought he'd lose his dinner. He could never figure out how people accepted living this way. He'd kill himself trying to find a way out.

Back to back, they proceeded down the hall to apartment 3C. When they reached the apartment in question, Louie spun away and faced the door, which was riddled with bullet holes and held open by a body sprawled against it. Their weapons drawn, radios in hand, Jake shoved open the door. The body didn't budge much. Dispatch had said to speak with a Blanca Santos.

Poised at the door, Louie heard a woman crying. He exchanged a look with Jake but continued their scan of the scene. A male dressed in loose-fitting pants and sweatshirt filled the doorway. Half of his face had been blown away, but he appeared to be in his late teens. Blood spatter decorated the floor, door, and walls. Blood also ran down the kid's neck. The overpowering smell from a puddle where his body had released its contents at the moment of death filled the air—the stench of death, the rusty metallic odor of blood, urine, and intestinal fluids burned his eyes as he blinked to focus.

Three bullet holes riddled the metal door. Jake would try to match them to the body wounds once they cleared the apartment. Trying not to disturb the scene, Jake shoved it open enough for them to get through. Louie swallowed hard. He pulled open the closet doors located by the door, while Jake covered him. From there they walked down a long hallway, back to back. The first room—the kitchen—opened into the living room, where they found a crying, pregnant young woman. Not a woman, a girl, if he was any judge of age. She looked to be no more than seventeen and ready to pop. She gripped the wastepaper basket, holding it to her face while she threw up into it. The girl appeared compact, with long black hair braided down her back. Her black eyes were red from crying. As though somehow making it worse, Louie discovered this was the apartment with the curtains in the window. The place appeared clean, though it smelled of burnt meat.

After a full search of the premises, Louie went back to the girl and helped her up while Jake returned to the body and called for the crime scene team. He and Jake had developed a rhythm over the years. He took the living. Jake took the dead.

Louie popped down the hall to inform Jake he'd called for the medics and a female officer because the young girl had gone into labor.

While Louie tried to calm down the girl to get her statement, Jake bagged the hands first, then the feet. Though crime scene techs would do the same, he liked to take his own pictures and the layout of the scene for further study. He took pictures of the body and the three spent shells that he had found out in the hallway. He circled them in chalk before bagging them. Rolling the victim to his side, Jake pulled the victim's wallet from the back-left pocket, removed his license, and studied it, shaking his head. It saddened him. The kid, Xavier Orlando, of this address, lived a short life. He was nineteen. *What a waste*, Jake thought.

The crime scene team arrived at the same time the M.E., Dr. Lang, did. Ms. Santos let out a bloodcurdling scream, startling all of them. The baby must have decided tonight was a good night to make its entrance into this world.

Jake almost laughed at the panicked expression on Doc Lang's face. "I haven't delivered a baby since medical school. Get her out of here, or you'll have another victim on your hands," Lang whispered to him.

The men let out a collective sigh of relief when Stella Fisher, the female officer, arrived, relieving them of the care of the girl. Nodding to Jake then Louie, she took charge of the situation and arranged transport to the hospital for Blanca.

Before Blanca headed to the hospital, she told Louie they'd been watching television when someone had knocked on the door. Xavier had gotten up to answer it. He always looked through the peephole before opening up. She had heard gunshots and had gone to see what had happened. She had found Xavier on the floor, bleeding. Not able to find a pulse, she had dialed 9-1-1.

"Did Xavier open the door, Blanca?" Louie asked as he timed her contractions in his head.

"No, I did." Leaning over, she grabbed the chair with one hand as she wrapped her other arm around her belly and took a deep breath.

"Why?"

"Because my next-door neighbor, Annie, called out, asked if I was all right. I let her in. When she saw Xavier, she screamed and ran back to her apartment. She's in 3D..." She yelled out in pain when another contraction came.

Lang's and Jake's heads jerked up as the girl in the living room let out a scream. Jake had the woman in his line of sight. She gripped Louie's arm. "Call my mother. I need my mother with me in the delivery room. She promised she'd be there."

"We have to get her to the hospital. I'll stay with her," Stella said. "Blanca, give me your mother's number. I'll call."

With no other choice, Jake let their witness go. Once she delivered they'd question her.

"Crazy night," Louie said.

"Sure is. How is she?" Jake asked.

"She's in good hands. Fisher will take care of her. What have you got?"

"The kid was shot three times through the door. Before Blanca could open for the neighbor, she had to pull the body out of the way first. I'm sure the exertion brought on her labor. This isn't where the body originally landed. Make a note to question her—how far did she move the body? Let's start the door-to-door with apartment 3D. See what this Annie person has to say. Make sure you take a uniform with you, Louie. I'll stay with the CSIs," Jake said.

Nodding, Louie walked away and grabbed the first uniform he saw.

"Be careful. We don't know if the shooter's still in the building," Jake called out.

"Okay, Mom," Louie said.

"So, Doc, what's it looking like to you?"

"Well, Jake, he's definitely dead." Doc Lang deadpanned and motioned for the team to take away the body.

"Good one."

"I'll let you know after I post him. Don't come around until after eleven tomorrow morning. I have a full house right now. I pulled in two shootings from the Hartford area, now this makes the seventh one I have in house. The natives are on a rampage. Check in before you come to make sure I'm still on schedule," Lang said, as he hurried out of there.

"Will do."

Jake needed information on his witness and when they'd be able to interview her. While waiting for Louie to return, he decided to give Stella a quick call for an update on Blanca's status.

Louie, with notebook in hand, walked back into the apartment as Doc Lang waved good-bye.

"I got the uniforms going door to door. 3D's Annie Darcy. She didn't want to speak with us. She's sorry she knocked on the door. She doesn't want to get involved. She feels bad she couldn't stay to help Blanca but she left her kids alone in the apartment to check out the commotion. Darcy didn't want the kids coming out to look for her or see Xavier. She heard someone knock before she heard the shots. They sounded like firecrackers going off. She looked out her peephole, but she saw no one in the hallway. She raced to her bedroom, grabbed her kids and hid them in the closet to protect them. Right after that, she heard Blanca scream and ran over to see if she could help. This is a direct quote from her. 'That's all I know.' Unquote." Louie flipped his pad closed.

"Let's finish our search in here. Doc said to see him tomorrow morning after eleven, not before. He hopes to have something for us. Oh, I spoke with Stella. The doctor said Blanca should deliver within the hour. If we try now we'll get nothing from her," Jake said.

"I got three kids. The doctor said Sophia would go fast for each one, remember? She was in labor for fifteen hours for the first one, ten for another, eight for the last one. What does the doctor know?"

* * * *

With little sleep, Jake plowed through his first departmental meeting. He reviewed everyone's caseloads. He looked over the file he and Louie caught the night before and decided to hand off the Wiggins Street shooting to Al Burke and Gunner Kraus.

"Burke, Kraus, where do you stand on the Rubino case?" Jake asked.

"It's basically wrapped, except for a few loose ends. We're waiting on the D.A. for a warrant," Burke answered.

"Who's going to be the lucky guest of the state?" Jake inquired.

"One Julianna Rubino, the wife. Seems Mr. Rubino stuck his zucchini where it didn't belong once too often." Kraus laughed, shaking his index finger at Jake, imitating Mrs. Rubino. "She warned him, but did he listen?"

"You have such a grasp of the English language, Gunner," Jake commented, unable to hide his grin. "Okay, last night's shooting on Wiggins Street. The victim, a young Hispanic male, age nineteen, was shot in the face through his door. He lived there with his girlfriend, Blanca Santos. She's in the delivery room at St. Mary's hospital as we speak. No witnesses except the woman in 3D, who heard everything. Burke, you and Kraus take this one. Girlfriend claims they don't do drugs or anything illegal. Here are the preliminary interviews. One's from the uniform who was first on scene, and one from Louie and me. I've also included a report of my observations and how it played out for me. Doc Lang said he'd have something for you after eleven today. Any questions?" Jake looked around at his team.

"Yeah. Overworked, Lieutenant? It's not like you to hand off a case," Kraus commented.

"We're bogged down with the Adams and Wagner cases. So, this one's yours. You have any questions, Gunny?"

"No, sir," Kraus answered. His guys knew when to joke and when to rein it in.

"Now, let's move along. Brown, what's the status on the hit-and-run? Also, do you have anything new on the high school shooting—a suspect or a solid lead?" Jake rapidly shot his questions at Brown and Lanoue.

"Not yet. The victim of the hit-and-run is still in a coma. The eyewitnesses didn't get a license number, though we do have the make and color. The witnesses are sure the driver was a kid. As for the high school shooting—the principal and the teachers are cooperating. The students aren't. I'm sure the kids know who did it, but no one's talking. It's obvious to me they're afraid. Right, Armand?" Brown turned toward his partner to confirm.

"Yeah, Kirk, those kids are afraid of someone. The victim didn't belong to any group or gang. He maintained straight A's and didn't do drugs, nothing. It doesn't make any sense," Armand Lanoue stated.

Kirk Brown and Armand Lanoue had been partnered since last year, when Joe Smith retired. Armand got promoted to detective. Brown's partner, Kraus, moved over to partner with Burke. Both were in their thirties. Kirk Brown matched his name—brown hair and brown eyes, height five-eleven. Armand Lanoue—thinning blond hair, brown eyes—stood a gangly six-three. Their partnership seemed to be working.

"Do you need any help on either one, Kirk?" Jake asked.

"No, we're still in the early stages. What if we grab a couple of uniforms for the door-to-door on the hit-and-run, to narrow down the list, is that okay with you?" Detective Brown said.

"Do what you need to. If you need more, come see me. Al, you and Gunner go over to the hospital, interview the live-in girlfriend after she delivers."

"We get all the choice assignments, don't we? Why couldn't she be a stripper?" Burke said.

Jake stared Burke down until Al turned away. "Gunner" or "Gunny," as everyone referred to Kraus, and Burke were the original odd couple. Gunner's suits, shirts, even his ties were matched and pressed with precision. Though married, he thought of himself as a ladies' man. Jake thought of him as a snake. He hated cheaters.

With Burke, Jake could always tell what he ate for lunch because he wore it on his shirt, which fought to cover his bulging belly. A red nose showed his penchant for alcohol. *A good cop*, Jake thought, though he'd seen too much in his years on the force. Years before, as the lead cop, Burke had worked the murders of seven children and their mother. It never let go of him.

Jake signaled for Burke to hang back when the meeting broke up. "You discover anything I should know about?"

Both he and Burke knew what he was asking. "No, but I agree that all the evidence points at Spaulding. You find anything?"

"No, my father was thorough, I agree, it all points to one person. But I still have more files to vet," Jake said.

Chapter 11

Jake organized his notes from the meeting then typed them into his computer. He sent an email with updates on each case to Shamus. Some of his other detectives missed the meeting and were out in the field handling the current crimes. He'd review their caseload later, when he caught up with them. The department's chits sat on his desk and needed his attention but Jake pushed them aside.

The murder book on each crime never left the station. Jake collected and organized his own notes on a large poster board at home to follow the evidence if a case didn't come together as fast as he thought it should. Now with an office at the station, he'd be able to set one up there and lock his door at night. He worked Chelsea Adams's board first. Most time, he tried to maintain a normal life and leave work at work. But some cases grabbed him and didn't let go. Louie stepped into his office as he wrote the timeline on the board as they knew it.

"She was a good-looking woman," Louie said, pointing to Chelsea's picture with his coffee cup.

Jake kept writing. "What've you got?"

"We need to update the information on the second wife. She left on Thursday from JAX and landed in Bermuda. Here's where it gets interesting. After she landed she took a connecting flight to New York. She stayed at the Radisson in Southbury on Thursday night, checking in around eight-thirty." Louie closed his notebook.

"You got her. Did you get the subpoena for Lola's cell records?" Jake reviewed his list.

"I'm waiting on Judge Eisenberg."

"I'll check to see what the holdup is. We put the request in two days ago. I bet you she called the first Mrs. Adams on her phone." Jake's intercom buzzed. "Yes, Katrina?"

"There's a Cara Adams on line two for you," Katrina said.

Jake picked up his phone. "Lieutenant Carrington."

"Lieutenant, I'm sorry to bother you. Is there anything new on my mother's case? We're burying her tomorrow. I wondered…" Cara said, tears hitching her voice.

"I'm sorry, Cara, it's ongoing. If something turns up, I'll let you know. Is your father coming in for the funeral?"

"He planned on it, but I told him to stay away. Seth's mad at me. He wanted him there. Did I do the right thing?" Cara began to sob. Jake found it difficult to understand her.

"That's between you and your brother. I'll call you with any new developments, I promise," Jake said.

"Thanks, Lieutenant."

Jake steepled his fingers as he turned back to Louie. "She told her father not to come for the funeral. I wish she'd checked with one of us first. It would've been nice to question him ourselves."

"Some of the lab reports came in. I'll look them over," Louie said as he left the office.

* * * *

He wouldn't admit it, even to himself, but Louie missed Jake sitting across from him, even though it had only been a week. Looking through the reports, he highlighted the pertinent information. He got up and made copies for Jake, then put the original reports in the murder book with his notes. The DNA results still weren't back from the lab. To move forward they needed to be sure all the blood belonged to Chelsea Adams. Next, he read the ballistics report. The M.E. had pulled a .40 caliber bullet from Chelsea's head. He stated it was from a Glock 26 handgun. It was the perfect gun for a range of twenty to twenty-five yards, in his opinion. Small, lightweight, easy to conceal, and it's a good fit for a woman, except for the recoil. It takes a firm wrist to hit your target. He checked his email. *Alleluia! At last, Lola's cell phone records.* He decided to get another cup of coffee before he started in on them. Reading while walking, he plowed right into Jake.

"What's up?" Louie asked.

"I should have Chelsea's cell records in a few minutes. You get anything new on your end?"

"Yeah, I got copies here for you on the lab reports, including ballistics, still no DNA results. I also got Lola's cell phone records, which I'm going to look over after I grab a cup of Joe. You want any?"

"No thanks, I'm going to check the fax machine. Chelsea's records should be here by now. Come in when you're ready. We'll spread out on my conference table. It'll be easier to compare Lola's records to Chelsea's there."

"I'll be right in."

* * * *

All the way back to his office Jake debated on whether he should try Mia's cell phone again before he got involved in the reports. *What the hell?* When he got in his office he placed the call. He listened to it ring. He was about to hang up when she answered.

"Hi."

"You sound out of breath," Jake said.

"I had to run for the phone, I left it on my desk. It seems no one calls me unless I walk away from it." He waited while she caught her breath. "How'd it go last night?" she asked.

"Tough. They're all tough. Two young kids living together, the boy gets up to answer the door and boom, someone shot him. Then his seventeen-year-old live-in girlfriend goes into labor with their first kid." He continued before she could speak. "I'm sorry for the late call. I feel bad about dinner. Can I make it up to you?"

Silence filled the moment. "Jake, we need to speak about a few things before this develops into something more. I understand about your job. It's a large responsibility being on call, directing a team—we need to lay out some grounds rules, though. What day do you want to do this?" Mia asked.

He checked his calendar. "I can do Thursday after work, or Saturday."

"Okay. I'll be in Wilkesbury on Thursday. Do you want to go out to dinner?"

"No, why don't I cook for us? It'll be easier to talk with less distraction," Jake said.

"You sure there'll be fewer distractions?"

"It'll be hard but I promise to behave," Jake joked, eyeing Louie eavesdropping in the doorway of his office. "Why don't you come from work—bring a change of clothes to relax in? I'll grill something fast for dinner." He didn't want to wait until Thursday to see her.

"Sounds like a plan. See you on Thursday." She hung up.

"Anyone I know?" Louie asked.

"You know who, Louie."

"Is everything okay?"

"I don't know. I guess I'll find out Thursday. She's coming to dinner to talk." He looked off into the distance, deep in thought. Out of all the women he'd dated, why was this one special?

Louie left it alone, no small feat for him, and changed the subject. "I have all Adams's records, including the lab reports. What do you want to start with?"

"Let's start with the phone records and see where it takes us. I also want to ask Cara Adams if either her mother or father owned a gun. I didn't find any record of one here in Connecticut. Maybe he didn't register it."

"I'm amazed." Sarcasm drenched Louie's words. "Some people don't follow the law and register them?"

"Don't bust my chops."

"You looked like you needed them busted," Louie said. "You want to talk."

"Yes, about our cases, nothing else."

"Don't be grouchy."

"Louie, please. I'm up to my neck in departmental reports. I still have to post the duty roster for next week. We have several active cases in need of leg work and no time to work Eva's case. Right now, I need you to back off."

Louie switched gears. "Fine. On Lola Adams's cell for Friday, April sixteenth, she had thirty-eight calls going out, fifty-two in, including fifteen voice messages. This woman lived on the phone. Most of these have 904, 305, or 941 area codes. I need to look those up. There are a few Connecticut codes in there also."

He reached for the phone book, thumbed through until he found the national area codes directory. "Okay, area code 904 is in the Jacksonville area, 305 is Miami's code, 941 is Ft Myers, on the west coast. She also sent a boatload of text messages."

"They live in Neptune Beach?" Jake verified.

"Yes, north of Jacksonville."

"Let's get the listing for all her numbers and see who she's been talking to."

"Got something there?"

"A hunch, nothing more, how long did she talk to her friend in Miami?"

Louie looked at the bill again. "She was on for over an hour."

"Well, she said she hadn't heard from her for a year. I guess they had a lot of catching up to do. Did Lola's credit card statements come in yet?"

"I haven't seen them. Was Lola married before?" Louie asked.

"Good question." It was one that had slipped Jake's mind.

An hour later, Louie looked up, frustrated. Not one number on Lola's bill matched Chelsea's cell, work, or home number. Neither he nor Jake believed in coincidence. If Lola visited Connecticut on April sixteenth, she either killed Chelsea or had set it up.

* * * *

Wednesday morning the DNA report came in along with some of the lab reports. All the blood on Chelsea belonged to Chelsea. The good news—there was no sexual assault. The bad news, evidence-wise—there was no sexual assault. Not one drop of body fluid was left behind to analyze. She hadn't scratched her assailant. No fibers or skin were found under her nails. The minute samples of hair and saliva found on the rug in the trunk of the car where she had been discovered turned out to be a bust. There were no matches in the database on the samples. Around midmorning, Jake sat back in his chair, put his feet up on his desk, and closed his eyes. He couldn't think of anyone else since he'd met Mia. Smart. Funny. Sexy. God, he wanted to explore every inch of her. Would he ever get the chance? Chloe was a problem, though he needed to be honest with himself, it was the job that turned off most women. Others pursued the uniform, not the man. He didn't know if the interrupted dinner on Monday night had put Mia off or if Chloe had. They'd talk on Thursday night, try to iron things out, but he wanted to see her sooner. No, he'd let her make the next move. For the rest of the day he processed paper.

Chapter 12

Apprehension kicked right in when he woke on Thursday morning. He couldn't wait to see her tonight but he needed to put it away for the day and concentrate on work. *I'll go nuts if I don't get this out of my mind today.*

Before he went into the station, he decided to open another folder in the storage boxes pertaining to Eva's case. Jake studied the lab reports. Doctor Jerome had been thorough. Each bruise, cut, and scrape was detailed. Semen collected had been placed in cold storage. Jerome had noted that he expected that new testing might be able to make a match to DNA on a suspect in the future. He'd been right about the new technology— but now would it exonerate Spaulding and raise more questions than it answered? His cell rang.

"Are you home?" Louie asked, with no greeting.

"Yeah."

"Can you give me a lift to the station? Sophia needs the car today to take the dog to the vet."

He looked at his watch. *Oh well, it's time to go to work.* He'd have to let the information on Eva's file stew in his brain until tonight.

Louie was ready ten minutes later when Jake pulled up in front of his house. "What's wrong with Sophia's car?" Jake asked as Louie climbed in.

"She doesn't want the dog in her car—she just had it detailed. Houston sometimes gets car sick. Plus we dropped her car at the garage last night for a brake job."

"What happens if the dog gets sick in your car?"

Louie laughed. "I clean it up."

* * * *

A little after seven AM, he turned on his computer and settled into his chair with a cup of coffee. Jake used the quiet time before the rest of his detectives arrived to review the Adams case and the new cases his team had caught yesterday. He and Louie had attended the service for Chelsea Adams yesterday. It had ripped at his heart, watching those two young people say good-bye to their mother on the cold, gray, rainy day.

A large crowd had gathered to pay its respects. No one in the group of mourners popped out, screaming 'I did it.' All in attendance seemed to be genuinely grieving. Burke stood in the background recording the burial, the attendees, and all cars and corresponding license plate numbers. Their next task would be the identifying everyone there. Maybe he'd delegate the job to Louie, have him set up interviews with anyone they hadn't talked to already.

He'd give the Adams kids a couple more days before he asked about Lola. Today, they were going deeper into Lola's life, her loves, her neighbors, her coworkers. Though progressing, he felt time slipping away—it had been a couple of weeks since they found the body. The evidence hadn't produced one solid suspect. Jake knew in his gut who did it but without evidence he couldn't get an arrest.

He'd find it. More than anything, he wanted to close the case for Chelsea's children. Nothing else in life made him feel more like a failure than a cold case. They creep into his every waking hour. None more so than Eva's case.

Without warning, he flashed back to a time on the beach in Rhode Island.

Eva scooped up a full bucket of water and charged at him with a vengeance right after he'd thrown her into the water. He laughed like a loon. They couldn't have been more than eleven and twelve years old. He let her catch him and dump her bucket of water over his head before he picked her up again and tossed her back in the water. His parents watched with amusement.

He tried to imagine the woman Eva would have grown into. Would she have chosen a career, or motherhood, or both? Would he have been an uncle by now? Would he have taken the sports scholarship? Played pro ball? Pursued a different career?

Jake understood he couldn't change the past. But his anger—always right below the surface—threatened to boil over. He could never picture Eva past the age of fifteen no matter how hard he tried.

* * * *

He looked up as Louie walked into his office and then stopped dead in his tracks. It was always awkward to be caught in these moments. Knuckling away a tear, he watched Louie try to back out of his office.

"You need something, Louie?"

"No, I wanted to let you know I found the addresses for Lola Adams's parents." Neither of them knew how to handle it when Jake slipped into the past. It didn't happen often.

"Give me ten minutes. And close the door on your way out?"

"Jake, if you—"

Jake cut him off. "I'm fine. Give me a minute here. Can you close the door behind you?"

He paced his office. How could he have let the beast out at work? If anyone other than Louie had walked in…he didn't know how he would have lived down the embarrassment. Most times he could control his thoughts, his emotions…at other times…they snuck up, whacked him in the balls, and showed no mercy. Going through the files again had brought it to the surface. He opened his office door and looked around. He didn't want to run into anyone else until he got himself under control. In the men's room, he stared at himself in the mirror before throwing cold water on his face. *Let it go*, he willed. On his way back to his office, he motioned for Louie to join him.

The minute Louie walked in, Jake started in on the evidence, outlining their time schedule for the day. "Any thoughts on the subject?" Jake asked, not giving Louie the chance to get personal.

"No. I called Lola's mother. Mrs. Gromme will see us in an hour. I'm still trying to get in touch with her father. Her parents are divorced, though they live right down the road from each other."

"I want to give the Adams kids a break. I'll touch base with them on Friday, unless they call us first. Do you have your report ready? I need to send both of ours together to the captain."

"No. I'm almost done. Give me another half hour," Louie said, always the perfectionist. It drove Jake nuts.

"I'm sure it's perfect, finish it up. Let me know when you're nominated for a Pulitzer."

"You're a funny guy, Jake. I like my reports to be exact."

"They always are." Jake buried himself in his own statement.

* * * *

Interstate 84, jammed with cars, trucks, and construction this time of day, slowed them to a crawl. After the long winter, Jake put his windows down to suck up the warm air. The noise from the construction took the pleasure out of it though. He shut the windows and put the air conditioner on. For as long as Jake could remember, this road had been under construction. It had become a longstanding joke. Another twenty minutes passed before he could make his way off the next exit where he switched to the backroads to make up for time lost.

Jake listened in while Louie called and left a message for Mrs. Gromme explaining why they'd be late for the appointment.

Not bad, Jake thought as they arrived at Mrs. Gromme's door only twenty minutes late. When Mrs. Gromme answered the door, Jake noted the resemblance between mother and daughter from the photos he'd seen of Lola. Lucy Gromme stood five-three, weighed about one twenty. Her bleached-blond hair appeared stiff as a helmet. Stuck in the seventies, she'd covered her eyes in thick, electric-blue eyeshadow, drawing attention to the deep lines around each one. She spoke in the hard, scratchy voice of a smoker. Jake put her around sixty, though she looked more like seventy.

"Show me your badges," Mrs. Gromme said as she reached out her creped hand. Jake kept hold of his badge as he held it up. Louie did the same.

"Mrs. Gromme," Jake said, looking around the apartment. The outside door opened into a mini foyer that preceded the living room. An umbrella stand stood off to the right, next to it a tray filled with shoes.

"Wipe your feet before you come in. I don't want my house messed up."

Jake scoped out the rest of the apartment while he stood in the doorway and wiped his feet on the rug. Louie did the same. Mrs. Gromme led them into the living room. On their way, they passed an efficiency kitchen on the left. Though the place was meticulous, it stank of stale smoke. A short overstuffed green floral sofa, a coffee table, one end table that sat at the right side of the couch, and an old recliner covered with a multicolored throw filled the room. The recliner had its own high-top table by its side, with a cigarette burning in the ashtray. In front of the sofa, a forty-two inch television tuned to a soap opera sat on a claw-foot drop-leaf table, offset with a fresh flower arrangement. *Cold, like the woman*, Jake thought. No pictures or knickknacks. An open door led into the bedroom off the living room. He didn't see a bath. He assumed it was in the bedroom. She stared at both their feet.

"Have a seat and tell me why you're here," she said. No niceties, no offer of a beverage.

"My partner, Detective Romanelli, and I are working the murder case of Chelsea Adams."

"So, because my daughter married her loser of an ex, you're here to accuse her? If you are, you're barking up the wrong tree," Mrs. Gromme said in her gruff voice.

"It's standard procedure to interview everyone who knew, or had knowledge of, the victim, Mrs. Gromme. We're not pointing any fingers at anyone at this time." Jake kept his voice neutral.

"You know how to do the dance, don't you, Lieutenant?" she asked, putting up a gnarled hand to stop his reply. "Ask your questions." She stared him down.

Jake respected her more for her directness.

"Your daughter Lola visited Connecticut the weekend of April sixteenth. Did she visit you?" Jake asked.

"No, she didn't." A frown dug deeper lines into her already wrinkled forehead. Hurt flashed across her face before she locked it down. Lola Adams had wounded her mother by not calling or visiting.

"Do you have a cell phone, Mrs. Gromme?"

"No."

"Why did you call her husband a loser?" Louie asked.

"Because it's what he is. She was stupid to marry a guy old enough to be her father."

"'Because he is' doesn't answer the question," Jake said.

"The man screwed around on his wife. A loser," she repeated.

"Wasn't your daughter also married at the time she started dating Adams? You don't put any of the blame on her for dating a married man?" Louie asked.

"A typical question from a man. It's always the woman's fault," she said with disgust.

"No, ma'am, I think it's both of their faults," Louie said.

Silence ensued as she eyed Louie. After a minute or two, she said, "I guess you're right. You can't be looking at Lola for this. My girl wouldn't hurt a fly."

"We're looking at everyone right now, Mrs. Gromme. Does Lola keep in touch with her ex-husband?" Jake asked. He and Louie alternated asking the questions. Mrs. Gromme needed to be shaken up. "I don't think they kept in touch. She pissed him off when she dated the old guy. His ego couldn't take it."

From his take, Mrs. Gromme didn't like the first one any better than the second. "Having one's wife date another man would be reason enough to be pissed off. What's his name, Mrs. Gromme?" Jake asked again.

"Nick Pilarski."

"Does he live in town?" Louie asked.

"Yes, he does, in their old apartment. He lives by the post office on Marion Road, in an apartment over the deli. He's listed in the phone book." She didn't offer up Pilarski's number. Jake was sure she had it too.

"Can you think of anyone else she might have visited when she flew in?"

"I can't think of anyone. You'd think she'd have learned. She dates losers like her father—no good, skirt-chasing, gambling bums. Why she keeps going for the same type, I don't understand." She stared out her window.

"Okay, one last question. Where were you on April sixteenth?" Jake asked.

"You're kidding, right?" she asked, looking from one to the other. "I was right here, where I am every night, alone." She lit another cigarette, blowing smoke in Jake's direction.

"No one can verify your whereabouts?" Louie asked.

"No, but you can ask my nosy neighbors. Maybe one of them was spying on me."

Jake let her answer hang in the air, stared for a second or two, then stood. They weren't going to get anything else out of this one. "Thanks for your time, Mrs. Gromme."

Outside, Jake asked, "What's your take, Louie?"

"I thought we'd need a cast-iron cup to protect the jewels. She doesn't like men."

"You got that right. Do you think she's telling the truth about her daughter not visiting?" Jake unlocked the car, folded his six-foot frame into the department-issued midsize car. "Who's closer, the father or the ex?"

"The father's right down the street here, on Main. It's number thirty-four. We'll hit the ex on the way back to the station. If he lives near the post office then he'll be at the bottom of Southington Mountain," Louie said. "And to answer your question, I think she was."

Jake drove down Main Street.

The father lived in an old, run-down building. According to the mailboxes, four families or individuals lived there. After ringing the doorbell, they waited a solid five minutes until Jerry Gromme answered the door and graced them with his presence.

Jerry sported a day-old beard, thin, dirty, straggly hair, and a pointed nose, which reminded Jake of a bird's beak. Gromme's wife-beater T-shirt showed off thin, boney arms with the flesh flapping in the wind. He reeked of cigarettes. Jake moved back, bumping into Louie to avoid the guy's foul breath. It smelled like the city dump on a hot summer day.

"Mr. Gromme, I'm Lieutenant Carrington and this is Detective Romanelli. Can we come in?" he said, staying back.

"Sure. The name's Jerry. I'm up on the third floor. We'll have to walk, there's no elevator."

Where the ex-wife's apartment was immaculate, Jerry's resembled a pig sty. And Jake thought this comparison insulted every pig alive.

Jerry pushed the racing forms off the couch to make room for them to sit.

"I told the other detective on the phone I don't see how I can help you. I haven't heard from Lola since her wedding. My daughter only contacts me when she wants something." He held up his hand and rubbed his fingers together—the universal sign for money.

"Lola visited Connecticut on April sixteenth. She didn't visit you, or even call?" Louie said.

"No, I told you, we're not close. Her witch of a mother always put me down in front of her."

"You two didn't get along?" Louie asked.

"You assume right. If you met Mrs. Gromme…" Jerry left it at that.

"Would Lola have contacted her mother instead of you?" Jake asked.

"Yeah, she would. They have a love-hate relationship, those two, because they're alike." Jerry shuddered. "I couldn't live with either of them—a pair of tough broads, one tougher than the other. They were always harping on my ass. I pity the guy who winds up with her."

"Jerry, do you know who she would have visited if not you or her mother?"

"She might've contacted her ex-husband. They go way back. She started dating him in high school. As for friends, she didn't have a lot of them."

"One more question, Jerry. Where were you on April sixteenth?"

He grabbed his calendar off the cluttered coffee table and looked up the date. "I attended the Tim McGraw concert at Mohegan Sun. They comped me the tickets."

"Thanks for your time, Jerry. If we have any other questions, we'll contact you," Jake said as he stood. Louie and Jerry stood. Jerry extended his hand. He had no excuse not to shake it, nor did Louie.

Outside Louie said, "I hope you have some antibacterial lotion in the car."

"I don't leave home without it. My God, how does someone live in such filth?"

"I couldn't, but I now understand his ex-wife and pity her," Louie said, opening his laptop to search for Nick Pilarski's address.

"What's the address for Lola's ex-husband?" Jake poured a generous amount of antibacterial lotion into his hand and passed the bottle to Louie.

"It's 345 Marion Avenue, second floor," Louie said, as he scrubbed his hands.

"Did she or didn't she contact her mother? What's your opinion?" Jake wiped his hands on a paper towel to get the excess antibacterial gel off before driving away from the curb.

"They might not be close, but mothers and daughters always seem to have a bond we men can't explain," Louie said.

* * * *

Nick Pilarski lived over a deli on the Southington/Wilkesbury town line. The aroma helped to wash out the stench from Jerry Gromme's apartment. It also kicked in their appetites.

"Let's grab a sandwich downstairs when we're through here." Jake knocked on the door.

Pilarski answered the door in a Hard Rock T-shirt and boxers. Scratching his belly, he yawned in their faces.

"What do you want? You woke me up." Nick complained.

"Are you Nick Pilarski?"

"Who's asking?"

"That would be us, Nick," Jake said as he displayed his shield.

"I'll ask again, who's asking?"

Jake braced, watching Nick lose his patience. *The guy's got a short fuse.* Something he could use if needed.

"I'm Lieutenant Carrington and this is Detective Romanelli of the Wilkesbury Police Department."

"Listen, I work nights, and sleep days. Can you say want you want to say and leave so I can get back to sleep?"

"We're here to question you about a recent murder. Can we come in?" Jake asked.

"Who got dead?" Nick said, opening the door wider to let them in.

"The murder victim is Chelsea Adams, the first wife of Jeffrey Adams, who is now married to your ex-wife, Lola," Louie said, taking a deep breath.

"What's it got to do with me? Shit—no way, man. I never met the woman. What are ya, crazy?" Nick looked around, found a cigarette, lit it, then took a deep drag before blowing the smoke in their faces. "You guys want one?" Nick offered.

"No thanks, we don't smoke." Jake swiped a hand in front of his face to dissipate the smoke. He wondered how much secondhand smoke he'd inhaled today. He hoped the cleaners would be able to get the smell out of his clothes.

"Did you see your ex-wife on April sixteenth?" Louie asked.

"No, she lives in Florida."

"On the sixteenth, she was here in Connecticut. You're sure she didn't contact you?" Jake questioned.

"I'm sure. Why would she?"

"Where were you on the sixteenth, Mr. Pilarski?" Jake asked.

"You're kidding, right?" Nick said, incredulous.

"No, we're not kidding. Where, Nick?"

He pulled his calendar from the table next to an old gray floral wing chair, while they continued to question him.

"What's your cell number, Mr. Pilarski?" Louie asked.

"Why?" He got up, started pacing around the dark, tiny apartment with the calendar in his hand.

"We need to check it against Lola's bill to be sure she didn't contact you." Jake observed him, finding no telltale signs Nick lied as he answered his questions. Nick handed Jake his calendar and pointed out his work schedule.

"I worked that night. You can check with the company. They'll verify it. You think she killed the woman?" Pilarski asked.

"At this time, we're questioning everyone who knew the victim, Mr. Pilarski," Louie said.

"Lola's a crazy woman, but she wouldn't kill anyone. I would know if I were—had been—married to a killer," he said with conviction.

"Sometimes people hide their true selves," Jake said.

"No, not Lola, she's a money-hungry bitch, not a killer."

"You still have feelings for her?" Louie asked.

"She's hard to get over. A great lay, but out of bed, she's a tiger with real sharp claws." He shrugged his shoulders. "We fought all the time. Christ, we were together since high school. No matter what I gave her, she wanted more. She's a tough woman who comes from hard stock. Have you met her parents yet?"

"Yes. I still need your cell phone number, Mr. Pilarski. Don't make us get a subpoena, because then we'll have access to everyone you called." Jake stared at Nick with no sympathy.

Pilarski got up, grabbed a pad, and wrote down a number, handing it to Jake. "I don't care if you look at all my calls, I don't have anything to hide."

"We like people who cooperate, Nick, it gets us out of their lives faster," Jake said. "Do you know who else Lola might have visited on her recent trip here?"

"Did you check with her best friend, Katy?"

"No, what's her full name, address, and phone number, if you have it?" Louie asked.

"It's Katy Bonita. Wait, I have to look up the number." He searched through his cell phone, wrote down the information, handed it to Jake. "Katy only has a cell phone."

"You keep in touch with her friends, Nick?" Jake quirked his brow.

"Friend. Yeah, after the divorce, I dated Katy a couple of times but there weren't any sparks. We remained friends though. You got a problem with that?" Jake braced as Nick went on the defensive.

"Nope. Anyone else we should look at, Nick?" *Nothing here*, Jake thought, but he had to go through the routine.

"Lola's not close to a lot of people. There's no one else she'd bother to get in contact with."

"Here's my card. Give me a call if someone else comes to mind. Sorry to interrupt your sleep." Jake handed over his card.

Chapter 13

A look at the bedside clock had her swearing. Mia jumped out of bed half an hour later than usual. Her luck continued to run downhill when traffic came to a standstill around Farmington, making her late for her first appointment. She needed to reevaluate her job. Work interfered with her writing. When she'd started, it had been a part-time job, three days a week as a way of giving back to society. Something her parents had stressed. Now she worked five days a week, with part-time benefits. Leave it to the state to get around giving benefits, though she didn't need them. Mia wanted to earn her own way in life. All the benefits she could ever ask for, as well as a high-paying salary, she got as an officer of her father's company. A writer-contributor slash vice president, she worked hard producing articles for each magazine every month. If seeing her name on a book was all that mattered to her, she could've easily published her mystery with their company ages ago. But she'd inherited her father's stubborn streak. It was important to her to make it on her own. It's why she used a pseudonym when she submitted. Logan Andrews didn't understand, never did, never would—and it caused constant friction between her and her father.

It was also the main reason she'd moved out of New York City. After the last argument, the idea to move out of state popped into her head. It took two days for the realtor to rent out her penthouse to a nice couple for a year. After she had the moving truck loaded with what she'd need for the year, she stopped by her parents, dropped the bomb, and didn't look back. The move to rural Connecticut was the best thing she'd done for herself in years. Like an omen, she had found the condo the first week at the right price. The owner had wanted a quick sale. She'd paid cash and moved right in. It gave her more time to write, plus it meant less bickering with her father. It wasn't time for her to take her rightful position at the company. Her dreams were hers and no one else's. She loved the seclusion and setting she had found in Connecticut. Now, three years later, she had a life here. One she wouldn't give up without a fight.

And she didn't need to work. The generous trust fund her grandmother had left her, and the income she drew from the various holdings and stocks the family owned, could support ten families. She wondered how Jake would handle it when he found out how rich she was. Would the depth of her portfolio bother him? Would he be man enough to handle it? She'd tell him in time. Where the relationship led would be anyone's guess. Too many men wanted her for her money. Jake seemed different from the others she had dated. Yet, he had a dark side to him, one she needed to explore more thoroughly. Whose baggage was larger, his or hers? When he'd spoken of his sister's death on Sunday, she realized he still carried a lot of survivor guilt around deep inside. Even with her degree in psychology she didn't think she could help him, or if she even wanted to begin a relationship with someone as damaged as Jake.

While waiting for her second appointment of the day, Mia wondered how tonight would go. She didn't need one of Jake's ex-girlfriends following her around. Did Jake bring it on himself? Would it be fair to blame him for a crazy woman's actions? It was rare she met a man she wanted to date. Would Jake Carrington be worth taking a chance on? Maybe she'd find out tonight.

Her cell phone rang. Looking at the readout, she almost moaned out loud when she saw Piper's name. Of all days, she didn't have the time or the patience to speak with her friend. Her husband, Darryl, had cheated on her and Piper wanted Mia to tell her what to do. Letting the call go to voicemail, Mia promised herself she'd call Piper back on her way to Jake's house tonight.

Her next appointment walked in with a big attitude and a foul mouth—a mean-spirited, boisterous thirteen-year-old girl who caused fights with the other students. The school had asked her to dig out the answer. Mia could tell them why before she even counseled her. Tessa threw herself into one of the chairs in front of Mia's desk and stared her down. Saying nothing, Mia waited her out.

Tessa said, "Hi, Doctor Andrews."

"Hello, Tessa. How are you today?"

"Why do I have to come here? It's a waste of my time."

"Well, consider it as a vacation from class," Mia said, with a smile.

"I don't need no vacation. I don't want to come, I don't come. Nobody cares one way or the other if I do or don't," she answered, an edge creeping into her voice as she tried to incite an argument.

"Don't need any vacation," Mia corrected.

"Whatever." Tessa waved her hand around.

Tessa picked up items from Mia's desk. The girl did it to irritate her. "Tessa, we spoke about you touching my things before. Put them down." Not giving an inch, Mia hardened her voice. She'd taken this job because she thought she could help kids. No matter how much she tried, she didn't see much progress. The job had started to depress her.

"Boy, you're grouchy today," Tessa said, dropping the crystal statue back on Mia's desk.

Mia cringed. "Would you like me to go through your handbag...touch your possessions?"

"You do, I'll kill you." Tessa jumped up.

Mia stared her down until she sat again.

"Are you ready for your session?"

"Why? It don't help."

"Tessa, in the last session you promised to explain why you're angry." Mia gave Tessa a gentle push.

"Fine. I ain't no white bitch who has everything. Or it could be I live in a hole where no one cares about me or what I do. Is that what you want me to say?" Tessa asked.

"I want you to be honest with me. I can help if you let me."

"Why should I?"

"To work toward your future to ensure you have a good life in front of you," Mia said.

"I hate my parents."

"You can't change who your parents are. If they're abusing you, we can address those issues."

"I hate them. They don't abuse me or anything." It was rare, but Mia couldn't read the kid.

"You need to tell more than that if we are going to root out and fix the cause of your feelings. Remember, you're the one who needs to take charge, implement the changes we spoke about in the last session to see change in your life. You have to want to change before I can help you. Dig deep, find the reasons why you hate your parents. Once you find the answer, work to resolve the issues. I can't help you until you tell me what they are." Mia made a decision and went with the personal touch. "I have problems with my father. I wish things could be different. I understand I'm not going to change him. I've accepted it and moved on in my life. I live it my way."

"What's his problem?"

Mia almost answered. Smiled at how easily Tessa could draw her in. "It doesn't matter. What matters most, Tessa, is you. You can work to be a better student, daughter or a successful businesswoman. Show the world you have what it takes to succeed, even against great odds."

"You make it sound easy." The girl slumped back in the chair.

"It's not. It's a lot of hard work. Anything worthwhile is."

"Why do you care? What do you get out of doing this?" Tessa spread her arms wide. "Does it make feel better about yourself?" A good manipulator, Tessa tried again to turn the session back on her. Mia wasn't allowing it.

"No, I like to help people. I see great potential in you. It would be a shame to waste it. Don't let them beat you down. You want power, Tessa? Real power is knowledge. Street smarts are good, but you need book smarts to accompany it to succeed. You're at a crossroads in your life—you need to make a choice. Are you going to be a troublemaker all your life and end up in jail? Or do you want to work hard to make something of yourself? It's your decision. What do you want?"

She pushed hard today. For Tessa, they were running out of options. Mia liked the girl. Even with all her sessions, she had never discovered the reason for Tessa's anger. A long time ago Mia accepted some kids couldn't be helped, though it killed her with this one, because Tessa had potential. A brainy girl with guts, Tessa could go far in life if she let herself.

"I'll have to get back to you with my answer."

"I'll see you next week at the same time. And dig deep to find your answer, Tessa." Mia dismissed her. Staring out her window, she didn't want to give up on Tessa but was she a lost cause? It annoyed her how much she wanted to sit there and cry. Cry for Tessa, cry for herself, and cry for the broken system that let these children fall through the cracks. Her work accomplished nothing. Mia understood that she was at the burnout point. It was a hazard of the profession.

Outside the window something odd registered in her brain—she recognized the red car parked next to hers as the Wagner woman's Jake had spoken about. Or was she projecting? Since their talk she'd spotted a dozen red cars at the grocery store, the bank, and on her way to work. No, this time she was positive it was her. Pissed, she hit number one on her speed dial.

"You're not canceling, are you?" Jake asked.

"No, the Wagner woman's sitting in my parking lot here at school, in Hartford. What should I do?" She paced as she spoke.

"Notify the resource officer there, but I want you to also call the police and explain you're dating a cop. Tell them about the other incident. No, never mind, I'll call a friend of mine at the Hartford Police Department and get him out there right away. Stay in your office."

She hung up, without a good-bye.

It took Sergeant Monahan and his partner Detective Perez five minutes to get there. Monahan knocked on Mia's door.

"Mia Andrews?"

"Yes?"

"I'm Sergeant Monahan." He walked over to Mia's window and stared down at the lot. "Which car is it?"

Mia joined him, looking down into the parking lot—gone. "The blue car's mine. The empty spot to the right is where she was parked." She pushed a hand through her hair.

"A red Honda, driven by a brunette woman, pulled out of the lot just as we drove in. What color car does the Wagner woman drive?" Monahan asked.

"It's a red Honda." Mia sat down. Monahan came over to her desk, pulled a chair around, and sat beside her and took her right hand in his.

"Miss Andrews..."

"It's Mia."

"Okay, Mia, most stalkers don't do anything. It's a form of intimidation to scare someone. They're cowards. I'm going to advise you to put in a complaint so it's on the record. This way if she continues to escalate you'll have enough for a restraining order. The next time take a picture of the car and driver with your cell phone."

"I did."

"Excellent, can you forward it to me. Maybe I'll be able to pull up the license number."

"This is ridiculous, Sergeant..."

"It's Mike, Mia. I know it's crazy, but let's go with the old saying, it's better to be safe than sorry. I'd bet Jake's on his way to Hartford right this minute. Let's give him a call and tell him everything's okay."

"All right, but what happens if I see her on the highway on my way home?"

"I'm sure she watched us pull in. Could she see you at the window?"

"I figure the answer is yes, if I could see her in her car."

"You're probably right. This is the second incident. Do you want to file a complaint? Next time, we'll use the picture you took to file a restraining order. Make sure to keep documenting the car every time you see it and try to get the license plate in all the pictures. It will make your complaint stronger." He let go of her hand.

Rubbing her temples to ease the throbbing in her head, Mia nodded at him.

"I can follow you home, if you like." Mike's partner had stayed silent throughout the exchange. He stood at the window as he scanned the parking lot. It unnerved Mia.

"No, thanks, I'm going to Jake's house after work. I'm sure she won't be stupid enough to follow me there."

"I'll write down my personal cell phone number on the back of my business card for when you're in Hartford. Don't hesitate to call me."

"Thank you for your kindness, Mike, I appreciate it."

"It's nothing. Jake and I go way back. Nobody stalks a cop's family."

She didn't correct him. She didn't know what Jake had told him about them and didn't care as long as it kept that nut away from her. She'd planned to change at work. After the cops left, she decided to change at Jake's house.

The day couldn't end soon enough for her.

* * * *

Jake got Mia's phone call right after he and Louie left Pilarki's house. He strung together a good array of curses.

"Hey, Jake, slow down, Mike will take care of her."

"That crazy bitch decided to stalk Mia instead of me. And Mia's coming over tonight to talk. I wonder what she's decided now that she picked up a stalker," he said, temper rising out of his frustration.

"I'm not going to guess what her verdict is and neither should you. You'll have to wait until she gets there to find out. If you want, I'll drive," Louie slipped in.

"No, I'm fine."

"Well, I'm not. Nor is that the old woman crossing the street over there. You took ten years off her life when she jumped out of your way. That'll teach her to try to cross the street with a green light."

"Funny, Louie." Though he didn't feel like laughing.

"What else is bothering you?"

"Everything. I feel we're almost there on the Wagner case, on the brink of something, if only we could unearth one piece of evidence that would swing us toward a suspect. We have to be missing something big, something right in front of our faces. Then there's Chloe and her antics. The Adams kids ripped my heart out yesterday, plus Spaulding's possible release. Now the trouble with Mia... It's piling up on me. How long am I going to have to pay for one indiscretion?"

It wasn't normal for Jake to give up. Louie didn't answer right away. He searched for the right words.

A block before they got to the station, Louie said, "Jake you can't control the actions of others. If Mia doesn't understand or won't accept it, then she's looking for an excuse not to be with you. No matter who you meet, she'll always be concerned you're a cop. Sophia still wonders if she made the right choice every time she hears a report of a cop being shot. The cases are the cases. Most times we solve them. You're the one who told me patience is a virtue. It's time to take your own advice. We'll keep working methodically and in time we'll get there."

"Wow, your logic impresses me. No, seriously, thanks. Chloe got me so angry. If anything ever happened to Mia, because of someone I dated, I wouldn't be able to handle it again."

And there it is. Jake always blames himself for Eva, Louie thought. "Jake, nothing's going to happen, chill out. And God forbid if something did, it wouldn't be your fault."

* * * *

Mia cancelled her other appointments and left before lunch. She also made an appointment with both her boss and personnel to discuss how her job and the hours had changed. After doing it for a couple of years, she realized it had led away from her life goals. She called Jake and told him she was leaving early. She liked how he rearranged his schedule to be there when she'd arrived. How he understood the seriousness of the threat. More than anything, even with the Wagner woman in the picture, she couldn't wait to see him. Though nothing had been resolved, she still got excited at the thought of him.

* * * *

Jake's cell phone started to ring as he packed up his briefcase. "Jake, the Wagner woman's sitting outside the school. Did Mia leave?"

"Yeah, Mike, she left about forty minutes ago." It was a good call on Mia's part to leave early it seemed. He owed Mike a bottle of good scotch.

He knew Mike would take care of Chloe. Before he left the station, Jake apologized to Louie, asked him to find his own ride home. He wanted to be there when Mia arrived at his house. As soon as her car turned into his street he hit the remote in his hand to open the extra bay for her to pull right in. Was he destined to put every woman he loved in harm's way? Deep down it was the reason he had avoided serious relationships in the past. He waited for her at the top of the short staircase leading into the house. As soon as she reached the top step, he took her into his arms and held her close. The afternoon's incident had frightened them both. Jake lifted her chin and studied her pale face. "Are you okay?"

"I'm a little shaken. If you don't mind, I'm going to lie down for a few minutes in the spare room. It's been a tough day all around and I need to make some decisions."

He'd seen that expression many times in his career. The dazed, confused blank-eye look of a victim peered out at him. And he'd put her in the situation that caused it.

Jake watched her walk down the hall to the spare bedroom. He checked on her a half hour later when she hadn't come out of the room. She'd fallen asleep, curled up in the fetal position. Two hours later he heard the shower running. Reaching into the fridge, he pulled out the white wine, uncorked it and let it breathe while he waited for her to join him in the kitchen.

Training taught him how to handle a victim. Did he handle Mia as one? Should he coddle her or come at the problem head on? Did he allow his emotions to get in the way of Mia's safety? He fought to appear casual as he leaned against the kitchen counter with his legs crossed at the ankles, sipping the cup of coffee he didn't want, as he waited for Mia to come out. Jake loathed Chloe for her vindictiveness. Every time he thought about it, his anger pulsated through him. He couldn't let Mia see the helplessness he felt. It wasn't what she needed right now—she was the one who needed comfort, not him.

"Hi," Mia said, standing in the doorway to the kitchen.

"Hey," he said, letting the silence fill the air, waiting for her to speak first.

"It's too early for dinner," she said.

"I have coffee ready if you want some, or wine." He fisted his hands at his side though he wanted to go to her and take her in his arms.

"No, the wine's good."

They were acting like strangers, each feeling the other out, the day's stress getting to both of them. He walked across the kitchen and kissed her to break the ice. He pulled back, looked down into her eyes as he traced his fingers over her brow, her nose, and her lips. The terror in her eyes when she had first arrived ripped a huge hole in his heart. For that alone, he could kill Chloe.

"It's nice out, why don't you sit outside and I'll bring out the wine. And, Mia, I won't let anything happen to you. I promise."

"We have a lot to talk about."

* * * *

She hesitated by the door, not wanting to go out by herself. It pissed her off how this Chloe person could scare the wits out her. A woman she didn't even know. Mia pushed her fear away and stepped outside, instead of waiting for Jake.

Handing her a glass of wine when he walked out, he placed some cheese and crackers on the table by her side. She gave him the once-over and liked what she saw. She felt warm and on edge every time she was around him.

"I don't know where to start." He stopped, searching for the right words before he continued.

She cut him off. "We need to talk about Monday night and Chloe. Is Chloe a side effect of your job? Or is it personal?"

"A combination, Mia, I'll explain."

* * * *

Jake thought that was a good starting place. After a lengthy time of back and forth conversation, he felt they had a better understanding of each other and their personalities, jobs, and what to expect from each other moving forward. The issue with Chloe was a wait and see. He couldn't predict Chloe's actions, even though Mia wanted some indication of what she'd do next. "Do you always analyze everything?"

"Guilty. It's the reason I'm a psychologist. My inquisitive mind never stops questioning."

"This is the only answer I have to everything that's been going on with us. I do know if you don't take chances in life and run with it, you lose all around. You'll miss out on what could be the most gratifying experience of your life."

She looked deep into his green eyes. "And if you lose?"

"You learn more when you lose. Life's an adventure. You gain knowledge and experience emotions—what more can you ask for?" He smiled.

"You're deep. What about the other factors, which will no doubt interfere with the experience?"

"It's called life, Mia. You deal with it or you turn away. What's your choice?"

"Let's discuss that nut. The woman frightens me. You never know when she'll lose it completely. And Monday night, I waited over an hour for you... then poof, you're gone. I understand it's your job but how often am I going to have to put up with your disappearing act?" While he contemplated his response, she let the silence fill the space between them.

"Mia, if I could control all the nuts in the world, I wouldn't have a job. As for my responsibilities, when I'm on duty the job comes first. Dating a cop is tough with the weird hours. On-call duty assignments screw with your plans. I'm a cop. I'll always be a cop. I don't know anything else, nor do I want to."

He stopped, giving her a chance to jump in, to voice her opinion, but the silence dragged on. Jake thought he'd lost her by the faraway look in her eyes, until she spoke.

"Jake, I'm spoiled, even self-centered. Growing up I always got whatever I wanted and never questioned my demands on other people. As I got older, I realized it's not how the world works for everyone else. I started to look inside myself and make decisions that would help me survive. You don't know anything about me, where I come from, who I am, or who my family is."

"I don't want to know everything about you today, or even tomorrow, Mia. I want to discover it all over time. Who your family is isn't important to me unless they're criminals." He gave her the fisheye.

For the first time since she arrived, Jake watched the tension drain from her body.

"No, they're not nor am I, though I do have a few outstanding parking tickets." She tugged his hands to her and raised them to her lips.

His stomach unclenched. "Are you hungry? I didn't realize how much time had passed."

"Yeah, I could eat."

Jake served burgers with a side salad. After dinner, Mia helped him clean up. He washed the dishes. She dried them. As she wiped the last the plate, she turned toward him.

"Do you have plans for Saturday night?"

"No."

"Would you like to come to my house for dinner and dessert?" With a coy smile, she lowered her lashes.

"Boy would I, and...we don't need food," he answered, smiling.

"Yes, we do."

Happy with the way the evening turned out, he couldn't wait for dinner on Saturday.

Especially dessert.

Chapter 14

Severe thunderstorms kept Jake awake most of the night. Up early, he brewed the coffee extra strong, almost equal to the consistency of mud. Tasting it, he was satisfied it would keep him from nodding off at his desk. He loaded up a thermos and headed into the precinct. At his desk, he decided to tackle his reports, including writing up the latest episode with Chloe, when Louie walked into his office, whistling. "What's up, Louie?" Jake asked.

"All manner of things, my boy, all manner of things, but I digress. I reviewed Meryl Drake's first interview again, compared it to ours. I didn't like her tone when she answered some of those questions about her relationship with Shanna. It was all over the board.

"First soft, then hard, and then back to soft. She got real nasty when Kraus asked if she and Shanna fought. Her attitude hardened again and never softened when she spoke of Chloe. Something's off with her. She hates Chloe. I got the impression Meryl would like to see her go down for this. Another interview is certainly called for," Louie said as he finished up.

"It's worth a second look. Before we talk to her, I want to talk with Kraus and Brown on it and make sure they verified if she did or didn't see Shanna the week she disappeared. We looked at her but there wasn't anything there."

"Okay, I want—"

Katrina, the squad secretary, buzzed in. "Jake, there's a call for you on line three. It's JC's Pawn Shop on Lakeview Road. Do you want to take it?"

Jake picked up the phone. He could hear Jessie Cerone, the owner of JC's, yelling at someone in the background.

"How's it going, Jessie?"

"It goes, Jake, you know," Jessie said.

"Yeah, I know. What's up?" Jake asked, before Jessie could go into one of his long spiels on the human race.

"You sent over a picture last week of an emerald ring. You said you were doing a follow-up, remember?" Jessie got to things in his own time. Jake waited.

"Yeah, I remember."

"Jake, this guy came in five minutes ago trying to hock it. I got it on my cameras. You want me to try to email you a picture?"

"You have cameras now?"

"Yeah, I got hit too many times last year. I now have surveillance 24/7."

"Good idea. Does this guy know you're calling me?"

"No, one of my clerks is still working with him. He called me up front to appraise the ring. I recognized it from your fax. I told him I needed to look up something in my gem book and walked back to my office, and called you. Don't worry, I played it cool."

"Can you stall him? We can be there in about fifteen minutes, if we don't hit traffic."

"I'll try."

"Don't make it obvious, Jessie. If he wants to leave, let him. Did he give you a name?"

"He didn't give a last name. His first one is Joe. Real original, huh?" Jessie laughed and hung up.

"What's going on?" Louie asked.

"Get your jacket. We're heading out to JC's." Louie walked to his desk to get his jacket. Jake followed. "Someone's trying to hock Shanna Wagner's emerald ring."

"Sometimes it just clicks."

Jake felt the buzz. Maybe they'd give the Wagners closure and get Chloe off his back at the same time.

"Oh, by the way, I'll need a ride home today. If you can find it in your heart to stop by the vet's I need to pick up Houston. Poor thing had to spend the night and Sophia's car is still in the shop."

"No problem," Jake said.

* * * *

Jake's jaw dropped when he walked into JC's. The guy called Joe—turned out to be Joe Wagner, Shanna's father. He'd aged since Shanna's murder.

"Joe."

"Sergeant." Joe Wagner avoided making eye contact with him.

"It's Lieutenant now," Jake said. "You remember Detective Romanelli?"

"Detective." Wagner looked down at his hands.

"Mr. Wagner?" Louie moved to Wagner's left side by tacit agreement. Jake walked to his right.

"Hey, Jessie," Jake said. "Can we use your back room for a couple of minutes?"

"Sure, no problem."

"Mr. Wagner…Joe, can you come with us for a minute?" Jake asked.

"Why? I've done nothing wrong!" His voice almost squeaked.

"It's either here in the back room or downtown at the station, Joe. Which do you prefer?" Jake asked.

"I guess here." Wagner's shoulders slumped as he pushed away from the counter.

Joe followed Jake down the hallway to the office. Louie boxed him in from behind. All of them crammed into a minuscule room designed to hold no more than two people at any given time. A desk, a small round table with two chairs, and a bookcase loaded with books narrowed the space even more. He pulled a chair out for Joe and stared at him until he sat. Jake saw a defeated man who'd lost everything, including his will to live. Wagner's hands were in constant motion—he was nervous and Jake wanted to know why.

"What has you so wound up, Joe?"

"I don't know what you want, Lieutenant."

"Yes, you do." Jake stared into Joe's eyes.

"I don't."

"Where'd you get Shanna's ring?" Jake asked.

"We found it in her room. We started to clean the room out in hopes it would help my wife move on. I'm glad I discovered it and not Anna. It would've killed her. I hid it from her. I figured I'd get rid of it before she found out," Joe said.

"Joe, it's a family heirloom. For the worth of Shanna's ring alone, I'd think you'd want to keep it or sell it at a jeweler's." Jake kept using Shanna's name to work Joe, to pull on his guilt.

"Her grandmother gave it to her. Anna couldn't bear to have it around. It would be a constant reminder of our loss." Tears ran down Joe's face.

Jake waited while Joe pulled a handkerchief from his pocket and swiped at his nose and eyes.

"Why, Joe?" Jake pushed.

"Because Shanna always wore it," he said, grief dripping off him.

"Joe, I'm going to ask you again. Where'd you get Shanna's ring?"

Joe didn't reply but continued to swipe at his tears. Jake didn't say a word. He struggled with his part in causing Joe's pain.

Jake sent Louie out to ask Jessie if he had any whiskey in the shop. Louie came back with his bottle of Jack Daniel's and poured Joe a drink.

"Here, take this," Louie said.

"Thanks." Joe chugged it down like medicine. When the liquor hit the back of his throat Joe started choking.

"You need to talk to us. You're not protecting her this way," Jake said.

"You don't understand."

"I do. I know this is hard, but it has to be done."

"No, you don't understand. Shanna's death—it killed our family. My wife has lost over twenty pounds. She doesn't participate in our lives. She's nags Chloe throughout the day to see where she is. I found a counselor for us, but she refuses to go. I don't know how long I can go on like this. I know this is going to sound horrible but...I...*we* need to move forward," Wagner said.

"When my sister was killed, my mother never got over it. My father, he tried to help her, but he couldn't. It ate away at him after a while. The stress killed him. My mother's in a home right now. She's not crazy. She either doesn't care, or just can't move forward. You can't make this right by trying to protect Chloe." Jake stared into Joe's watery eyes.

"Chloe's all I have left."

"Joe, you knew, or you suspected, Chloe might be involved in Shanna's death. You didn't want to face it. Finding the ring made you realize Chloe might be a big factor in how Shanna died. You're trying to protect her. It's the reason you're here today, trying to sell it. You know if Anna saw the ring, and found out where you got it, she'd make the connection to Chloe too." Jake kept using Anna and Shanna's names. *Press harder.*

"Are you going to leave us with nothing? I lost one daughter forever, now you want to take the other one away. I don't understand how you do what you do."

"Don't you believe Shanna deserves justice? Don't you deserve closure? Someone ended her life, when she should've been starting to make her own way in the world. She was excited about her future. She was smart, kind, beautiful, and focused on what she wanted. The killer needs to pay for the crime he or she committed against her. Every crime's cruel, but this one demonstrated an extreme brutality. He raped her, then beat her, then he dumped her naked in a field for the animals to find. He left her with nothing." Jake watched his words land like fists in Joe's face.

"I understand that. We love our daughters, both of them, Lieutenant. We didn't create the monster capable of this horrendous crime. I won't, no I can't, accept it was Chloe. Chloe's had some problems dealing with things since Shanna died, but she loved her sister. You can't judge her for her lack of common sense, Lieutenant." Louie poured Joe another drink.

"I'm not judging her, Mr. Wagner. Envy's a terrible thing, it can lead to actions in the heat of the moment that we can't take back," Jake said. "We need you to come with us to the station to make a statement. We've confiscated the ring as evidence. Here's your receipt for it. We're not questioning Chloe solely based on you hocking the ring. We've been reviewing the case, going over statements. Joe…the evidence is pointing to her. The ring only adds to our suspicions."

"I don't believe you. What kind of evidence?"

"We can't tell you that at this time."

"Do I leave my car here?" Joe asked, looking around the office for the first time.

"Yes. When we're finished, we'll give you a ride back."

"Should I call my wife?"

"No. Do you know where Chloe is today?" Jake asked.

"She should be at work. She knows I have the ring."

"How does she know?" Louie asked.

"I confronted her with it. She denied it, but I saw something in her eyes that hurt me." Joe wiped his nose on his sleeve. "No matter what you tell me, I'll never believe she killed her sister."

Chapter 15

"Jake, you got a few minutes?" Burke asked.

"Sure, come in." Jake said as he looked up.

Al took a seat. Kraus took up a position by the door. "We wanted to catch you up on the interviews and play back my meet with my snitch. My gut says we have to act fast." Al turned to Kraus. Gunner nodded his agreement.

"Play it," Jake said.

"This is in the diner."

Jake listened as Burke set up the scene along with his commentary on Sniff Lee. Al described Sniff's fondness for cocaine. When he started in on how his nose dripped like a faucet Jake cut him off.

"Al, play the tape. You can give me Sniff's full description afterwards."

Nodding, Al hit the play button.

Sniff: Hey man, you know when you talk with Spike you can't use my name. He'll kill me dead.

Burke: If he's that bad, why are you talking with me, Sniff?

Sniff: Well, you know the kid who got killed...it ain't right. I saw him every day at the store. He treated me real nice. With respect even. No one else ever did.

Burke: Come on, Sniff, you want me to believe you're a humanitarian all of a sudden? What gives?

Sniff: Man, Spike's out of control! You know he cut one of his whore's faces the other day because she refused to go out on account of being sick? When I got my medicine, it was weak. Then the bastard charged me double! It ain't right, you know. I pay his price, and I don't give him no trouble. Why'd he do that?

Burke: Times are tough, Sniff. Everyone's got to make a living.

Sniff: Yeah, I hear ya, still...

Burke: No one's around, Sniff, finish up your story. Give me facts, not bullshit.

Sniff: This ain't no bullshit, man. One of his customers lives in the building, or he did. He took off after the shooting. No one's seen him since. His name's Leroy Kale. You know Leroy—big dude. He hangs out at Berkley and Wiggins. Leroy's a badass. He's always harassing the girls going in and out of the building. Well anyway, I heard he bought some black tar. Leroy starts spitting some junk about how bad the stuff is. He set it up to pay Spike on Thursday, when he got paid. Gives him his address, with the wrong apartment number—I bet he did it on purpose. He gives the kid's apartment number for when Spike comes around to collect. Leroy's nowhere to be found. Then Spike comes back at night, and starts shooting through the door, don't even wait till the kid opens it.

Burke: You got any witnesses?

Sniff: Ain't nobody gonna talk against Spike, you know—they value their lives.

Burke: This isn't going to do me any good without witnesses, Sniff.

Sniff: Hey, man, where you going? I give you a lead! What, you don't wanna follow it?

Burke: It's not enough, Sniff. I need more. Did anyone on the floor see the shooter in the hallway?

Burke hit the stop button. "LT, Elmore Wilson, otherwise known to us as Sniff, holds back sometimes, like he was a big deal businessman. I had to entice him with my billfold."

Jake nodded, Burke hit the play button. *Sniff: Man, I'm telling ya—I ain't got no more. Spike wouldn't just kill me, man. He'd cut me up first. I'm taking a chance being here now. Why don't ya give me some for the information I already gave you?*

Burke: Come on, Sniff. You know it don't work like that. You gave me nothing. Everyone's saying the same thing about Spike, no one's giving details. It's all in the details. When you have them, call me. We'll negotiate then.

Sniff: Hey man, come back. If I be dead, it be your fault, you know?

Burke: You're not going to be dead. Who saw it, Sniff?

Sniff: The lady in 3D, the one with the three kids—she won't talk, 'cause she knows Spike would kill the kids.

Burke: How do you know this?

Sniff: I know. I hear things. She's scared he gonna kill her anyway. She don't change her mind. You go visit her, you'll see. She all beat up and afraid to come out of her apartment. She's keeping the kids in, stopped talking to everyone. I heard he raped her. It's the word on the street. Some said he told her after he killed her kids she'd be passed around to his friends and his clients. She ain't gonna talk.

Jake pressed the off button and thought for a few moments. "We'll need to set up a safe house for Darcy and her kids right away. You know this guy Leroy?"

"Oh yeah, and badass is a kind word for that piece of shit. He's on parole for rape, assault with a deadly," Kraus said.

Jake scratched his chin. "I know Vice has been after Spike for years. Maybe we can lock him up for good this time. I'll set this up. Hang around, this is going to go down fast."

Jake outlined the operation in his head as he made the necessary calls and set up the meeting.

* * * *

Everyone crowded into Jake's office. Mike Testa of Special Operations worked out the details for the safe house. Jake ordered round-the-clock protection for the Darcy family. The officers involved would be Burke, Kraus, Romanelli, and himself. They wanted to keep this quiet with no leaks. Other than them, only Mike Testa, Special Agent Franklin of the FBI, and Captain McGuire knew of the operation. After Wilkesbury got Darcy and her kids away and to the safe house, the FBI would take over. They wanted her and the children alive with no complications. Each member of the team would wear vests, two drivers waiting outside would protect the inside team with long range rifles. Jake felt it was enough fire power along with their departmental issued side arm.

They chose a house owned by the FBI in Watertown off Guernseytown Road. The old white farm house with the wrap-around porch was in need of a paint job. It also gave them a three-sixty view. A thousand-foot-long driveway would give the team a clear view of anyone approaching from the front. Open fields to the right and woods to the left merged into the back-property line sixty feet from the house. It would be easy to monitor anyone approaching.

The captain wanted to wait until morning. Burke felt the longer they waited, the less chance the Darcy family had to survive. He didn't trust Sniff Lee to keep his mouth shut. In the end, the captain agreed.

Jake handpicked two officers to go in with them. No one got the address until they were on their way. Everything was on a need-to-know basis. He stressed the need to be on high alert. They took three identical cars—Jake and Officer Sherman in one, Louie and Officer Burrows in another, with Burke and Kraus out front. Once in the cars, Jake gave the drivers the address. Louie and Burrows went to the back entrance when they arrived at Wiggins Street. Burke and Kraus drove up to the front of the building. Jake and Sherman pulled in behind them. They got out with their rifles locked and loaded.

Jake went in with Burke and Kraus. He let Burke do the talking and kept his back to him to view the hallway. Burke knocked on the door to apartment 3D. "Police. Open up, Ms. Darcy."

"No, go away, I don't know anything," she pleaded.

"Ms. Darcy, you can bet someone has already called Spike. It would be wise to open up or we'll take down the door," Burke said.

They all knew the longer they stayed in the building, the longer they were exposed. Jake felt they had a target on the center of their backs as he scanned all the apartments on the floor.

A pale, shaking woman with her right eye blackened and her lips bruised and swollen opened the door a crack. Burke pushed his way in. Jake stayed outside in the hall with his rifle at the ready.

"Why can't everyone leave me alone? I made a mistake when I opened my door. I don't care about the other people. I want my kids safe. Go away," Ms. Darcy begged.

Jake thought it best to let Burke do the talking. She was more familiar with him. "We're here to keep your kids safe. How long do you think Spike's going to let you stay alive? Get the kids. We'll supply whatever you need. We don't have time for you to pack anything. Move it." Burked looked around. "Where are the kids?" Burke asked.

"They're in the closet in the bedroom." She wrung her hands.

Kraus, the third man in group, went back into the bedroom. He picked up the three-year-old, and took hold of the five-year-old's hand. Burke got the one-year-old, who screamed in his ear. Jake continued to scan the hallway as he listened in.

"Ms. Darcy, follow my directions exactly and no one will get hurt. Take the young one in your arms and hold on tight. We're going out in a tight formation, you in the middle, between me and Detective Kraus. We'll each carry a kid. You're going into my car with the youngest. The other two are going with my lieutenant, who's standing guard in the hall. Got it?"

"You can't separate us. You'll scare them," she said.

"This is the safest way. Ready?"

Jake heard Burke cock his gun. He swore he could see the thick, heavy tension fill the air as they all started to leave the building. Darcy's fear crawled over his skin.

"Oh, my God!" She wiped the tears running down her face as she snuggled the baby to her chest.

"Are you ready, Annie?" Burke asked as he looked up and down the hallway and gave Jake the nod to start out.

"Yes." Jake heard her whisper under her breath. "Please, God, protect my babies."

Jake hoped He was listening, because they needed a miracle to get out of there alive.

Since he, Kraus, and Burke went into the apartment building, clouds had formed, threatening rain. Jake hoped the gray overcast sky wasn't an omen. He led the team out of the building, Burke in the middle and Kraus bringing up the rear, shotgun poised to fire, covering Ms. Darcy as they marched to the cars. Sherman protected their flank. They hurried Ms. Darcy and the youngest into Burke's car. Jake shielded the other two kids into his car, gently pushing them onto the floor, telling them to stay down. Sherman climbed in back with the kids, making sure they did what they were told. Jake gave Louie the all clear to come around the front.

He saw Louie's car come around the corner first before he heard the squeal of tires. A black Cadillac raced toward them, swerving to the curb. Burrows and Louie flew out of their car, guns aimed. Jake saw the barrel of the rifle hanging out of the black car's passenger side window and took his shot through the front windshield. Louie shot at the front tires, Burrows at the back. The Caddy veered off the street and drove into a lamp post head-on. The driver and shooter rambled out of the car as they shot at them over their shoulders, running in opposite directions. The first car had already left the area. They were two blocks away, trying to make the highway before anyone had a chance to follow them. Jake jumped into the second car with Officer Sherman and took off.

"The kids are okay, Lieutenant," Officer Sherman said.

In his car, Jake gave the rear-view mirror a constant check to be sure they weren't being followed. He called for backup to support Louie and Burrows and hoped it arrived in time.

* * * *

Louie's heart pounded in his chest, his veins constricting as the sounds exploded in his ears. God, he wished it would slow down. Looking over to the passenger seat, he checked on Burrows and gave a sigh of relief when he saw the kid was okay. It took a few moments to catch his breath. He used the secured channel they were assigned to for the op and notified McGuire of their status. His backup had arrived. They started combing the streets for the driver and the shooter. Louie didn't talk with Jake. They'd agreed beforehand radio silence would be maintained to ensure the safety of the witness and her children. An hour seemed like an eternity, but it was the agreed-upon time. Lord, he hoped Jake was okay.

The time dragged on for Louie. At a minute to the hour, he pressed in the cell number for the operations. "Hey, everything all right, there?" Louie used no names.

"Yeah, everything's fine. No injuries?" Jake asked.

"None, but they got away. We're combing the neighborhood now. Don't expect we'll find them, unless someone gives them up."

* * * *

A little drizzle had started to fall. Jake hung up with Louie as he patrolled the perimeter of the house. His adrenaline hadn't returned to normal yet. On the deck outside the dining room window, he sat and listened to Burke and Special Agent Franklin outline the program to Ms. Darcy. They told her the relocation gave the family a fresh safe start wherever she wanted, with money in her pocket and a nice neighborhood for her kids. His phone vibrated in his pocket.

"Carrington."

"Jake, I thought you'd like to know that Spaulding's request for DNA testing has been approved. They're taking the samples sometime this week," McGuire said.

Lousy timing, he thought. Jake hung up with Shamus. He'd be there for the collection and delivery of the specimen. You could go months with nothing major going down, then you got hit with weeks like this one: two deaths, one crazy bitch stalking him and Mia, information that might lead to an arrest on a cold case, and someone forcing him to face his demons.

His thoughts rolled back to last night's conversation with Mia.

He settled onto his couch, put his feet up on the coffee table and dialed Mia's number. "Hey, what's going on?" Her hesitation had him sitting up. "Mia?"

"Jake, there was a package on my front steps when I got home. It was a skunk."

The tremors in her voice undid him.

"Mia, was there a note?"

"No."

"Did you call the police?"

"No, I was sure it was kids goofing around until I thought about it."

"What did you do with it?"

"I shoveled it into the garbage bin."

"Mia, call the police and have them retrieve it."

"You're scaring me, Jake."

"Mia, call the police. It might turn out to be kids, but let's be safe, rather than sorry. Okay?"

"All right."

The police came, retrieved it, and let her know she was right. It was a dead skunk with its throat slit.

Jake's first thought was it had to be Chloe Wagner. But something bothered Jake about the sender. Would Chloe be stupid enough to put it there on the same day she received a written warning to stay away? They'd have to wait on the lab reports to see if there were any fibers or solid evidence linking it to her.

Damn it, he didn't need another obstacle in his relationship with Mia. It would be a miracle if they made it past all this. He loved his job, but it did screw with his personal life.

Burke interrupted his thoughts. "Lieutenant, could you come in, please?"

"What's up, Al?"

"She wants to talk to my boss," Burke said with a smile.

"Why?" Jake asked.

"She's having a hard time processing all this. Here's the clincher." Burke yanked his pants up. "Her old man's in prison in New York. She wants him to know where they are."

"Great," Jake said, walking into the house. "Ms. Darcy, do you remember me?"

"Yes." She was pacing, her hands in constant motion as she pushed at her hair in the stark dining room.

"Please, sit down and stay away from the windows. I'll go over this again." Jake waited until she sat and looked over at the FBI guy, getting the nod to talk. "You can't notify anyone right now. If you choose to go into the witness protection program, you can't let anyone know where you are. I mean no one. If you want to be with the kids' father, we'll see if he can be relocated with you. After removing you from the apartment today, we can't let you and the kids go back there. You wouldn't last more than a day." Jake stopped to take a breath and watched Darcy. Annie shuddered as she fought back her tears. But the children had a strong mother. She'd make sure they survived. It was his job to see they did.

"Ms. Darcy—Annie, you can't believe that Spike would let you and the kids live?" Jake looked deep into her eyes as he asked the question.

"I wasn't going to say anything," she whispered.

"Did he give you those bruises?"

"Yes."

"Did he do anything else?"

"Yes." She started to cry—tears poured down her face as she brought her hand up to hide her shame.

With gentle hands, Jake took hers away from her face. "There's no reason for you to feel ashamed. He forced himself on you. Detectives Burke and Kraus will make sure he pays for everything he did to you and Orlando. Okay?"

"No one's been able to touch him before. Why are you certain you can?"

"We have you to help put Spike where he belongs. This officer is Caitlin Moss. She specializes in sexual assault counseling. She's going to stay with you and the children. Talk to her, she'll help. There are other officers who are assigned around the clock to watch over you. Detectives Burke and Kraus will patrol both inside and outside at various times. I promise, we'll keep you and the children safe." Jake took one of her hands, lifted her chin to look her in the eyes. "Hold your head up, Annie. I know you'll do whatever needs to be done to protect your children."

"Thank you."

"In a day or two you'll be in FBI custody. This special agent here has his men patrolling the woods for your safety. He'll be your best friend until you're all settled in."

Darcy left the room to find the kids.

"You know, Jake, you could be a counselor." Caitlin smiled.

"No thank you. I'd kill the bastards. I couldn't deal with it day after day. They take so much from the women."

The bruised and bloody body lying on a morgue table alone and broken jumped into his thoughts. He coughed into his hand, massaged his brow to ease the memory, and headed out for another look around. When he caught Spike, he'd give him a few punches for Annie.

Chapter 16

The warrant to bring Chloe in for formal questioning came through while they were in the field on Burke's operation. Jake checked his watch—four PM. He figured they'd catch her when she got out of work at five. A female officer followed in a patrol car and waited along with them for Chloe to get out of work. He parked as close to her vehicle as possible in the hopes of avoiding a scene. A half hour later he spotted her walking out the front door of the building. Chloe had on a blue raincoat with the hood covering her head as she hurried to her Honda. As she drew near to him, Jake climbed out of his car and stood beside it, waiting before he approached her. A light rain fell and the dampness seeped into his clothing, chilling him to the bones. "What's up?" Chloe asked, eyeing him as she stopped in front of him.

"Chloe Wagner, information has been uncovered in your sister's murder case. I'm going to ask you to accompany this officer to the station for a formal interview."

Louie stepped out of the car and walked to Chloe's left. She looked up at Louie, then back to Jake.

"What are you talking about? I didn't kill my sister and you know it. You're doing this because I hassled Mia. You won't get away with it." Chloe started swearing at the top of her lungs.

So much for not creating a scene, Jake thought.

"Chloe, to cover both you and me, I'm going to read you your rights. Afterward you'll be escorted to the station by this female officer." Jake read her Miranda rights.

"Do you understand these rights as they have been explained to you?" he asked.

They had enough evidence, the ring, her controversial relationship with her sister, her father's statement, and her whereabouts at the time of the murder—though most was circumstantial, this would give him time to find more. Deep down, his gut told him it wasn't her. But the ring troubled him.

"What, do I look stupid? Of course I understand my rights. This isn't over, Jake. I will prove you set me up because you didn't want to date me anymore," she screamed.

Walking a fine line, he decided not to cuff her. Huge mistake.

She lunged at him, scratching his cheek, the grooves from her nails left a burning sensation in their wake. And she didn't stop there. Chloe kicked him in the shins, right on the sensitive area of the bone. Still not finished, she bit him. Jake recovered enough to help the female officer get the handcuffs on her. Louie stood by with his hands on his gun and a grin on his face.

She held up her cuffed hands and put on a nasty grin. "Bring back memories, Jake?"

The officer pushed Chloe into the patrol car and drove away

* * * *

"I didn't recognize the patrol officer, did you?" Jake asked.

"Yes."

"Who was she?"

"Tara Jones," Louie answered.

"I liked her."

"Me too. She handled Chloe well. We're not interviewing her right away?"

"No, I want her to sit and stew for a while, and contemplate her actions. When I'm good and ready, we'll take her. She won't be as calm or as in control as the last time," Jake said.

Back at the station Louie couldn't help but notice the cold look in Jake's eyes—he decided they needed a third person to witness the interview. "Jake, I'm going to pull in Burke. Why don't you watch from behind the glass?"

"Nope, I'm under control, Louie. We got called out before you scheduled the interview with the Drake girl, right?" Jake asked.

"Yeah, you still want to interview her?"

"Yes, I still want to speak with Kraus, and Brown. Something's off with her answers. If Chloe did it, she didn't do it alone. Oh, I also want to re-interview the ex-boyfriend, Mark Cavilla. We can hold Chloe for up to forty-eight hours. Line up your questions in case she hires a lawyer."

"What do you mean if? She had the ring."

"No, she didn't. Joe found it in Shanna's room, not in Chloe's room or on her person. It doesn't mean she had possession of it. You told me to keep an open mind. Now, I'll tell you the same thing. When we close this thing, I don't want the evidence coming back to bite us on the ass. We tie up all loose ends, got it?"

"I got it. I'll schedule the rest for tomorrow," Louie said.

He thought Jake was being too cautious, but he was the boss. When he turned to leave the office, Jake stopped him.

"You got anything at your desks for cuts? This hurts like a bitch." At his desk, Jake sat and touched his face.

"Yeah, I do. You should have cuffed her right away. Human bites and scratches are the worst."

"Hindsight's great, Louie. Get me the disinfectant?"

"The vet closes at six tonight, we'll be cutting it close. Should I tell the doctor to keep Houston overnight?"

"We'll try to get there, but no promises. This interview could be ten minutes, or ten hours."

Jake's phone rang as Louie left his office. "Lieutenant Carrington," he answered.

"It's Shamus. Come into my office."

The captain handed Jake a piece of paper with the test results for the sergeant's exam, and lo and behold, Louie placed twenty-first out of seventy-five.

"Thank God. When are you telling him?"

"You're his lieutenant now, Jake, you get the honors." Shamus smiled.

"Thanks. I'll do it now, before we interview Chloe Wagner."

"I thought you interviewed her Monday. She's still stalking you?"

"No, we brought her in for a formal interview and are holding her on the suspicion of murder. There are a couple of things I need to clear up before charging her. You'll have my report tonight. I'll send it to your office and home email." He noted Shamus questioning look. "Her father tried hocking the ring the victim always wore. Said he found it in Shanna's room. He also said besides himself, his wife, and Chloe, no else had access to the room. But the fact is, anyone could have stowed it there. They've had other visitors in the last three months. Who to say they didn't put it there? I understand Meryl, and even Cavilla, visited her parents since Shanna's death. We're not stopping there. Shanna Wagner's best friend, Meryl Drake's, statements were inconsistent, changing what she said first to Kraus and Brown, and four days later to me and Louie. We're pulling her in tomorrow, along with the ex-boyfriend." He lined the pieces up in his head as he spoke.

He needed to cover all his bases if he planned on getting a conviction. "I want you to go by the book here," McGuire said, his tone stern.

"Don't worry. This has nothing to do with the stalking incident," Jake said over his shoulder as he walked out. He flagged down Louie on his way to his office.

"I set up Drake's interview for tomorrow morning at ten o'clock," Louie informed him. "Cavilla can't make it in until two o'clock. He works a half day on Saturdays. Are we interviewing Chloe now?"

"Nope, I need you to come into my office and take a seat." Jake kept a concerned look on his face. Louie chose to stand.

"What now?" Louie asked.

"I've been informed you passed the sergeant's exam with flying colors. You're twenty-first out of seventy-five applicants. They're promoting thirty detectives to sergeants. Congratulations, Louie, you deserve it." Jake held out his hand, took a firm hold on Louie's and pulled him into a bear hug.

"Don't bust my chops, Jake. Are you shitting me?"

"Yes, Sergeant," Jake said, using his new rank.

"Oh, my God, I have to call Sophia. She won't believe it." He turned and started to run to his desk. He almost tripped, turning back to Jake. "Hey. This isn't fair. We can't celebrate so soon after yours. Sophia would kill us both."

"Oh yeah, she would. Go give her a call. Chloe can wait, it'll do her good"

* * * *

Mia took a personal day to unwind after the crazy week she had. Writing always cleared her mind. She'd been so scattered over yesterday's incident that she'd forgotten to call back her friend Piper until this morning. She made plans for them to have lunch in town today. *Put on your compassion hat, Mia, Piper needs a shoulder to cry on.*

Mia had never understood how someone could forgive a lover or a spouse of infidelity. It was the ultimate betrayal. The same way Bart had betrayed her. He'd created her trust issues—the psychologist in her knew the cause of her fear of commitment, but the woman couldn't forgive or move past it. Since she'd begun to date Jake, Bart's lying, cheating behavior played on her mind. Could Jake be trusted? Would he be faithful?

When she got to The Eatery at noon she looked around for Piper. Spotting her in one of the booths, Mia slid into the seat across from her friend. Without waiting for a greeting, Piper started talking and Mia listened as she looked around the restaurant. The place had a country-flair with bronzed roosters hung on the blue and white floral wallpaper. More importantly, the food was good. Turning her attention back to Piper, it was unclear to her if Piper was trying to convince herself or Mia of Darryl's worth.

"You don't throw away the baby with the bathwater," Piper said in between sniffles.

Mia had always thought it was the dumbest statement in the world. She understood Piper was afraid to be alone at her age.

Darryl and Piper had been married for twenty years and last week she'd caught the bastard cheating on her with a twenty-two-year-old woman. Mia didn't know where or who to direct her anger at—Darryl or Piper. Piper said she never confronted him, thus reinforcing the bad behavior.

She chose her words with care. "He betrayed the most sacred trust. Didn't he promise in front of God and family he would honor, love, and cherish you?"

I couldn't stay in a marriage after that, I'd always be looking at him—wondering if he broke his vows again. I could never trust a man who cheated. Bart's cheating is the reason I broke it off with him in the first place. But Piper isn't me. Still, I don't understand how Piper would want to stay married to Darryl.

"You never liked him," Piper said, reading her mind.

"It's not true. I never trusted him. He's always flirting with every woman in the room."

"Real nice, thanks, Mia." Piper swiped at the tears pouring down her face as she scooted across the seat.

"Wait...I want you to look at this from all angles. Why are you going easy on him? Can you trust him again? Do you want to make love to him after he's been with another woman? You need to look at everything in depth. Then ask yourself again if you can live with it and his actions. I don't want you to be a victim. Are you forgiving him because you don't want to be alone at forty-two?" Mia finished up, searched Piper's eyes for understanding.

"I don't know. I have a family to consider. I haven't worked outside the house in twenty-three years. How will I survive? I'm twenty pounds overweight. Who'd want to date me? Look at you. You're thirty-one, gorgeous, and you hardly date, because you know there's nothing but garbage out there—men who want free sex with none of the responsibilities. I don't want a free-for-all lifestyle. All I want is my family intact," Piper said.

Mia had a lot of sympathy for Piper and her fears. She scooped up a spoonful of chocolate chunk ice cream, stalling as she gathered her thoughts. In the silence, tears continued to fall down Piper's face. Piper swiped them away in between eating her favorite frozen treat.

Mia broke the silence. "I love you, Piper. I don't want to see you hurt or used. I will support whatever decision you choose. You have choices. Please look closely at everything before you decide. Question everything. This way, in the end, you'll have peace with your decision, no matter what it is. You're a beautiful woman. Weight means nothing. If you want a relationship, you'll find one. I don't want you to rush into anything. But before you decide, maybe you and Darryl should go to marriage counseling," Mia said.

"Oh, he'd never go." Piper looked away.

"Ask him, see what he says. What are you afraid of?" Mia asked, hating that Piper was a victim and not able to take control of her life.

"That's he'll leave me," Piper said.

Heavy sobs burst from Piper's throat as she cried harder. It had the entire restaurant looking their way. Piper turned away from her ice cream and pulled a tissue from her purse as she blew her nose. "Is that such a bad thing?" she asked, holding up her hand when Piper tried to defend Darryl. "Are you so afraid to be alone, Piper, that you'd allow someone to walk all over you? You're one of the strongest women I know. You did a great job raising your children. You volunteer at the children's schools and at church. You're the greatest friend a person could ask for. When someone's in need of support you're the first one to offer help. You're a gift to those of us who know and love you." Mia ended with a smile.

"I don't know how to respond." Piper smiled for the first time.

"I mean everything I say."

"I know you do."

"What have you always dreamed of doing, when the children were grown and out on their own?" Mia asked, changing tactics.

"I always wanted to go back to school. I love interior design. Oh, and I want to take piano lessons. Stupid, huh?" She laughed.

"No, it's not. Let's go over to the community college after lunch, pick up the brochures for next semester. We'll check out the curriculum and see if anything appeals to you. In the beginning, maybe you should audit the course. Auditing without the upfront cost will let you know if you like school or not—"

Piper interrupted her. "Are you telling me to leave Darryl?"

"No, that's up to you. No one else can decide that for you. You don't have to make a decision today or tomorrow, or even next week. This is a big decision. Consider everything before you make up your mind. Understand?"

"I want you to tell me what to do. I respect your opinion. Please. I need help," Piper begged.

"No, you don't. What you need is the support and friendship I can give you. In the end, it's your life. You pick how you want to live it or who you want to love. I'll be there no matter which way you go."

"I know you will. If I stay with him, how will you treat Darryl?"

"The same as I've always treated him. He's your husband, Piper. I wouldn't jeopardize your marriage." Mia picked up the check.

* * * *

Jake gave Mia a quick call while he waited for Louie.

"How are you today? See, I asked first." He laughed.

"A rough day. How was yours?"

"The same, I'll fill you in later. We picked up Chloe Wagner a little while ago on suspicion of killing her sister. I wanted you to know."

"You're kidding, right?"

"No. When's a good time to call you back?"

"Anytime, I'll be home working." She sounded upset.

Chapter 17

On their way to the interview room, Jake asked, "So, what did Sophia say?"

"Oh, you know. The usual—she wants to have another party. I told her to let me pay off the last one first." Louie laughed.

Sophia had shouted with joy when he had told her. Her exact words brought a smile to his face—*I'll be waiting for you, Louie, with a big private party for two with lots of champagne. I'll even be wearing the little red number you gave me for Christmas.* No, he wasn't sharing.

"I'm sure she said more."

"Why?" Louie asked.

"You got the biggest grin on your face. On second thought, please don't share. I'll be jealous."

Slipping into interview mode when they reached the door, Louie pushed the door open. With a somber expression, he blanked his face. Jake thanked the officer inside the interview room. It was a CYA move to have her there. With the way Chloe had been behaving, he thought it was wise to cover his ass in case Chloe tried to pull a sexual harassment charge on him.

* * * *

First thing Jake noticed, Chloe hadn't lawyered up—either brave or stupid on her part.

"Chloe, let's get started," Jake said, handling this stage of the interview.

"You arrested me for a murder I didn't commit because you couldn't control your dick. What do you expect to accomplish here, Jake?"

Ignoring her, Jake said, "We didn't arrest you, we picked you up for questioning in light of new evidence discovered today, and we're holding you until we can verify a few things pertaining to that evidence. I'm going to reread you your rights, record, and videotape this interview." Jake reread the Miranda rights. "Do you understand your rights?"

"As I stated before, Lieutenant, I'm not stupid. Of course I understand my rights. Once again, I didn't kill my sister or anyone else. Do you hear me?"

"I hear you. Let me record who's present in this interview before we move forward." Jake read all the pertinent information into the recorder. When he finished he asked, "Do you understand you're under suspicion for the murder of your sister, Shanna Wagner?"

"Yes, I understand my freakin' rights. I'm telling you again, I didn't do it. Why are you doing this to me?" She pounded her fist on the table as she spoke.

Jake continued. "We understand you've waived your right to an attorney at this time?"

"Yes." Realizing the seriousness of her situation, Chloe's answers were subdued. *About damn time*, he thought.

"We're here today because the ring belonging to your sister, Shanna, turned up in her room, in the home you share with your parents. Do you know how it got there?" Jake never took his eyes off her face. He looked for telltale signs of deceit.

"No, I don't."

"No explanation, Chloe? This would be the time to come clean. Your parents have been through enough."

"They have, but you can ask all you want and I'm still going to tell you the same thing each time you ask. I didn't put the ring there. I don't know how the ring got there. Yes, I want this to be over for my parents and myself. We need to get on with our lives. If that's selfish of me, so be it," she said with passion. "My sister and I didn't always get along, but I loved her. Loved her, Jake. I would never hurt Shanna. You don't have a clue who Shanna was. You've learned nothing in all this time you've investigated her case. You've missed the most important aspect of her," Chloe said, cocking her eyebrow at him.

"What do you mean?" Louie asked, taking over the questioning.

"It means what it means. You've never questioned what I thought should be a flag." She shrugged.

"Not good enough. What does it mean?" Louie asked again.

"In my parents' eyes Shanna was a Miss Goody Two Shoes who did nothing wrong. She wasn't. Shanna enjoyed a different lifestyle than us.

She was confused about her sexuality. Right before her death she had started to experiment by dating men." Chloe didn't elaborate.

"Please state for the record what you mean about her lifestyle." Jake understood the direction of Chloe's statement. He wondered what game she was playing.

"Oh, Jake, do I have to spell it out?" She waved a hand in the air.

Her voice quavered, and her eyes filled with tears. Jake ignored it as an act. "Yes."

Silence filled the room. For the first time since he'd known her, Chloe seemed withdrawn, even contrite. Dropping her head, she refused to meet Jake's eyes.

"Chloe?"

She looked up, tears clinging to her lashes. "Lesbian, Jake. She was a lesbian. Or maybe she was bisexual. Shanna was experimenting with both men and women. She was confused."

It annoyed him she'd stoop to this level, acting as if she was protecting her sister's reputation. Did she have no boundaries? Not once in the last few months did anyone even hint that Shanna played for both teams, and even if she did, what did it matter?

"There's nothing wrong with being gay. Attitudes have changed about it. But in all our interviews nobody's ever hinted at her being bisexual. Why are you saying it now?" Jake asked.

"The great investigator missed an important piece of information!" She flung her hands out, mocking him. "I'm shocked. Attitudes here in Wilkesbury have not changed. In the business world, Shanna wouldn't get hired if she flaunted it. Plus, she never would have disappointed our parents. That's why she never outed herself. We didn't get along all the time but mostly we argued about one subject."

"What subject?"

"We fought about her choice of partners."

"Who were they?"

"Her friend Meryl—now there's one vicious bitch, if you ask me. She thought she owned Shanna. She went nuts every time Shanna dated a guy. I'd say she even hated Mark Cavilla."

"Did she date anyone else?" Louie asked.

"One or two of the girls at school until it started to be a problem. The girls, from what I understood, stayed friends."

"Who were they?" Jake asked.

Before Chloe could answer, he threw out another question, "Why didn't you tell us this at the beginning of the investigation? Why now?" Jake's mind kept circling around the statement.

"I didn't want you to label her—push the case aside. More important, I didn't want our parents to find out. I never thought it caused her death, but now I'm not sure." Chloe started to cry.

Jake had no sympathy for her. "Chloe, your father believes you put the ring in Shanna's room."

"I know," she whispered.

"Did you?" Louie handed her some tissues.

Officer Jones continued to stand at attention inside the door. Her face void of expression.

"No, I didn't. Jake, please look at me. Yes, I get crazy sometimes. But I didn't kill my sister. I didn't put the ring there," she said, pleading with him to understand.

"Who did then?" Jake asked.

"I don't know. Why don't you ask Meryl? She was over last week visiting my parents. She cozied up to my mother. Mom told me Meryl wanted to hang out in Shanna's room for a while because she missed her. Mom thought it odd. She considers Meryl a sweet person." Chloe said with disgust.

"You don't like Meryl?" Louie asked.

"No, I hate how she controlled Shanna. It began when they met in the first grade. Most of our fights were about Meryl."

"What day did she visit your mother?" Jake said.

"I'm not sure. You'll have to ask my mother."

"Will she remember?" Louie asked.

"Oh yeah, she loved the distraction and Meryl." Chloe looked off into the distance.

"Did you see your sister on the night she disappeared?" Louie asked.

"No. I saw her on Thursday night. I told you in my original interview and again in our other interviews. I went over to her dorm on Thursday. Mom made Shanna some food she wanted me to take to her. After I dropped it off, we went out to McDonald's for a bite. Shanna insisted we make it an early night because she needed to study for an exam the next morning. I never saw her again." Jake saw Chloe become lost in the memory of her sister.

He cleared his throat twice before Chloe looked up at him. "We're going to break at this time." He and Louie stepped out. He motioned for Officer Jones to follow him. "Officer Jones, Ms. Wagner may stay in this room until we return. Will it be a problem with your sergeant?"

"No, sir," Officer Jones replied.

He stepped back in with Jones. "This interview has ended. It's now seven twenty-five PM on May eighth. This interview will resume at a later time."

He and Louie left the interview room. Louie started to speak. Jake held up his hand. "Not until we're in my office."

The minute they were in his office, Louie started in. "You don't believe her, do you?"

"I don't know what to believe. We have the interviews tomorrow with Meryl and Mark. We'll wait until we complete them all before we make a decision. In the meantime, I want to verify with Chloe's mother that Meryl did visit her last week. It's strange a week after Meryl's visit, the ring shows up. Or maybe Chloe had waited for the perfect opportunity to hide the ring. Or Meryl planted it when she visited the last week. This could go in either direction. It still points to Chloe for hiding pertinent information. Perhaps she hoped it would turn up when her parents cleaned out Shanna's room and they would give it to her. Most parents know their children and her father had doubts when we asked him. You have to wonder why. What are your thoughts?"

"I don't know. Maybe Meryl's playing them against each other? She said she considered them more her parents than her own. For what purpose, I don't know." Louie scratched his head.

"I know this is going to make you crazy, Louie, but I don't want to hold her overnight." Jake watched his words land. Prayed Louie would come onboard.

"What are you, nuts? Of course it's gonna make me crazy. After all the trouble we went through to get the damn warrant. What's your logic here?" Louie looked at Jake as if he'd lost it.

"I jumped the gun. Go ahead and say I told you so. I've got a doubt niggling at the back of my head. I don't want her locked up if she doesn't deserve to be. Let's keep her here while we go to her parents' house. See if anyone visited them tonight, or if anyone called the station."

"Who could've called?"

"Let's wait and see. I want to talk to dispatch before we leave. I also need to leave Shamus a voice message."

Jake went back to the interview room, called Officer Jones out and gave her instructions. Next, he went in to speak with Chloe.

"Chloe, I'm going to verify a couple of things in your story. We'll be back in an hour or so. You might want to reconsider whether you want a lawyer or not. You can wait in this room with Officer Jones, or you can go back to holding. What'll it be?"

"I'll wait here. I don't need a lawyer. Why are you being nice?" Her eyes filled with suspicion as she studied him.

"I'm not being nice. I'm being thorough and want to clear up a few things in your statement. Maybe you won't have to spend the night here."

"I'm telling the truth, Jake," she said, her expression filled with hope.

"We'll be back," Jake said.

Outside the room, Jake checked his watch. "Damn, Louie, the vet's closed."

Chapter 18

Jake pulled up outside a modest, yellow ranch house built in the eighties, before the era of big colonials. It had a well-manicured lawn, edged with flowers in the first stages of bloom. He found the flowers hopeful, and maybe the Wagners did too. The door opened before they got to the top step.

"Lieutenant, Detective," Joe Wagner said with a dour expression plastered on his face as he blocked the doorway.

"Hi, Joe. Can we come in?" Jake asked.

"I don't want to disturb my wife. Can we talk out here?" Joe continued to block the doorway.

"No, Joe. We need to speak to you and Anna," Jake said.

"Why? It's after eight o'clock. This can't wait? I don't want you upsetting her," he fumed. "I can't take any more of your questions or your accusations today, Lieutenant."

"I'm sorry, but this is important," Jake said.

"Jesus, will this never end?" Joe slumped his shoulders.

"Will what never end?" Louie asked.

"The pain, the suspicion—I don't know, everything." He held out his hands, palms up.

"You didn't ask about Chloe. Why?" Jake asked.

"Why? I don't understand."

"Don't you want to know where she is?" Louie asked, jumping in again.

"It's Friday night, she goes out after work with some of the girls."

"No, Joe, we brought her in after work tonight. She's down at the station, being questioned." Jake watched Joe's reaction, registering shock and surprise simultaneously.

"I should've been notified. She needs a lawyer. Why didn't she call?" He bombarded them with questions. "You can't tell her mother you suspect Chloe. It would kill her. I know what I said today. I was distraught. But I know in my heart, I know she didn't do it. She couldn't." He stared them down.

"What we have to ask your wife is important," Jake said. "Did you have a visitor today or tonight?"

"Yes."

"Who?" Louie asked.

"Meryl Drake dropped in. She left about five minutes ago. Why? Will Chloe be home tonight?"

"What did Meryl want?" Jake asked.

"Oh, to visit, she said she missed us," Joe answered.

"Did she visit last week?"

"Yes. Why?"

"Did she go into Shanna's room for anything?" Louie asked.

"She needed to lie down. Why?" Jake continued to ignore Joe's questions.

"How long did she stay last week?" Jake asked.

"I got home after she'd been here for a while. She visited for a little over an hour. Meryl's visit picked up Anna's spirits."

"Do you know what they spoke about?" Louie asked.

"She talked about Shanna, their childhood, how much she loved us," Joe said.

"How much Shanna loved you?" Jake asked.

"No, how much she, Meryl, loved us. How she'd always be there for us. Why?"

"Let's go in the house and talk to your wife." Joe stepped back. Jake steered him into the living room. Louie trailed behind them.

When the three of them entered the room, Anna asked, before looking up, "Did Meryl forget something, honey?"

"No, Anna. Lieutenant Carrington and Detective Romanelli are here," he said in a controlled voice.

"Oh? Why? Hello, Lieutenant, Detective," Mrs. Wagner said as her head came up, glasses perched on her nose.

"It's Sergeant now. Please don't get up," Louie said.

"Why don't you take a seat and explain why you're here." Anna folded her hands together. Her knuckles whitened as she braced to hear them out.

"We have a few follow-up questions for you if you don't mind?" The woman looked fragile. Jake didn't want to be the one who pushed her over the edge.

Anna nodded, pointing to the chairs.

"When Meryl Drake visited you last week, what did you speak about? How long did she stay?" He sat in the overstuffed blue chair.

"She talked about Shanna, as she always does, and the childhood they had, which for Meryl wasn't great. The girls fought sometimes. Of course, they'd always make up later, like children do. Meryl's parents are both alcoholics. She spent a lot of time here. Like the rest of us, she misses Shanna." A tear spilled down Anna's check.

"Anything else? Did she ask about anything in particular?" Jake pushed.

Mrs. Wagner thought for a few moments. "Meryl did ask me if she could lie down in Shanna's room for a while. It was a strange request that bothered me at first. I asked her why. That's when she explained that she had a headache."

"Did she come here a lot in the past few months?"

"No...no, once or twice maybe, to see Chloe, but then they'd get into arguments. They'd stop fighting when they saw it upset me."

"When did they argue? What did they argue about?" Jake asked.

"Girls, they argue one minute then they're friends the next. Chloe would never tell me why they fought."

"Did they make up after they argued?" Louie asked.

"I don't think so. The second time Meryl came over, Chloe wouldn't see her. I tried to talk to Chloe, ask her why—again she wouldn't say, told me to drop it." Anna looked tired.

"I have a couple more questions then I promise we'll get out of your hair," Jake said.

She nodded. "I miss Shanna terribly, you know. I know my girls aren't perfect. Shanna was sweet, but a little too driven. She needed to be top of her class, A's in everything. She wouldn't accept anything less for herself. All I ever wanted for my girls was happiness. Now, none of us can be happy, because we're incomplete."

"A little driven, Anna?" Joe's smile never reached his eyes.

"I guess you're right, Joe. A lot driven would best describe our Shanna." She smiled back at him.

"Mrs. Wagner, who do you think killed her?" Jake asked, watching Joe flinch.

"I can't say, but it was no one in the family. We all loved her. I know you think she and Chloe didn't get along. That's not true. They were siblings. Don't you have a brother or a sister, Lieutenant? They argue sometimes, but that doesn't mean they don't like or care for one another. They fought more when Meryl hung around. Odd, isn't it, that I never thought of that before?"

"No, sometimes things pop into our heads with no rhyme or reason. One last thing, how long was Meryl's visit last week?" Jake asked.

She pushed back her graying hair. "She was here about forty-five minutes before Joe got home. And about another thirty minutes afterward. In fact, we asked her to join us for dinner, but she declined our offer."

"Why?"

"She wanted to leave before Chloe got home."

"Mrs. Wagner, if we find Shanna's ring, will it go to Chloe?"

"Why, of course. My grandmother gave me her jewelry. My mother gave her jewelry to her granddaughters. I'll give mine to my granddaughter, if I have one. It's always been our tradition. Why do you ask?"

"I was curious. Thank you for your time." Jake nodded at Louie, and stood. Joe pushed out of his chair to join them. When Anna started to rise, Jake said, "No, please don't get up."

At the door, Joe asked, "When can I bring Chloe home? Can I ask why all the questions?"

"I can't answer your questions at this time. Yes, she'll need a ride. Give me an hour to clear the paperwork and talk with her. I'll call your cell when she's released.

"Okay, Lieutenant. I know Chloe didn't do it."

"Take care, Joe," Jake said.

Jake didn't say anything else. He didn't remind Joe of their conversation today at the pawn shop, when Joe had his doubts.

They left the Wagners, drove straight to Captain McGuire's house—he lived in the same neighborhood a few blocks over. Jake called before heading over. When they knocked on the door Shamus answered. He led them into his study, bypassing the living room crowded with people.

"It must be important if you're both here at this hour. What's up?"

"I'm not second-guessing myself, Shamus. I don't want to hold Chloe Wagner in lock-up tonight."

An aggravated Shamus said, "I told you to tread carefully there, Jake. Why the sudden change of mind?"

"New information came in through the interview with Chloe Wagner. Before you interrupt, Cap, it has a ring of truth to it." Jake filled Shamus in. Louie said nothing. "I'm putting her under surveillance and will keep it on her all weekend."

"Besides her sexual orientation, what else came to light?" Shamus asked.

"It played a big part in her death, if I'm reading the players correctly. It might not. Chloe said she didn't want her parents to know." Jake lined it up in his head as he filled in Shamus. "Shanna and Meryl dated for years. She got jealous when Shanna dated Mark Cavilla. Chloe felt both Meryl and Mark were applying pressure to Shanna for her to pick a side. Confused, Shanna didn't know where to turn for answers. The reason we decided to re-interview Meryl in the first place was she lied to us in the original interview. She told Kraus she saw Shanna the night she disappeared. Four days later, she told us she didn't see Shanna all week because of exams. Tonight, Chloe let us know Meryl visited her mother last week. She claimed to have a headache and asked to lie down in Shanna's bedroom. Now a week later, Mr. Wagner finds the ring in Shanna's room." Jake stopped, took a breath, and shrugged his shoulders.

"Who killed her?" McGuire asked.

"At this point, I want to re-interview everyone involved and go from there. Are you on board, Cap?"

"Yes, but I want to judge her reactions for myself. I'll be behind the glass tomorrow when you talk to Meryl and Shanna's former boyfriend. Come to my office afterward. I'll give you my impressions," Shamus said.

"You're on board to let Chloe go for the night?" Jake asked.

"Yes, but make it very clear she's still a person of interest and can't leave the state. Also, explain if she fails to report when summoned, she'll be arrested. She'll have to wait in jail until the judge decides if he'll grant her bail. What do you have to say, Louie?"

"Ah, someone remembered I'm here."

"Louie," Shamus said, looking over the top of his glasses.

"I agree with Jake. We might've jumped the gun, but the evidence led that way. We'll put a tail on Chloe tonight and on the other two tomorrow, see what shakes out."

"Get it done."

"Cap, tomorrow night—I have a special dinner engagement. I'm going to assign the night guys to watch them all."

"You're in command, Jake, utilize your team. Good night," McGuire said, leading them to the door.

"Good night," they said in unison.

Outside, Louie said, "The plot thickens."

"Go ahead, Louie, get it off your chest." Jake could almost see the steam coming from Louie's ears.

"What?"

"You know what. How I didn't listen. How I jumped the gun because she annoyed me."

"I didn't say anything, but if I did, it would be part of it. The other part is you feel desperate to close this particular case because it hits too close to home," Louie said.

"If you think I acted inappropriately, Louie, call me on it. But leave my personal life out of it."

Louie's comment had hit the mark. Jake drove in silence. At the station, they went right to booking and explained to the officer on duty what they were doing. Next, he called Mr. Wagner before he went to the room where Chloe was detained. Jake took a seat across from Chloe when they walked into Room Three. Louie turned the video and recorder on and took up a position by the door. Jake explained the reason for her release and her obligations in the matter. He let her know her father would be outside waiting for her.

"You're an asshole, Jake. You did this to teach me a lesson." Chloe trembled.

"No, I didn't. The evidence pointed to you. Now it points to a couple of others. I follow the evidence. It's not personal. Right now, I'm giving you a break. So, you don't have to spend time in lock-up with the hookers. Say thank you and go home."

"Well, excuse me for not being grateful, you bastard." She stormed out. Together he and Louie trailed behind her. In the lobby, Chloe ran right into her father's arms and cried.

Mr. Wagner looked over Chloe's shoulder and mouthed 'thank you' to them.

Nodding, Jake turned his back on them and spoke with the officer. "Did she give you any trouble?"

"No, she's scared. It dawned on her she could lose her freedom. She believes you did this because she stalked you. I'd watch your back. She's trouble. Good night, sir."

"Good night, Tara." *Sound advice*, he mused as he turned toward Louie.

"Sometimes a case sticks with you. This one grabbed me. Not because of Eva. Everyone wanted a piece of Shanna. She didn't have a chance as they pulled her in all directions. The brutality is the only similarity. You know what I mean? I'm sorry I jumped at you back there."

"It doesn't help that we don't like Chloe."

"You're right, it doesn't. I want to play a hunch. Let's go over to dispatch, see if anyone called in asking for information on the arrest."

"How would anyone know Chloe got arrested tonight?" Louie asked.

"I'm guessing it would be the person who planted the ring, if it wasn't Chloe."

The dispatcher gave Jake the printout for the evening calls, complete with each caller's phone number and name. Jake looked at it. "Well, well, well…"

"What?"

Chapter 19

Jake handed Louie the printout. "Look at the list."

"How'd she know?"

"Good question. We'll ask her tomorrow. I'm going to take your car, you take mine. I'll stake out Chloe's place tonight."

"Not alone, you won't," Louie said.

"Why not?"

"Because."

"That's a stupid answer, one I'm sure you don't accept from your kids," Jake said, mocking Louie.

"I'm not leaving you. This is a touchy situation, Jake. CYA is important here. Shit, there goes my celebration." Louie frowned.

"I know how to 'cover my ass.'" He saw the look Louie gave him and added, "We'll compromise. I'll talk with Officer Jones's supervisor. If he agrees, I'll have her ride along with me. I liked her style tonight. Is that acceptable? This way you can get home to the celebration Sophia's planned for you, Sergeant."

"Yes, it's acceptable, Lieutenant. I'll walk with you down to the squad room, and say my hellos to Sergeant Kline."

"Don't trust me?"

"You've been known to go off on your own. And I stress, this is not the time," Louie said with emphasis.

"Let's go, Dad," Jake joked.

Officer Jones's sergeant cleared her for the ride-along.

"Take off, Louie. I'm all set. And I'll pick you up at nine tomorrow."

Jones got in the car with Jake and sat at attention. Her uniform had been pressed. Her hat was at the correct angle, and her shoes had been polished to a high sheen. Her mahogany skin showcased black eyes and her dark hair was worn in a regulation bun under her hat. At five-eleven, Jones carried her hundred fifty pounds in a well-toned body.

"Tara, you can take your hat off in the car. I know it gets hot with them on. It's going to be a long night."

"Thank you, sir," she said. She never made a move to remove it.

"Please, call me Jake while we're on a stakeout. Do you wish to be addressed by your rank or by your first name?"

"Tara's good, sir."

"Do you want coffee?" he asked, pulling to the curb at the donut shop.

"Thanks, I take it black."

"Okay, any special kind of donuts you like?"

"I can't afford to eat donuts, sir. A minute in the mouth is years on my hips."

"You don't look like you need to worry," Jake said.

"That's because I don't eat them." When she smiled, it lit up her whole face.

"You want a bagel or something?"

"No, I'm good. The coffee's enough."

"Okay, but I'll guarantee you'll be sorry in a couple of hours." He got out of the car.

"Sir, I'll get the coffees." She jumped from the car.

"It's Jake. And Tara, I get my own coffee and a lady's. My mother raised me to be a gentleman."

He saw the look of confusion on her face and figured her partner made her get the coffee all the time. It was hard for a woman on the force. Add to the fact she was a black woman, she fought harder for the respect she'd earned. The old prejudices never died here. Jake knew some of the other cops still thought women and minorities didn't belong on the job. He wondered how they passed the personality tests for the academy. Jake never took advantage of rookies or uniforms. He gave respect where it was earned, no matter what the rank or color.

He returned to the car.

"Here you go. One large cup of black coffee for you, and for me I got a cup of coffee and a whole bag of donuts." He laughed, opening the bag, sniffing its contents.

* * * *

They pulled across the street from the Wagners' house. Jake was happy to see the skies had cleared. In the driveway, Chloe's red car and

Joe's gold one were parked next to each other. He pointed to the right corner of the house.

"The one with the light on is Chloe's room."

"Are we going to stay out here all night?" Tara asked.

"No. It's nine-fifteen now, I figure we'll watch until ten-thirty. You go off shift at eleven, correct?"

"Yes, sir."

"Tara, it's okay to call me Jake while we're on the stakeout. Do you have a problem with me?" Something behind her formal manner bothered him. What had he done to earn her scorn?

Jake studied her as she processed the information, "Is it my past relationship with the suspect that's bothering you?"

"Sir, it's not my place to question you. You have rank over me and can make my life a living hell," she said, an edge to her voice.

"Is someone making your life harder than it should be, Officer Jones?" He switched to her rank, addressing her formally as she addressed him.

"Politics, sir."

"Ah, politics—I hate politics. Tara…" He switched to her first name again. "I don't explain myself on a regular basis to a subordinate but I will tonight because the situation's unusual." He stopped to gather his thoughts. Tired of telling his story, he wondered if the questions would ever end. Cops were the worst gossips. He wasn't going to give Officer Jones the full story. Rank did have some privileges.

"Tara, I had—note the past tense—a brief personal relationship with Chloe Wagner, which could cloud the issues in this case. Since the relationship has ended, she's been harassing me. In recent weeks, she started to stalk me. I filed a formal complaint against her this week. If you'd like to check, I'll give you the file number. I'm sorry if you're uncomfortable working with me. I heard you were professional, discreet, and looking for a place in homicide. I'll return you to the station, no hard feelings," Jake said, annoyed.

"I'm sorry, Lieutenant. As I said, it's not my place to question you. The way the suspect spoke to you seemed odd. It's also unusual to release a murder suspect."

"It's an unusual case. Several things didn't add up from the beginning. Today we recovered an emerald the victim always wore. Tonight, for the first time, her sexual orientation came to light. Whoever planted the ring in the room made the first actual mistake in the case. Also, after reviewing all the previous interviews, Sergeant Romanelli and I discovered discrepancies in her best friend's statements."

"They didn't show up in the beginning?" Tara asked.

"No, sometimes, you can bang your head against a wall, then one day Lady Luck comes into play and the case takes on momentum. It seems to have happened with this one. We had scheduled interviews for tomorrow with Shanna's best friend and the man she dated prior to her death. Every case has to be treated uniquely. They don't always go by the book. The book's there as a guideline, not as an absolute—one needs to use common sense. The officer who survives is the one who sticks to the book, and yet can be flexible enough to get results. Do you understand?" Jake turned his head to look directly at her.

"I've been on the job now for three years. I know it doesn't always go by the book. You have to admit, it's one for the records."

"Yep, I'll admit it."

"So, why are we watching her?" Tara asked.

"To see if she goes anywhere tonight. If she did kill her sister, she didn't do it alone."

"Why do you say 'if'?"

"Because with this new evidence, it doesn't make sense she killed her. Overkill's the word to best describe this crime. Each bruise, each assault on her body, showed the killer's anger with the victim. He or she beat her to a pulp. Love and hate aren't that far apart for some. With no current or serious lovers in the picture, we went in the wrong direction. It's part of the reason we couldn't figure it out. She had no serious relationships, or so we were told. Now we find there were two. Tomorrow or Monday, we'll verify what Chloe told us tonight. Search for the other women she dated at school. Of course, we still can't rule out her sister. The ring's worth over fifty thousand dollars—a real motive for murder."

"Fifty thousand dollars? For a ring?" Tara's brown eyes opened wide in shock.

"Yes. I've learned emeralds are worth more than diamonds. This ring has both, increasing its value."

"I'd love to see a picture of a fifty-thousand-dollar ring," Tara said.

Jake reached into the back seat and pulled his briefcase up front. He skimmed through it until he found the folder he was looking for—he took the picture of the ring out and handed it to her.

"My God, the emerald's huge. It's beautiful." Tara let out a low whistle.

"Yes, it is. It's insured for its full value, but you still don't want to lose an heirloom."

"I wouldn't want to lose it, no matter what the circumstances."

They called it a night at ten-thirty. Chloe never left the house. The light in her room went out at ten-fifteen. They circled the block a couple of times to make sure she wasn't on her way out. He dropped Officer Jones at the station at ten forty-five.

"Thank you, Lieutenant."

"Good night, Tara. It's been nice working with you."

"Same here, sir," she said, getting out of the car.

Chapter 20

Jake pulled up outside Louie's house, an old Victorian, at eight forty-five. Louie barely got his ass in the seat before the door closed and Jake took off.

"We need to pick up Houston before noon. I promised the vet. We have to do it before the interviews."

Jake agreed and drove to the vet's office. Two cars were in the parking lot. Jake hoped they belonged to the staff. He had to get to the office and had no time to wait around. Jake pulled his collar up to block the wind as soon as he climbed out. Once inside, Louie walked right to the desk. The receptionist led him to the back of the place. Restless, Jake paced the waiting room until a dog with sad, chocolate-brown eyes came out of the back. When the puppy saw Jake, she cowered in the corner and started shaking, peeing on the rug. Jake approached it, holding out his hand. The dog sniffed it and drew up into itself further.

Poor thing. He stroked its back and neck until the dog started to relax a bit.

"Sad, isn't it," Doctor Glass said from behind him. "Some idiot abused the poor thing. She shies away from men. But she seems to be taking to you."

Rubbing the dog's back, he got lost in her brown eyes. "I find people are crueler than animals, Doc."

"People, animals—cruel is cruel—I guess we both see it in our professions. Louie's still in the back with Houston. He'll be right out."

"Thanks. Are you giving the dog back to the abuser?"

"Not in a million years. After I finish treating her, she'll have to go to the shelter. I hope and pray someone will adopt her before they have to put her to sleep. She's a good, gentle animal—she's a beagle mix with a little Dalmatian in her." He eyed Jake. "Do you want a dog?"

"I'd love one, but I work long hours. It wouldn't be fair to her."

Doctor Glass walked to the treatment area, leaving him with the dog, who now rested her head on his knees as she looked up at him begging him for a home.

"I wish, but you'd be alone all day. What kind of life would that be for you?" The Gaelic girl's name Brigh popped into his head. It stood for strength, power, and force, things she'd need in order to survive. His heart opened a little wider.

God! I'm already naming her.

No, he couldn't take her. It would be an injustice to her. Taking her face in both hands, he looked into her eyes. "I'm sorry."

He hadn't had a dog since his and Eva's had died. Their dog, Roger, died less than six months after Eva. God, he swore the dog had died of a broken heart. Jake pushed up as Houston came bouncing out before Louie and jumped up on him. The dog in the corner backed away and tried to make herself smaller. Jake grabbed Houston's collar with his left hand as Brigh inched over to reclaim him.

"A new addition to your house?"

"No, Louie." *She is beautiful, though.* "Let's go. We have a lot to do."

But Brigh was on his mind for the rest of the day.

* * * *

Saturday night while dressing for dinner, Jake looked back over his day. In today's mail, he received his notification letter from the parole board. Spaulding would come before them on October fifth. There was no mention of the DNA test he had requested. *I guess the family's not privy to such information. Blindside them when they come to testify. What rights do they have?*

Thank goodness Shamus let him know Monday would be the collection of the specimen. He hadn't slept a full night since Shamus had told him about Spaulding's request. Every time that bastard came up for parole it affected every part of his life.

The interviews with Meryl Drake and Mark Cavilla had given him few answers and more questions. He would listen to them again tomorrow, or maybe Monday.

According to the detectives who followed Chloe around all day, the only time she went out was to the grocery store with her mother. For the remainder of the day she stayed at home.

The detectives on shift also reported in. She was still home at seven. Jake figured if she went out, it would be around nine or ten o'clock, what he considered the normal time for a Saturday night adventure. He told the detectives to call his cell phone and leave their updates in a message, because he wanted no interruptions this evening. By ten tonight, he hoped to be immersed in dinner and dessert.

The letter sat atop his dresser as he got ready for dinner. Jake tried to shake his morose thoughts from his head. Tonight, nothing was going to distract him from Mia. Or at least he hoped not.

At seven-thirty, he headed out to Mia's condo. Hitting no traffic, he arrived at eight. A whole week had gone by, with a heavy caseload, mounds of paperwork, and new leads. Every spare minute he could find he'd spent it with her for a quick lunch, dinner, or a fast phone call. They talked about everything, and never hit a low in the conversation. He was glad her concerns were behind them and wouldn't present any issues to interfere in the actives he had planned.

Woodbury, a small, quaint New England town located fifteen miles outside of Wilkesbury didn't fit in with the cosmopolitan woman in his head. Why Mia had settled here was food for thought. She owned a condo/townhouse in one of Woodbury's exclusive areas. As he raised his hand to ring the bell, the front door opened. His cop's eyes missed nothing as he absorbed his surroundings. He stepped into a generous foyer done in shades of gray. A huge vase filled with various types of colorful flowers in the far corner sat on the gray slate floor.

To his right, the living room caught his eye. Furniture done in bold reds and whites accented a big bow window dressed in red drapes and long, white flowing sheers, and lots of red throw pillows strewn about on the white leather furniture. Green leafy plants scattered throughout the room. The hardwood floor, polished to a high gloss, poked out from under the oriental area rug, which was white and red, with specks of yellow and black. A tidbit of information slipped into his thoughts from his last case. The psychiatrist told him red stood for blood, fire, and emotions. Didn't psychologists shy away from it?

The room was beautiful, but it was the woman who drew and held his attention. Mia wore a black, sleeveless, body-hugging dress, which emphasized each and every curve. The wide v-bodice further heated his blood. His eyes took it all in, from the skinny belt accenting her waist to the sexy, black strappy high heels adding to her height. *I'm a goner.* He leaned in for kiss.

In her response, he felt the promise.

She pulled away and said, "Hello."

"You look amazing."

"Thanks, come into the living room." Jake followed her into the room.

"What smells so good, besides you?" He rubbed his hands down her arms and took her hands in his, not wanting to break contact.

"I went simple with steak and potatoes, and a side salad. You must smell the appetizers. It's a pastry stuffed with spinach and cheese."

"It sounds great. Do you want me to grill the steaks?"

"No, I've got it. What would you like to drink?"

Their voices stretched as tight as strings on a violin as they performed the mating dance. They both knew where tonight would lead, dinner, a prelude to the ultimate event. Food would not quench the hunger each experienced.

"I'll have what you're drinking." He didn't sit down.

"White wine?"

"Yes. Is there anything I can help you with?"

"No. I have it under control. Instead of the living room why don't you come in the kitchen and keep me company while I put the finishing touches on the table?"

He followed her down the hall. One wall was covered in photographs both in color and black and white, offering a glimpse into her life. His training kicked in as he took in everything he saw, including the teasing sway of her ass with each step. In the huge kitchen/dining area, three large windows faced the woods in back, giving him a full view of the deck and yard. Mia walked to the center island and began chopping lettuce for a salad.

Jake continued to scan the room for exits before banking the contents in his head. The oval mahogany dining table could seat at least twelve people, but was set for two. An easy elegance that was Mia was reflected in the bone china and crystal, along with fresh flowers and the low lighting that set the mood.

Mia set the tray of appetizers on the island, then poured the wine and handed him a glass. Jake clinked his glass to hers, took a sip, and never took his eyes off her.

"You shouldn't have gone to all this trouble," Jake said, eyeing the fancy table.

"It wasn't any trouble. I like to entertain and don't do it enough. And it's a special night." With a seductive smile over the rim of the wine goblet, she brought the glass to her lips and took a sip.

He set his glass down and went to her. He wrapped his arms around her waist from behind. She shivered in his arms.

"What makes it so special?" he whispered, nibbling on her neck.

She leaned into him and moaned. "Your first time here, and..." She blushed, all of a sudden shy.

"And..."

Disengaging his arms from her waist, she walked to the fridge "Here, I changed my mind. Why don't you cook the steaks? It'll keep your hands busy." She smiled.

"I liked where my hands were," he answered.

"Mmm."

"Mmm, that's it?"

"Yep."

"Mia, you have to give me a little more encouragement." He shot her a grin.

"If I gave you any more encouragement, we'd be on the floor right here, right now, having sex like dogs." She fluttered her lashes.

"It works for me," he said.

"Well, it doesn't work for me, Jake. So go out and cook."

"Boy, you're tough." He took the steaks outside, fiddled with the grill until it lit, and then placed the steaks in the center of it.

She had timed everything to the minute. Mia put the salad on the table when he walked back in with the steaks. She grabbed the bread off the counter and set it on the table between them before she sat down next to him.

Jake broke off a piece of bread, buttered it, and handed it to her. Though the food was good, he had a taste for other things tonight and couldn't wait to sample them. Her arctic-blue eyes drew him in until he was lost. With her it was easy to speak about his caseload. He told her as much as he could without stepping over the line.

Mia spoke in depth about her book, piquing his interest. He asked to read it, but she told him no, not until it was finished. She spoke about an article she'd written and sold to *Cosmo* magazine. The excitement in her voice pleased him.

Again, it bothered him how she skimmed over her family. It left him curious but he figured in time she'd talk about them.

Through the meal, they ate, talked and laughed but most of all, they flirted. The sexual tension in the room grew to the bursting point.

"You've enchanted me. I've got nothing on my mind but you." He rubbed his hand over hers.

"You don't know how much I've looked forward to tonight, to having you all to myself for the entire evening..."

Jake stood, his plate in his hand.

"No, don't, Jake. I got it."

"No, I'll help, it'll go faster."

"Why, are you in a hurry for dessert?" Mia looked at him from under her long black eyelashes.

He pulled her up from the chair and cradled her in his arms. "Oh yeah, if you mean dessert is being served upstairs."

"You're so transparent. Put me down or the kitchen will never get cleaned."

He put her down. "As I said, let's work fast."

"Do you want some coffee with your dessert?" She grinned.

"You're serious. You're serving dessert?"

"I am, unless you have a better offer." With a coy twist of a strand of hair, she batted her eye lashes at him.

He chuckled as she had intended. "Oh, you bet. Do you have any whipped cream?" He picked her up, threw her over his shoulder fireman style, as he raced up the stairs. Mia giggled. "No."

"It's a pity. What I can do with whipped cream would make you crazy." He laughed, hoping he could slow down, because he was as hard as the dining room table.

"I'll hold you to it for the next time."

At the top of the stairs, he asked, "Which way?"

"To your right and down at the end of the hall." Mia pointed.

His trained eyes took in everything and nothing as his blood pounded through his veins. *I need to make love to this woman*, was his only thought. He wanted his hands and mouth on her. In this moment, nothing else existed for him but her.

With care, he laid her upon the bed, caressing her body with his eyes as he sank in next to her. The black dress exposed her toned arms and full breasts. Good God, those legs drove him crazy strapped into those sexy shoes. He hoped he could exercise some control, because he felt sixteen again, and he needed to remind himself to slow down and breathe.

He ran his finger over her throat, tracing a path to her cleavage, circling around the bare skin. Mia shuddered under his touch as he continued to run his fingers down the length of her. Rolling on top of her, he followed the path of his fingers with kisses. He laid his head on her breast and listened to her heart gallop as it almost pushed him over the edge. The dress needed to go. He grabbed the hem and inched it up over her thighs. The garter belt would be his undoing if he didn't get a grip on the emotions swirling around inside him. Slipping the dress over her head, he locked eyes with her. Now, all she wore was the garter belt, stockings, and heels.

Mia was the fantasy he didn't even realize he had.

Not wanting to rush his exploration of her body, he'd bring her to the edge, then back off before he sent her there again. Rolling to his side, he ran his hands and eyes over her. Her body invited him to experience more. The time she spent in the gym showed in every muscle and curve of her body. He traced circles over her biceps, down to her hands, over to her flat stomach as he explored each indent and flare of her body. On overload, he was ready to take her. Reaching for her, she dodged him and pushed him onto his back.

* * * *

Her lips parted as she watched him through half-closed eyes as she gripped the sheets in her fists, panting, arching into him. Each sensation more tantalizing than the last as his gentle touch floated over her. If he didn't take her soon she'd go mad. When she thought she couldn't take more, he sent her flying higher. In a fog, she heard a husky voice begging him to finish it. Realizing it was her own, she increased the motion of her hips, shuddering with need—hoping he'd join with her and shoot her up and over to heaven.

Then it was her turn to discover. Undressing him, she glided her hands over his exposed flesh, teasing to the point of no return. His taut body excited her as he reacted to her touch. At the silky, hard muscle pointing straight up, she stopped, admired and caressed as it vibrated in her hand. His body felt warm. Oh yes, a well-disciplined body. She loved his reddish-brown hair, which surprised her—she always went for blondes. When they were together, she got lost in his green, green eyes. When they weren't together, she dreamed of them. His intelligent eyes always looked at her as though they could devour her. As if no one else existed or mattered but her. No one had ever looked at her with such passion and need. His focus was all-encompassing and she loved it. She trailed kisses down his body. When she took him in her mouth she felt the power as he begged her to finish him off.

She was ready when he reached down and lifted her on top of him and glided into her with a slow, steady rhythm, her need building with each stroke. She thrusted her hips to match his as their rhythm synced, until at last, together they jumped over the edge—the orgasm shredding them both. The act of love was completed with their eyes and bodies locked on each other.

She stretched out on top of him, spent but wanting more.

She felt the wild beat of his heart against hers. Looking down into his eyes, she moaned and in a husky voice said, "Wow."

"I don't have words for it."

"I'm looking forward to the next time." Mia rolled onto her back and pulled Jake on top of her as she laughed. "So, are you ready?"

"You bet."

"You're a man of few words." She cocked her head.

"Let me show you how a man of action speaks." Jake wiggled his brows.

Jake woke at six o'clock on Sunday morning, thrilled to find Mia spooned into him. He pressed his body closer to hers as he nibbled his way down her neck.

She stirred, turning toward him. "Good morning."

"Morning, I didn't wake you, did I?"

"No."

When he kissed her on the mouth, she pushed him away. "I have to brush my teeth."

He grabbed her, kissed her again. "Don't go."

* * * *

Sunday they stayed in, made love, and then made love again. Content in each other's company, they kept the world at bay.

Having no choice, he checked his voicemail throughout the weekend. Chloe didn't go out on Saturday night. Meryl Drake and Mark Cavilla did. Meryl had gone to a friend's house in New Britain and stayed until eleven. Mark drove over to a country and western bar in Southington and hung out until one-thirty. Both went home alone. On Friday, Jake had subpoenaed Chloe's phone records. The subpoena covered both home and cell, something he'd follow up with on Monday. He'd also request one for Drake and Cavilla's phones.

He looked across the bed at Mia, who had her nose buried in the Sunday Funnies. He leaned in and rubbed his hand on her thigh while nibbling on her neck.

She put down the paper and looked at him over her reading glasses. "You can't possibly be ready again?"

"Is that a challenge?"

Chapter 21

At seven-thirty on Monday morning, Jake walked into the bullpen. He bypassed Louie's desk and his attention-grabbing rendition of "That's Amore" and continued on to his office. As he took off his jacket and turned on his computer, Louie stepped in.

"Did Sophia throw you out this morning?"

"And good morning to you too, Lieutenant. Did you have a nice weekend? Oh, and yes, thanks for asking, mine was wonderful. Sophia and I celebrated all weekend long," Louie said, with a wide grin.

"The celebration went well? Mine did too." Jake wiggled his brow.

"Yep. How was your dinner?"

"Terrific," Jake said as he turned toward the coffee machine.

"So what time did you get home?" Louie pushed.

"It's none of your business."

Louie changed the subject. "Hey, have you made a decision on the dog? I know Doc Glass is shipping her to the shelter later this week."

"I haven't thought about it. It's been a busy weekend." That wasn't totally true. He kept trying to talk himself out of the idea, but the more he remembered those sad brown eyes, the more he wanted to claim Brigh. Maybe Brigh would heal him as he healed her. "Oh, I received my notice from the parole board. Spaulding's hearing is next fall. His DNA results might not be back by then. We'll see. This year I'm going in with more crime scene photos and evidence to keep Spaulding behind bars for the rest of his natural life."

"I'll help," Louie said.

"Let's review all the interviews from both Friday and Saturday. What do you have planned for today?"

"Well, I set up an interview with Katy Bonita for noon."

"Great, on the way there we'll stop at my house so I can change. It's on the way."

"Change? What's wrong with what you have on?"

Jake watched his comment hit, counted to three. He sipped his coffee to hide his smile.

"You spent the night?"

"That's incorrect. I spent the last two nights at Mia's"

"I'll be damned. I like her, Jake, so does Sophia," Louie said.

"I do too. Let's get to work."

"It must be spring, lots of *amore* in the air." Louie started singing again.

"Please, for the love of God, stop singing. And Louie, my romance is not for office gossip. Got it?"

"You're no fun. I was gonna run the pool on how long it would last. Killjoy."

"Work, Louie."

"You're absolutely no fun." They'd been friends too long for him to flinch as others did when Jake looked at them that way. "I already listened to the recordings. I figured you'd want to, so I set them up on your machine. Meryl, she's an odd duck. You know?"

"She is. What about Cavilla's statement?"

"We took him by surprise when we told him she liked girls. Hey, maybe we should arrest Meryl too! Have her sit in a cell for a while so she gets it's not a game. It certainly worked on Chloe."

"I deserved that. Let me listen to them alone first. Later we'll go do the interviews on the Adams case. When we get back, we'll listen to them together and dissect their statements."

"Sounds like a plan," Louie said, turning to leave Jake's office.

"One more thing, Louie, I want to take you and Sophia out to dinner, to celebrate your promotion. Is Friday or Saturday good for you?"

"Thanks, but you don't have to."

"I want to. It's a big accomplishment. I'm proud of you."

"Alright, I'll check with Sophia."

At nine o'clock Jake stepped out of his office and into the bullpen. He waited until he had everyone's attention.

"It's my honor to announce Louie Romanelli is one of thirty detectives being promoted to sergeant. The ceremony's this Friday at noon at city hall."

Everyone clapped as they walked up to Louie and slapped him on the back. Louie ate it up. Jake stood back and watched. No one deserved the promotion more than Louie.

"Hey, where's the celebration going to be?" Burke asked. "Have you picked out a bar yet, Lieutenant?"

"No, Al. Louie wants to pass this soon after my celebration. Sophia would kill him if he came home soused again."

"Hey, that's not fair, Louie. We're all proud of you. You can't take this celebration away from us. I'll talk to Sophia," Al said.

"Well, good luck with that." Louie smirked.

* * * *

To give Jake time to change, they left the station at eleven-twenty. The ride from Jake's house to Katy Bonita's would take about fifteen minutes, even with traffic.

"So, let me get this straight. You arrived for dinner Saturday night and what, never left until this morning?" Louie asked when Jake got in the car.

"Yep."

"Remind me not to invite you to dinner," Louie said.

Jake flashed him a wide grin.

"That's it, no details? What's going on?"

"I'm not giving you details. What are you, a pervert? Or are you looking for instructions on how to perform?"

"Very funny, I'm busting a damn rib over here. I want to know how you feel about her. Is it a long-term thing or are you two ships passing in the night? You know Sophia's going to asked me for deets."

"Gee, Louie, want to set each other's hair too?"

"I'm not kidding, Jake."

"I can't answer your question. Yeah, I like her. She's beautiful, smart, funny, and I love being with her. About the rest, we'll see. I don't know much about her. But I'm sure it's going be fun finding out."

"I'm sure." Louie smiled to himself. He waited in the car while Jake changed and figured he had enough time to call Sophia before Jake came back out. Louie relished gossip. Sophia picked Saturday night for dinner. He hung up with her as Jake climbed back in the car.

"Sophia said Saturday night's good."

"Okay, I'll tell Mia."

* * * *

Jake got off Route 8 at exit 34, which put them onto Watertown Avenue. Louie constantly brought up the dog, though Jake hadn't told Louie he'd already named her or even wanted her. He was still unsure, especially now with a new relationship developing. Right after they passed Municipal Stadium, Louie spotted Bonita's address and pointed it out to him. Katy's building stood on the town line between Wilkesbury and Watertown in a two-family house. Before they jumped out of the car, Jake's cell phone rang. Not recognizing the number, he hit talk.

"Jake, it's me."

His mother? *Oh no, what's happened*? "Are you okay?"

"I got a letter this morning about Spaulding. Are they allowing that pig to go free?" Maddie Carrington's voice shook, almost squealed as she spoke.

"No, Mom, it's only a hearing. I'm going to attend like I do every time he comes up for one. Please try to relax. I promise I'll take care of it." He hoped it was a promise he could keep.

"If they let him out, you have to kill him, Jake," Maddie said in her shrilled voice.

"Mom, no one's going to kill anyone. I promise I'm on top of it. I'll see you this week." Jake hung up after he was sure she had calmed down.

"She got her letter, huh?" Louie asked.

"I thought I took her off the list. She'll be nuts until this is settled." Jake opened his door and climbed out of the car. He needed to focus his attention back on the case at hand. The mailbox out front directed them to the second floor. Long narrow steps led up to her apartment. Louie went first, Jake followed behind him as they ascended the staircase. Louie knocked on the door while Jake scanned the area.

Katy Bonita answered the door right away, eyeing them through a slit in the door, held closed by a security chain.

"Katy Bonita?" Louie asked.

"Yes?"

"I'm Sergeant Romanelli. I spoke to you on the phone this morning." He held up his shield.

"Hi, Sergeant, come in." Closing the door on them, she released the chain then opened it wider to let them in.

As they walked in, Louie introduced Jake. "This is Lieutenant Carrington, my partner."

"Ms. Bonita." Jake shook her hand.

"It's Katy. What can I do for you?"

In the tiny morsel of a kitchen, Jake bumped into Katy as she pulled out a chair at the round table. She sat down then pointed to the other chairs. From his research, he knew the house was built in the nineteen forties, and the kitchen looked like the original. Butting up against the door on a small counter area sat the dishrack, next to it an old-fashioned, deep, sparklingly white porcelain sink. There was more counter space to the right, with cabinets over the whole area. The refrigerator stood on the other side of the door, a narrow counter separating the stove from the refrigerator, barely leaving enough room for the table and chairs. The floor, covered in worn, dull gold and beige swirled linoleum, reminded Jake of his grandmother's house back in Ireland.

Louie took the lead. "Ms. Bonita, you're a friend of Lola Adams?"

"Yes."

"Did you see Lola recently?"

"Yes. Back in April she surprised me and showed up unannounced. I was a little annoyed but I let her spend the night."

"Lola never called to say she'd be in town?" Louie asked.

"No."

"Did she give you a reason for being in Connecticut when she showed up?" Louie asked.

"Not exactly, though she did say things were starting to go her way."

Louie asked again. "She never told you exactly why she came to Connecticut?"

"No. I fished around to see if she showed up to reclaim Nick. She said no."

"Did she know the two of you were dating? Did you tell him you had a house guest?" Louie asked.

"No to both of your questions. I didn't tell him until after she left on Sunday."

"Why?" Jake asked.

Embarrassed, she said, "Well, she left early on Sunday because she had to catch a flight out of New York. At the time, Nick and I were dating. She would've gone out of her way to cause trouble for the both of us if she'd known. Lola's a selfish person."

"Did you know the first Mrs. Adams had been murdered on the sixteenth?" Louie asked.

"No, I didn't know about the murder until a week ago. I didn't realize it happened the weekend Lola was here until you mentioned it. Are you telling me you suspect Lola?" The woman was visibly shaken.

"She's a person of interest right now. Anyone who knew the victim is," Louie said.

"You have to tell me," she said, her voice shaking. "If she shows up again, do I let her stay here?"

"I don't know what to tell you, Katy. You have to use your own judgment," Louie said.

A clearer picture of Lola Adams began to emerge in Jake's head. A woman who trusted no one, cared only for herself, and who never formed a strong bond with anyone, including her supposed best friend.

Jake jumped in and asked, "Katy, in your opinion, is Lola capable of murder?"

He watched her process the question in silence. After a few moments, Katy whispered, "Yes."

"Well, then you have your answer about whether to let her stay here," Jake said.

"Is there anything else you can tell us about Lola?" Louie asked.

"She didn't act weird or anything when she visited," Katy offered.

"Here's my card. Call me if something else pops into your head. Or if Lola shows up again." Louie handed her his card as he stood.

Outside in the car, Jake said, "Interesting."

"Yep."

* * * *

When they got back to the station, Louie requested a subpoena for the Delta Airline records from April sixteenth through April eighteenth. Jake debated. Should he have Katrina book flights to Florida or wait?

He called the forensics department to get an update. A snippy secretary told him if the lab reports were completed, they would've already been in his email. The DNA results were holding up the investigation. Skin cells, sweat, or saliva from Chelsea Adams's attacker might lead them sooner to the killer but Jake had no choice but to wait until the lab finished up.

After his call to forensics, Jake decided to wait on the flight. The forensics guys told him he should have everything by the end of the next week. He needed to keep his patience in check.

His voicemail showed he'd received three calls from Cara Adams looking for results on her mother's case. He also noted one from Detective Burke. Burke and Kraus were out following up on a lead on the Xavier Orlando case. Burke gave him the list of officers who replaced him and Kraus on the protection detail in case he wanted to make any changes. For now, he was happy with Burke's choices. Al also noted that this past weekend had gone smoothly. Jake couldn't wait until they passed Darcy and her family over to the FBI. That should happen sometime this week.

Once they were in the witness protection program they'd be safe. In the meantime, Jake needed to make sure everyone kept their guard up. When it came to revenge, Spike was known for his patience.

He also received a call from Kirk Brown, updating him on his cases. A car fitting the description for the hit-and-run showed up in a body shop on Meriden Road. Kirk and Lanoue were checking it out. They'd send an email to update him if they didn't see him later at the station. The hit-and-run victim died yesterday from his injuries. It upgraded the case to a vehicular homicide. He also informed Jake that they were at a dead end on the school shooting. Brown thought if he interviewed the kids at the station with their parents present, they might get more out of them. Brown wanted to know if Jake would be onboard with the idea and available when they set it up.

Realizing he hadn't given Mia a call as promised, he grabbed his cell phone and dialed her number.

"This is the first chance I got today. How are you?" Jake asked in way of a greeting.

"There's nothing like a weekend of great sex and food to energize a woman," Mia said.

"A man also. I asked Louie and Sophia out to dinner Saturday night, to celebrate Louie's promotion. Is Saturday good for you?" He realized he'd made the plans without checking with her first.

"I have to be out of town starting Wednesday. I don't know if I'll be back in time," Mia said.

"Oh." He heard the disappointment in his own voice.

"I'm sorry, it's business."

"Well, we'll do it another time with them. Do you want to come over for dinner?"

"Not tonight. I didn't go into work or even get dressed today. My book needs some polishing before I present it to who I hope will be my new agent. It's the reason I'm going out of town on Wednesday."

"Excellent, when did you finish it?"

"I didn't, but I'm working on it. It should be completed by Tuesday. I sent him the first fifty pages. He wants to meet and review the rest of it. I'd ask you to join me if I thought there was a chance you'd come. You don't want to go, do you?"

"I wish I could. You know I'll be with you in spirit, sending my good wishes to you. I won't see you until you get back?"

"Do you want to come over tomorrow night for dinner? We can hang out here."

"What kind of wine should I bring?"

"I have everything we need here."

"And Mia... I enjoyed the weekend," he said.

As he hung up, Louie knocked on his door and walked right in without waiting for an answer. "Ready to review those interviews now?" Louie asked.

"Yeah, come in. Mia might not be at dinner Saturday."

"What did you do? You guys are done already...?"

Louie's comical expression lifted his mood. "Calm down, Louie. I found out she's leaving for a business trip on Wednesday. She doesn't know how long she'll be away. I still want to go out with you and Sophia. We'll do the couples thing the following weekend."

Louie looked relieved. "Okay. Let's get to work."

Chapter 22

Louie rewound the tapes and hit the play button. He and Jake listened to the tones and inflections of the voices, taking notes. Next, they viewed the video again, this time watching for nervous tics and following the eye movements as they looked for signs of deceit.

"Meryl is one cocky woman, isn't she?" Louie asked.

Jake hit pause. "Why?"

"Listen to her. Her tone's flirty—then hard—then soft—like she's playing us. It's all a freaking game with her. There's a change again when she realizes she could be in trouble. It took a while but now she knows we're serious," Louie finished.

"Yeah, I got the same thing. Next up is the part where we confronted her about dating Shanna. Okay, turn it back on."

Louie rewound the tape back to the last sentence then hit play. As they listened to the rest of it, it became clear Meryl was one angry woman, but clever. The interview took over two hours, ending with Meryl requesting a lawyer.

Jake remembered assessing Meryl a few months ago. At five-three, Meryl's long black hair matched her empty black eyes. Meryl had a sturdy, athletic body wrapped around a tumultuous attitude. She was always on the verge of exploding—the complete opposite of Shanna. He'd have never put them together. Was Meryl strong enough to carry Shanna? He thought about it. Yes, she could've carried her the short distance to the woods. Jake read Meryl Drake her rights. "Do you understand these rights as I've read them to you?"

"Yes. Why am I here? I know you arrested Chloe yesterday. And let me say, it's about time," Meryl said.

"How do you know we arrested Chloe yesterday, Meryl?" Jake asked.

"Her parents told me." She shrugged.

"When did they tell you?"

"It was last night, when I stopped in for a visit."

"No, they didn't, Meryl. Chloe's parents didn't know she'd been arrested until well after you left," Jake said, pinning her with a look.

"What can I tell you? They're the ones who told me," she insisted.

"What else did they tell you? What time were you over there visiting?" Jake asked

"I got there around six o'clock. I left around eight. What do you mean, 'what else did they tell me'?"

"Did they tell you anything else?" he asked again, watching her process his question. He didn't want to lead her on, so he didn't mention the ring. He waited for her reply as silence filled the room. Over the years he had found silence often unnerved a suspect and she didn't disappoint.

"No, they didn't," Meryl said.

"When they told you about Chloe's arrest, they didn't tell you what generated the arrest?"

"You mean evidence?" she asked.

"Yes, or a statement, something like that," Jake said nonchalantly.

"I can't remember. I'll give it some thought," Meryl baited him, treating the interview as if it was a joke. Well the laugh was on her. It was obvious she couldn't wait to see Chloe locked up for good.

"Okay, what did you mean when you said, 'it's about time' we arrested Chloe?" Louie asked.

She looked over at Louie, who stood by the door. "We both know she wanted Shanna's ring. Chloe knew her grandmother gave the higher value piece of jewelry to Shanna. Chloe's a jealous woman. My God, it's not only beautiful, it's worth a fortune."

"How do you know the value, Meryl?" Jake asked.

"Shanna told me, and after Shanna died, Chloe mentioned it. Chloe asked me if Shanna wore the ring the last time I saw her."

"When did she ask you that, Meryl? Give me dates."

"Oh, I saw Shanna the night she disappeared. We hung out."

In Meryl's expression, he could see her mentally going back in time. Her black empty eyes filled with tears. False tears? Who knew? Either way they didn't affect him. As they fell, Drake continued to wear the smile she had plastered on since she'd walked in the door.

Meryl gave him his lead-in to the next line of questioning. Jake opened the file in front of him. Louie took the seat beside him.

Jake asked, "Meryl, I have your original statements to both the Sergeant and me here, along with your statement to Detectives Kraus and Brown. Detective Kraus asked you two days after Shanna went missing if you saw her the day she disappeared or anytime within the week. You answered, 'Yes, we hung out on Friday night and went for pizza and beer with some of her friends from the dorm.'" Jake handed her a copy of her statement.

She read it and agreed. "Yes, I remember giving a statement. I don't remember what I said. Should I?" She frowned.

Ignoring her question, Jake continued. "Here's a copy of your statement four days later to us. I'll read it to you." He handed her a copy of her previous statement. "Is this your statement to us after we found Shanna?"

"Yes. I remember speaking with you. Again, I don't remember what I said. Why are my statements so important, especially now if you have Chloe in custody?"

Jake ignored her. "In your statement to us, you said you didn't see Shanna the week of exams. Your statements, each within days of each other, are contradictory. Which one's correct? When someone lies to us we have to ask ourselves why, right, Sergeant?"

"You got that right. Meryl, the lieutenant asked, why did you lie? Which one is correct?" Louie's cold, hard stare could scare a gorilla into turning over his bananas.

Meryl sat in silence for a few minutes before answering. "I told you, I don't remember what I said."

"Look at the copies I gave you and read each one out loud," Jake demanded.

Meryl picked up the copies but didn't look at them. "I'd never help Chloe kill her sister. You're nuts. I wouldn't do anything to help Chloe or hurt Shanna."

"I don't remember saying anything of the kind, Meryl. Please read both statements. When you're done, we'll reread your statement from today."

Meryl went silent again and then after a few minutes began to read the statements aloud.

Kraus: Did you see Shanna the week she disappeared?

Drake: I saw her on Friday night.

He stopped her there. "Now please read the second set of sheets I gave you."

Meryl put the sheets aside and grabbed the other stack. She looked it over first, before she read aloud from it:

Carrington: Thanks for coming in, Meryl.

Drake: Anything I can do to help. It doesn't seem real that she's dead. Heavy crying noted here.

Carrington: I'm sorry for your loss, Meryl. When did you see her last?

Drake: The week before exams, I'm sure. The following week we both stayed at our own dorms to study.

Carrington: You didn't see her at all last week?

Drake: No.

Before she went any further he interrupted her. "Meryl, which one of these statements is correct?"

Meryl thought for a few moments. Shrugging her shoulders, she said, "The first one I gave the detectives, Kraus and Brown, and the one I gave you today."

"Why did you lie when we interviewed you a few months ago?"

"I didn't lie. My emotions were all over the place. You had found Shanna the day I spoke to you. I always thought she'd be found alive. I thought she needed her space. I was confused, definitely upset and grieving. I'm still in shock over her murder. I didn't lie on purpose, I must've forgotten."

Louie jumped in, changing tactics. "Were you and Shanna lovers?"

Ah, a question that wiped the damn smile off her face, Louie thought. The one she'd worn since she entered the room, even when she cried.

"What do you mean?"

"I thought the question was self-explanatory, Meryl, but I'll repeat it. Were you and Shanna Wagner lovers?" Louie pressed, leaning across the table, inches from her face so she focused on him.

Meryl whispered, "Yes."

"Did you and Shanna quarrel on the Friday night she disappeared?" Louie asked.

"Yes," she whispered again.

"Meryl, please speak up. I can't hear you," Jake said.

"I said, yes. Yes, we were lovers. I loved her," she shouted.

"Did you kill her?" Louie asked.

"No."

"What were you doing at her parents' house last night?" Jake jumped in, switching it up again.

"I went to visit them. I miss them."

"Why did you want to get into Shanna's room last week? What did you put in there?" Jake continued his line of questioning.

She gave Jake a calculated look. "I had a headache. I asked if I could lie down. Why would I put something in there?"

"You surprised the Wagners with your request. It shook them. When Mrs. Wagner asked why it was only then that you said you had a headache. Correct?" Jake asked.

"No. No, I had a crushing headache."

"Meryl, that doesn't answer my question. Mr. Wagner said he told you he thought your request to go into Shanna's room was odd. It was after he said that is when you mentioned your headache, not before. Now, I'll ask again." Jake's voice hardened as he pounded the point home. "What were you doing in Shanna Wagner's room last week?"

"I want a lawyer," Meryl said.

"Meryl, once you lawyer up there'll be no deals on the table. We're breaking the interview, subject has requested a lawyer. Time is twelve-ten PM on May ninth." Jake stood, gathered his file, and reached out to take the statements back from Meryl.

"No, wait. What do you mean deal? A deal for what?" she asked.

"Sorry, Meryl, you requested a lawyer. This interview has ended." Jake continued packing up his files.

"No, wait, I don't want a lawyer. What deal?"

"You're requesting we continue this interview without your lawyer, Meryl?" He raised an eyebrow.

"Yes. Yes. What deal?" she asked, clearly aggravated.

"Okay, Meryl Drake has requested this interview continue without her lawyer," Jake read into the record.

"What deal?" Meryl repeated.

"If you know anything about Shanna's death, this would be the time to tell us. Give us the details, like it happened while you were fighting, not preplanned or premeditated. Meryl, lovers quarrel all the time, sometimes an argument gets out of control and you can't take it back."

"What deal?"

"We'll talk to the D.A., see if he can offer manslaughter in the first degree, instead of murder in the first," Jake said.

"That's it?"

"What were you expecting? I can't make a recommendation until I know your involvement in Shanna's death. I need details before we speak with the D.A."

"I've changed my mind, I want a lawyer. I didn't kill Shanna. You're not going to trap me. I'm not stupid, you are." She violently pushed back her chair, knocking it to the floor, and stood.

"Interview has ended at twelve-twenty PM."

"You got nothing. You're—"

Jake interrupted her. "You ended this interview, Meryl. Remember, anything you continue to say is being recorded. It will be used against you in a court of law. You've been warned. Do you understand?"

"Yes." She continued to walk to the door then turned back to them. "You guys are fishing. You're like the cops in those comical police movies." She walked out the door.

"Well, Ollie, wasn't that fun?" Louie foot shuffled his feet from side to side, imitating the Keystone Cops of the silent films. Jake started laughing.

"Yeah, we pushed some buttons. What time's Cavilla's interview?"

"Two o'clock. Let's grab some lunch. I'm starved."

* * * *

Their interview with Mark Cavilla didn't turn up anything new. Cavilla remembered his answers verbatim. They had seemed rehearsed then and now. His arrogant attitude stayed until they asked their last question.

"Mark, did you know Shanna was a lesbian?" Jake asked, gauging Mark's reaction.

Mark flew to his feet, his fists clenched, and took a step toward Jake. Louie walked around behind Cavilla and applied pressure on his right shoulder until Cavilla sat.

"You don't want to do that, son, sit down," Louie said.

"I won't let him label her," Cavilla shouted.

"It's not a label if it's true, Mark," Louie said quietly.

"She's not a queer," he said adamantly.

"The new term is LGBTQ, Mark. We have it from reliable sources she was," Jake said.

"She never gave a hint... I mean, we made love. I would know if the girl was gay," Mark said. "Which one told you this nonsense, Meryl or her sister? They were both jealous of her sweetness, her brains, and especially her looks."

"It doesn't matter who told us, Mark. She was. Do you know who killed her?" Jake asked.

"No. If I knew who killed her, I'd kill him."

"I'd watch what you say, Mark. Someone will take you seriously," Jake offered.

"It's the truth. I loved her. I wanted to marry her. Are you any closer to finding her killer?" *Mark's eyes don't hold the passion of his words*, Jake thought.

"We have some new leads we're following. The investigation's ongoing." Jake gave the standard answer.

"You'll let me know?"

"Not if you intend to kill whoever did it," Jake said.

"It's a figure of speech. I've been so empty since she died."

"I thought she broke up with you, Mark?" Louie asked.

"She did. She wanted to wait until she graduated, got settled into a job. She would've come around." It bothered Louie that Cavilla used pronouns instead of Shanna's name.

"You didn't know there was something between Shanna and Meryl?" Louie asked.

"Not what you're implying. They were close, best friends since childhood. A sick mind would come to your conclusion."

"Do you think her sister Chloe knew?" Jake asked.

"If she did, she wouldn't have been happy about it. She hates Meryl. She always felt Meryl controlled Shanna's life. I've kept in touch with Chloe. She's lost without her sister."

"Anything else you can offer, Mark?" Jake asked.

"No. I want to go home. Why would you even bring this up?" Mark asked.

"It needed to be discussed, Mark. It could be a motive. We needed to see if you knew," Jake said.

"Because she dated me?"

"No, it's not about you, Mark."

"Am I done here?" Cavilla asked, pushing to his feet.

"Yes. If we need to ask you any more questions, we'll give you a call." Jake gave him the same spiel, asking him to contact them if something or someone came to mind.

They watched Cavilla leave. His shoulders hunched, tears washing down his face. Jake hated when the job crushed the innocent, though sometimes it was the only way to find out the truth. He wondered how Cavilla would regard Shanna in the future.

Louie turned off the tape and said, "Okay, did Mark, or didn't he know Shanna was gay?"

"I couldn't tell. He seemed upset. Could you date a woman and not know if she's gay or bisexual?"

"Can't say. We weren't given radar on something like that." Louie said.

"I guess you're right. The question is, did she tell him? It had to be hard to keep it a secret like that."

Chapter 23

"Let's head up to the UConn campus at Storrs. Re-interview the girls on Shanna's floor in her old dorm. When we get back into town, we'll interview Meryl Drake's friends. This way we'll be in town for end of shift," Jake said.

"Have big plans tonight?"

Jake didn't answer. Louie smiled at him and then headed to the car.

* * * *

They did the recanvas of the dorms and hit pay dirt when they talked to a girl they'd missed in their first sweep back in March. Jake knocked on the door of room 4-15. A petite, five-foot-tall brunette who couldn't have weighed more than ninety pounds if she weighed an ounce, greeted him. She had a fine-boned, sculpted face, sloe-brown eyes with long, dark lashes. She wore no makeup. "Yes?" she asked.

"I'm Lieutenant Carrington and this is Sergeant Romanelli with the Wilkesbury Police Department. Were you here a few months ago when Shanna Wagner was killed?" He held up his shield.

"Yes, please come in." She stood back to let them in. She sat at her desk and offered them a seat on her bed. He and Louie chose to stand.

"And you are?" Jake asked.

"Donna Star."

"I don't remember interviewing you before." Jake ruffled through his notes.

"No, you didn't. I had to go home for a family funeral." She grabbed her calendar. "I left for home on the Monday after Shanna went missing. I didn't come back to school for over two weeks."

"Who died?" Louie asked.

"My father," she said quietly.

"I'm sorry for your loss," Jake said. "Did you know Shanna?"

"Yes. We hung out sometimes. Are you any closer to finding out who killed her?"

"We are. Did you hang out with her on the night she disappeared?"

"No, she asked me, but I didn't feel up to it. My mother had called earlier in the day to tell me my father was in a car accident. I didn't want to be with anyone."

"It must have been a shock," Jake said, not indicating which event he thought had shocked her the most.

"It was. Some idiot drunk driver killed him. My father was forty-four years old."

"Did you know they found Shanna before you got back to school?" Louie asked.

"Yes, my roommate called. I was devastated. First my father, then Shanna—it was too much."

"Did you know anyone who ever bothered Shanna?" Jake asked.

"I know the guy she used to date from work hung around all the time. Shanna humored him to avoid arguing with him. I mean, wherever we went, he was there." She frowned.

"You mean Mark Cavilla?" Jake's brow creased.

"Shanna only introduced him as Mark. She never gave a last name."

"Would you recognize him, if you saw him again?" Jake felt the buzz in his blood. Knew they were getting close. Maybe this was the lead they were looking for.

"Yes. He was completely shocked when she dumped him. He had a 'no woman dumped him' attitude, like he was something special, and he wasn't, take my word for it."

"Why?"

"Why, what?"

"Why wasn't he something special?" Louie asked.

"I don't know. It's hard to put your finger on. He's one-dimensional, like he bought a magazine, picked out the outfit, read an article, and then quoted it verbatim. Not original in his words or actions, almost like he was a robot. He had a superiority complex, as if it made him a big man because

he had already graduated. The guy's a real a-hole. Shanna said he was a
bossy son of a bitch. It's the main reason she blew him off."

"Did you know Shanna was gay?" Jake asked, watching her closely.

She stood up, started to pace around the room.

"Donna, did you?" Jake repeated the question.

"There'd been some talk. I don't pay attention to gossip…"

"And?" Jake questioned.

"Yes, I did. Shanna had started to question her orientation,
experimenting—it confused her. Her friend Meryl is a lesbian and pushy.
She didn't like it when Shanna dated Mark."

"Shanna told you this?" Jake understood what Donna wasn't saying,
but he wanted her to say it aloud for the record.

"Am I going to have to testify about this?" She looked concerned, sat
back down, this time on her bed, holding her head in her hands.

"If it helps close the case, yes," Jake answered honestly.

"This would kill my mother if it got out. It's been a rough year for her.
Shanna and I kind of hooked up for a couple of weeks. I'm not gay. We
were experimenting. I always wanted to see what it would be like with
another woman and…"

"What happened?"

"It wasn't my thing. Shanna understood. She was curious how I
could be so sure."

"What did you tell her?"

"I wasn't comfortable being with her as a lover. I wanted to be friends.
I'm in love with this guy back home I plan on marrying."

"Did Shanna tell Mark she was a lesbian?" Jake asked.

"Yes, she did. She gave it as the reason for the break-up. She felt he'd
leave her alone if she didn't play on his team."

"She told you that?" Louie asked, taking over the questioning.

"Yes. One night when we went for pizza, she needed someone to talk
to. I asked her what was wrong. Shanna pointed to the other side of the
street. The creep sat outside in his car and watched us for hours. Shanna
stressed to me never to be alone or go anywhere with him."

"Did she think he'd hurt you?" Jake asked.

"She never said. When I asked her, she said she told him she was gay.
She didn't want him to get the impression that I was her girlfriend."

"Do you have any other information that might help us to catch her
killer, Donna?" Jake scribbled in his notebook.

"No."

"Thanks for your time," Jake said, giving her his number as he turned to leave the room.

"I will. Shanna was a great person, though a little confused. Meryl and Mark weren't helping any with all the pressure they put on her. Shanna would've been better off getting away from both of them," Donna said sadly, as she stood. "Did you find her diary?"

"Diary?" Jake turned back.

"Yes. Shanna kept one in her purse. She wouldn't leave it in her room because she was afraid someone would read it. She put all her thoughts and feelings down in it."

"No, we didn't find one. Who else knew about it?" Jake asked.

"Basically, everyone on our floor, her sister, and her friend Meryl."

"Did Mark know?"

"I'd say yes, though Shanna wouldn't write in it in front of him. She said he was a snoop."

"When did she tell you that?" Jake asked.

"About a week before she died. I don't want to get anyone in trouble, but if he killed her I want him dead."

"Thanks for your insight. Good-bye," Jake said as they walked out.

Outside the dorm, Jake turned to Louie. "It's amazing none of this came out sooner."

"Yeah, it is. Every time we think we have a suspect pinned, it turns around. Do you think we have one or two killers?" Louie scratched his chin.

"Not sure but we're going back and asking all three of them, Meryl, Mark, and Chloe, about the diary," Jake said, frustrated. "Cavilla's a good actor. He fooled me."

"He fooled me too. I think his ego's in denial. Not admitting it—in fact, lying about no knowledge of her preference—put him at the top of my list. I can see him for it."

"I hate liars."

"Jake, would you tell someone if the girl you were dating turned out to be a lesbian? I mean, being dumped by a woman for another man is one thing. Being dumped by a woman for another woman? Man, that's the ultimate insult," Louie said.

"I don't see where it would make any difference. Dumped is dumped."

"Oh, come on. It wouldn't bother you?"

"No, it wouldn't. I'm secure in who I am," Jake said.

"Well, once it got out I think the ridicule would be worse. Don't you think?"

"It could be, depending on what type of person the guy is. If someone insulted me or carried on, I'd probably punch him out."

"See, it would bother you." Louie laughed.

"It would bother you more."

"Yeah, it would. It's the Italian macho thing, which I think Cavilla has going on too," Louie said, his tone turning serious.

"I agree. I can't wait to question the bastard, see how he reacts."

They re-interviewed all the girls from the dorm. Donna turned out to be the only new witness.

Next on the list would be tracking down Meryl Drake's friends. Before subjecting himself to Meryl's anger, Jake decided to try the Wagners. He wanted to see if they knew who she hung out with. Jake climbed in the driver's seat and dialed Chloe's cell phone before pulling out of the parking lot.

She answered on the third ring. "What do you want?"

"Chloe, who besides your sister did Meryl hang out with?"

"I can't tell you, we don't go to the same bars. You know—straight, lesbo," she said sarcastically.

"Did Shanna keep a diary?" Jake asked.

"Yes. You didn't find it.?"

"No, it only came to light today. Why didn't you mention it before?"

"I assumed you had it, she always kept it in her purse."

"We didn't recover her purse. What did she do with the old ones?" Jake hoped Chloe had them.

"She kept them under a floor board in her room. She thought no one knew about it. Why?"

"Are you home?" Jake asked.

"Yes."

"Can you check to see if her diaries are still there?"

"Hold on."

Jake figured Chloe put her phone down to go check. After a few minutes, she started talking. "They're all here, except for the current one she would have had with her."

"When's the last entry in the diaries you have there?" he asked, excitement building.

"About a month before she disappeared," Chloe said.

"Can I pick them up, or do I need a warrant?"

"Come get them. I'll be home for another hour." She hung up without another word.

"Did she have the diary?" Louie asked

"Chloe has the old ones. The one current to Shanna's death is missing. She's going to give them to us without a warrant."

"Were you expecting her to confide in you if she still had the current one?" Louie smirked.

"No."

"Then we'll do it the old-fashioned way, with feet on the pavement detecting until we find the last one."

"First, we're going through every gay bar in the city tonight."

"It'll be a reminder to you that not every woman is after you." Louie gave him a toothy grin.

"You're right. It'll do my ego good. Tonight, I'll read the diaries and makes notes for you, unless of course you want to read them too," Jake said.

"No, reading a young girl's inner thoughts would drive me crazy. Boy, I hate this drive," Louie said switching topics as Jake started to drive back to Wilkesbury.

"I like it this time of day. It's a quiet and scenic trip when the sun's out. It's also good thinking time. Put your seat back, take a nap."

"Sounds like a plan." Louie hit the release switch. His seat glided back into a reclining position.

"Nighty night, sweetheart," Jake teased.

In no time at all, Louie fell asleep, giving Jake some thinking time. He rearranged all the new pieces of the evidence, mixing them up with the others they had, hoping for a clear suspect to emerge. He and Louie had originally thought it would be the motive that solved this case. Right now, there were too many of them and nothing supporting them.

He started arranging each person's reason to commit the crime in his head while Louie snored away. Chloe's would be the ring, valued at fifty thousand dollars. Meryl felt threatened when Shanna dated Mark, thinking she was changing sides. Mark Cavilla, shot down because after spending time with him, Shanna preferred the company of women. A damaged ego would be a strong, powerful motive—one that pointed right at Mark. Cavilla's lie moved him to the top of the list. A question popped into Jake's head. He'd need to interview the head of the accounting firm, see if everyone knew about Shanna's sexual orientation.

They'd been on the road for about fifty minutes when Louie stirred.

"Well, good morning, darling. Did you sleep well?"

Louie cleared his head, looked around. "Where are we?"

"We're coming into Southington."

"Wow, I slept the whole way?"

"Yep, and Louie, your beauty sleep didn't help." Jake laughed.

"Cute. You should be half as handsome as me, you'd be a star. Did your quiet time pay off, or did you spend it all thinking about Mia?" Louie asked.

"No, I spent it working the case." At Louie's mention of Mia, his thoughts diverged toward her.

"Oh, is the mighty Jake pulling back?"

"No, we need to close this case and move on."

* * * *

Jake's cell phone rang. Looking down, he recognized his friend Dave's number from the Woodbury Police Department. He answered and listened to Dave talk. The lab reports had come back on Mia's package. The skin cells on the package Mia had received didn't match the sample Jake gave them.

"Thanks, Dave. Can you email me a copy of the report?"

"Sure, I'll get it to you in five minutes. Oh Jake, she's one hot woman," Guerrera said.

"And she's all mine. Remember that." Was she his? Time would tell.

"Maybe," he said, laughing. "Bye."

"Asshole," Jake muttered.

"Who's Dave?" Louie asked, as he hung up.

"Dave Guerrera from the Woodbury PD."

"What's going on there?" Louie asked.

"I told you about the package on Mia's doorstep Thursday night. Dave called with the lab results."

"No, you didn't say anything about a package," Louie said. "What was in it?"

"Someone left a package at her front door. It contained a dead skunk with its throat slit."

"Oh, is that all? And you didn't think to mention this?" Louie asked, miffed. Jake knew he hated to be left out.

"I thought I did. So much has happened this week, my mind's reeling."

"What sample did you give them?" Louie asked.

"I gave them Chloe's DNA sample, but it didn't match," Jake said.

"Well, that makes sense. Wasn't she in Hartford the day the restraining order was issued? Mia doesn't have clue who's leaving them?"

"No, she doesn't."

Switching up the conversation, Louie asked, "You're not seeing her tonight?"

"No, she's packing for her trip. I'll see her tomorrow night. But I'll find out if someone who could be doing this popped in her head."

They stopped at the Wagner's house. Chloe had packed the diaries in a box and made him sign a receipt.

"Thanks, Chloe," Jake said.

"I want them back. It's like talking to her, so make sure nothing happens to them."

"We'll keep them locked up." He took a minute and studied her. It appeared she hadn't slept in days.

"Are you any closer, Jake?" Chloe looked at him with hope in her eyes.

"I want to think we are."

Chapter 24

They left the Wagners' and headed to the station. On the way, Louie started in on him again about Brigh. Jake brushed him off. He didn't bother to tell him he'd already called the vet with a few questions. Though he knew owning a dog wasn't practical at this stage in his life, he couldn't get Brigh off his mind.

After parking the car, they parted ways. Louie went to his desk. Jake went to the coffee machine in his office where Detective Brown caught up with him.

"Lieutenant," Brown said.

"What's up, Kirk?"

"The body shop turned out to be a solid lead on the hit-and-run case. I have an arrest warrant. Lanoue and I are on our way to execute it now. It's a shame. The kid got scared, left the scene, and screwed up his life. He's seventeen." Jake heard the sympathy in Brown's voice.

"Pick him up. If you need anything from me, give me a call. I'm tied up on my cases, but I'll make whatever time you need." Jake turned away, though Kirk kept talking.

"Lieutenant, we still don't have anything on the school shooting. And we still haven't turned up anything that would've gotten the kid killed, but he's still dead," Kirk said.

"I liked your idea to bring everyone in here with their parents. It's tough to turn kids, but I've found intimidation works. Hopefully bringing them in will get the students and their parents to cooperate. Keep me informed. If you need me in any of the interviews put it on my calendar," Jake said.

"Will do, sir."

Jake took his coffee to his desk then updated the Wagner murder book with the new information. Then he put his feet up on his desk and closed his eyes. He let the information on the Wagner case roll around and rearrange itself. It was going in too many directions. He needed to rein it in.

* * * *

Louie settled into his chair, stalling for a few minutes before calling Meryl Drake. On Saturday, she'd displayed some animosity toward Jake. So, he got the chore of calling her.

"Meryl Drake?" Louie asked as the call connected.

"Who's asking?" she replied snottily.

"It's De…" He caught himself, "This is Sergeant Romanelli, Ms. Drake."

"What do you want?"

"We have a couple of follow-up questions for you. I need to inform you this call's being recorded."

"Well, I told you to talk to my lawyer, not me," Meryl said.

"Okay, Ms. Drake. Give me your lawyer's information for the record, and I'll give him a call."

Silence.

"Ms. Drake, are you still there?" Louie asked.

"Yes, what questions?"

"You pulled out the lawyer card so I can't speak with you. I need his or her name and number." Louie held his breath while he waited for her reply.

"I don't have a damn lawyer. They cost too much money."

"For the record, you'll now speak with me without a lawyer? You do understand your rights, if you can't afford a lawyer, one will be provided for you," Louie said, wanting to make sure he covered his ass.

"Yes, ask your questions. I didn't kill Shanna. I loved her."

Louie's silence hung in the air for a few moments. Call him old-fashioned but he didn't have a reply.

He went right into his questions. "Ms. Drake, I'll need all your friends' names and phone numbers, anyone who hung out with you and Shanna. I'll also need the name of the place you worked back when Shanna disappeared, including all your bosses' information."

"Why?"

"These are follow-up questions to your interview. It could be pertinent to the investigation," Louie said, surprised when he started to feel sorry for her.

"It's a long list, Sergeant. Give me your email address and I'll send it to you."

"Fax it, please." Louie gave her the number, then hung up and got a cup of coffee while he waited for it to come through. Faxes gave him a number connecting the information to the sender. Email addresses took more time to trace. So whenever he could, he had people fax him.

* * * *

Before he started in on the diaries, Jake looked over the lab reports Dave had emailed over from Woodbury. The DNA turned out to be male, not female, so definitely not Chloe's. He wondered whose it could be. He reached for the phone and dialed Mia's cell number. She answered immediately.

"Hey."

"Are you all packed?"

"Not quite. I'm still choosing my wardrobe, but I'm almost there." She laughed.

"Mia, I need to ask you some questions. I got the lab report back on your...package. It's not female DNA. The sample came back—it belongs to a male. Have you ever met a Mark Cavilla? Is there anybody who's angry at you?" He threw out Mark's name hoping for a hit.

"No, who is Mark Cavilla?"

"Seriously, Mia, has anybody been threatening you? Have you gotten any unusual phone calls or someone hanging up when you answer? Has anyone been following you?" He bombarded her with questions, ignoring hers.

"No, no, and no, Jake. I've been in contact with you, my friend Piper, and the people at work."

"Okay, make sure your doors are locked when you're home."

"They always are, Jake. I'm a New Yorker. It's one of the major life lessons you learn growing up in the city."

"Okay, if you think of anyone, even a minor player in your life, give me a call right away and I'll go talk to him."

"What are you going to do, beat him up?" Mia asked.

"No, there are ways you can scare someone without beating him up, or leaving any marks."

"You're scary, Jake. I'll take your word for it. Right now, I need to get back to this."

"See ya." He hoped it would turn out to be a childish prank, though his instincts told him different.

Louie walked into his office, helped himself to a seat, and handed Jake a copy of the list Meryl Drake had sent over.

"I called Meryl Drake. That's her list of friends. It looks like we'll be busy tomorrow," Louie said.

"What do you mean tomorrow? There's plenty of time to start dialing today," Jake said, looking at his watch.

Louie raised an eyebrow. "We're not doing these in person?"

"No, let's start with phone calls, now before Meryl can warn them. If anything pops, we'll give them a visit."

"I didn't get any new reports from the lab, did you?"

"No, I'll call again. They said this week."

"Today's only Monday, Jake."

"It feels like Friday. It's aggravating." Jake rubbed his temples where a headache was forming.

"Sophia said I'm driving her crazy. I think of something, jump out of bed in the middle of the night, and grab the file and start looking for it—but it slips away. It's right at the edge of my mind while I sleep and it disappears when I wake up."

"I got the same thing going on. I don't believe we missed anything. We need to uncover everything associated with the new information we got this weekend. The diary's the key. Find it, we find the answers. See if she accepted any other job offers outside her current firm. Also check if she made plans to leave the state," Jake said.

"Shanna might've confided in Donna, but if she did, Donna would've mentioned it," Louie said.

"Agreed, but ask her outright. I'll take half of Meryl's list, you take the other half. It shouldn't take us long to cull through it."

* * * *

One new piece of information resulted from all the calls—Meryl's jealousy had become a problem for Shanna, and Meryl had become more and more controlling. She let no one near Shanna and they stopped going out to clubs. When they attended parties, Meryl never left her side. Meryl's friend, JD Whitney, stated they argued a lot while out in public. If they did at home, she wasn't privy to it. She'd seen Meryl's jealous rage out of control, especially when someone approached or talked to Shanna.

"I made an appointment for ten o'clock tomorrow to speak with J.D. Whitney. She lives in town," Jake said. He checked his email next. The reports on the Adams car were in, including DNA results. The lab found skin cells in the trunk. They also found sweat deposits. The DNA belonged to one female, excluding Chelsea Adams, and one male.

Jake updated Louie after he hung up. "They left behind their DNA. Unfortunately, they're not in the system. I'm going to apply for a subpoena for samples."

"Well, it's about time something came through. Who are we going to subpoena?"

"I'm going to request Lola Adams, Jeff Adams, and Nick Pilarski. Can you think of anyone else?"

"You're not going to request Chelsea's son or daughter?" Louie asked.

"Not at this time, according to the DNA report, there's no relation with the deceased."

"If it's the father's, there'll be a relation to the kids," Louie stated.

"You're right, but we won't need it if Jeff supplies his sample and it matches the one in the trunk. I don't want to upset the kids. Let's hit up Judge Eisenberg again to get everyone's?"

"Might as well, he's familiar with the case. I'll take it over now, see if I can get a rush on this." Jake walked back to his office to grab his jacket. Louie followed him in. Slipping on his jacket, Jake asked, "You coming?"

"So much for leaving on time," Louie said.

"You want to leave on time, get a desk job."

"Yeah, like I'd be an asset in an office."

"You? Of course, you would. You're so anal with your paperwork, they'd love you." Jake slapped him on the back.

"That's true, but you'd miss me."

In the lobby, Jake headed for the front door. Louie grabbed hold of his arm. "We're not driving over?"

"It's two blocks, Louie. It would take us a half an hour to find a parking spot at this time of day. Suck it up."

They walked up from the precinct toward the center of town. Jake spotted two drug deals going down. If time had permitted, he'd have busted them for having been so bold. But he needed the subpoenas. Picking up the pace, they reached the courthouse with fifteen minutes to spare before the courthouse closed.

The judge's clerk made them wait in the outer office for ten minutes before the judge opened his door and called them in. Eisenberg's chambers reflected the judge's personality—rich and formal, unlike the outer office, which had the standard governmental décor—gray everything. But in here his personal tastes showed in both art and color. The wall behind his desk, painted in a forest green, played off the window drapes of green and ivory. A large desk in a dark wood—Jake thought cherry—took up half the room. The office demanded respect, as did the judge himself. His steel-gray hair matched the outer office. Martin Eisenberg stood five-eight. His nose had been broken in a college boxing match, giving his face a mean perpetual expression. The judge presented a fierce, authoritative figure even while seated at his desk.

"Jake, Louie, what can I do for you today?" Judge Eisenberg asked as his pale blue eyes narrowed. He pointed a finger to the clock on his wall. "At this late hour?"

"Thanks for seeing us, Your Honor. We got the DNA report from the car on the Chelsea Adams case. There are two sets of DNA found in the car, besides the Adams woman's. One's male and one's female. We'd like a subpoena for the ex-husband, his new wife, and the new wife's ex-husband. Their names are Jeff Adams, Lola Adams, and Nick Pilarski," Jake added.

"Why include Chelsea Adams's ex-husband and his new wife? I thought they lived in Florida?" Eisenberg asked as he stood and removed his robe, revealing a black suit with a fine gray pinstripe, a white shirt, and a gray tie with black stripes. Jake guessed him to be about sixty years of age, though he looked younger. Eisenberg kept himself in shape. The judge's reputation intimidated a lot of detectives and criminals alike in the court room. The judge worked with the police to get results if they minded his time. Jake liked and respected him. He was betting on getting his subpoenas.

"Jake, how'd the other warrant go last week on the Wagner case?" he asked. Eisenberg seemed to pick up on every little tidbit of gossip in and out of his court room pertaining to a case or the cops. This slap on the wrist was to remind him not everything needed to be expedited.

"We brought in Chloe Wagner for questioning, but released her while we investigated the new allegations." Jake danced around the fact he'd also pushed Eisenberg for the other warrant.

"Pending further investigation of what new evidence?" Eisenberg asked.

"We recovered the victim's ring. We also found out she was either a lesbian or bisexual. We didn't even pick up a hint of this in our initial investigation. Everyone kept quiet for their own reasons. We also discovered today she kept a diary. The one covering the month she died is missing," Jake said.

"How did you get this information?"

"Her sister Chloe revealed Shanna's orientation in her interview last week. Her father tried to hock the ring at JC's Pawn Shop on Thursday. We learned of the diaries from a witness we missed in our first round of questioning at Shanna's school."

"How did you miss a witness?" The judge looked over his glasses at Jake.

"Your Honor, the witness's father died unexpectedly the same weekend Shanna went missing. She headed home to Nebraska for the funeral. She didn't return to school until two weeks later. We discovered her today when we re-interviewed everyone at the school." Jake looked over at Louie.

"Your thoughts, Sergeant?" Eisenberg asked.

"It's frustrating when we don't have all the pieces up front. I'm glad they're now starting to fall into place. Maybe before the month's over we'll put this one to bed," Louie said.

"I'll sign your subpoenas, Jake, but from now on do try not to make everything an emergency."

He signed the subpoenas and handed them to Jake as he held open his door for them to leave. He followed them out without another word.

Together they walked back to the station at a more leisurely pace and passed city hall on the way. The night was mild with temperatures in the seventies. Jake scanned the streets as he watched for the dealer he'd seen on the way to the judge's chambers. Not spotting him, he stopped in Vice to talk to Detective Max Carey. He gave Carey a description of the dealer.

When he and Louie stepped into Homicide, he turned to Louie. "Why don't you call it a night? I'm going to call Chief Taylor in Florida and tell him to expect the subpoenas."

"Katrina's already gone home for the day, so she won't be able to do the overnight package or print the labels for the vitals. Doris is on the desk for the nightshift. You have twenty minutes to make the overnight drop for today otherwise it'll have to be driven to the facility in Watertown. I'll take care of it and save you a trip. Call the chief," Louie said, walking toward the copy machine.

"Thanks, I forgot the time."

"You always do." Louie started to make copies for Doris before he headed to her desk with the original subpoenas.

Jake dialed the Neptune police chief. "Hi, Sammy, do you work twenty-four seven?"

"It sure seems like it. Let me guess, Lieutenant Carrington from Connecticut? I expect you want to talk to the chief?" she asked.

"Please."

"Hold on a minute," she said. Taylor didn't keep him waiting.

"Hey, Connecticut, what can I do for you today?"

"Beau, we got the lab reports back on the car Chelsea Adams was found in. It contained DNA for one female and one male, besides the victim. I have two subpoenas I'm going to overnight to you for DNA samples of Jeff and Lola Adams. Are you able to execute them and save me a trip?"

"Oh, sure, I look forward to seeing that delicate creature with the gutter mouth again," He joked. Jake recalled Taylor's description of his last encounter with Lola.

He appreciated Beau's sarcasm. "Sorry, next time I'll try to get a sweet-mouthed beauty."

"I hope there won't be a next time, Jake," Taylor said, his tone serious.

"Me too, Beau."

"Do you want our labs to process the samples or overnight it back to you?"

"Please overnight the samples back to us. They'll go to UConn Medical Center. It's where all of our state autopsies on suspicious deaths are performed. The overnight envelope will already be addressed for you. The case number will be on all the vials so you don't have to label them but you'll need to mark whose specimen is contained in each. I'll give you the results as soon as I get them. Thanks," Jake said.

"Not a problem, Connecticut. We don't want any murdering bastards here either. I'll send you an email when the samples are on their way back to you."

Chapter 25

His cell phone vibrated in his pocket as he was packing up for the day. Looking down at the caller ID he almost didn't answer it. *This woman just doesn't get it.* "Chloe, do I need to remind you that you're required to go through the switchboard to talk to me?"

"I'm not harassing you. I couldn't wait until tomorrow to tell you. I got a weird phone call from Mark Cavilla. He wanted information—asked what you guys told me when I was arrested. Who told him I got arrested?"

"I'll look into how he found out. What else did he want?"

"I'll run through the phone call for you...if you have the time now?"

"I do, go ahead."

"First, he said he heard about the arrest and figured I needed a friend. He's not my friend, I haven't heard from him in a couple of months. I asked if he was nervous and told him you were closing in. He wanted details about the case and my arrest. He asked what evidence you had against me in order for you to charge me. When I wouldn't tell him anything, he caught an attitude with me. What do you think?" Chloe said.

"It's interesting, Chloe, but it doesn't help the case. Make sure you don't go anywhere alone with him or Meryl."

"I won't. He spooked me and he's running scared. Do you think he or Meryl killed my sister?" She was asking for comfort, but he had none to give. She could still be the killer.

"I don't think anything. I think it's prudent to stay close to home. We'll talk again." Then Jake added, "At the station."

"I can't tell you how much I miss my sister. You of all people should know, Jake, I live with the pain of her loss each day. I swear on my parents' lives I didn't kill her. Don't waste time investigating me when her killer is still out there."

* * * *

Jake arrived home at seven-thirty. He slung his jacket onto his bed and then locked his guns in the safe before he headed into the kitchen to grab a beer. At the kitchen table, he reviewed his files, wrote up his notes on the call from Chloe and also wrote up his notes on his conversation with the Police Chief in Florida.

Cavilla's call to Chloe occupied his mind. What did he want and how did he find out about Chloe's arrest on Friday? They'd kept it off the books on purpose. Meryl was the caller asking for information. Someone at the station had to have notified Cavilla, but who?

Meryl wasn't happy to hear from him when he called. "Meryl," he said when she answered.

"Yeah, what do you want?"

"It's Lieutenant Carrington." He identified himself.

"I said what do you want? I already spoke with the sergeant."

"I understand. Meryl, this is important. It's for Shanna. Have you spoken with Mark Cavilla lately?"

"No. I don't talk to the bastard. I can't stand him. He thought he owned Shanna." *She always sounds angry*, he noted. "Why are you asking?"

"Nothing, I'm putting all the players in order, assessing their relationships to each other. We'll talk soon."

"For some reason, I don't believe you. I have no relationship with Cavilla. He's a dickhead. Are you going to give me anything else on this?"

"All I can offer you is the investigation is ongoing, Meryl. Thanks again. Good night." She hung up on him. He got that a lot lately. He must be hitting some nerves.

Jake knew he'd perked Meryl's curiosity though it couldn't be helped. Until a definite suspect emerged, was arrested, and locked away based on the evidence, he couldn't give any one of them information. He needed to put his prime suspect at the scene—so far he hadn't been able to. He was sure the killer had kept the diary as a souvenir. *Find the diary. Find the killer*, he thought again. It sounded so simple—he wished.

Jake pulled a couple of burgers from the fridge and sat them on the counter to come to room temperature. He grabbed another beer, walked out to his deck, and sat in a chair and watched the sun as it started to set. He took a sip of his beer then pressed one on his cell phone to speed dial Mia's number.

* * * *

Louie sat down to dinner with his family. As usual, he couldn't get a word in edgewise with the chatter of the kids, and Sophia breaking up arguments. That was okay with him. The case, along with the new evidence, occupied his mind. No clear individual stood out. Too many people wanted a piece of poor Shanna. He blew out a breath when Sophia cut into his thoughts.

"You okay, Louie? You seem distracted."

"Yeah, I'm fine. So much has come down the last few days. I'm trying to put it in order."

"Why don't you do it later? For now, you can reintroduce yourself to the kids." Sophia smiled at him.

"Funny. Hi, kids. I'm your dad." He laughed.

"Oh, really?" Marisa said, reminding him of her mother.

"Yes, really. So, I take it you missed me?"

"I didn't. Mom brought this other guy over to fill in for you. A great substitute and he's much better looking," Marisa said, flashing him a grin that had cost him thousands of dollars.

Yep, just like her mother. "Well, I'm glad to hear I wasn't missed. So next week, you can go to him for your allowance," Louie said with a straight face.

"Jeez, Dad, I was only joking," she complained.

"How are you doing, LJ?" he asked his oldest son.

"Dad, Mom said I needed to ask you first if I could borrow the car Saturday night. Her curfew's eleven," LJ said.

"Your mother's curfew is eleven? Good to know." Louie laughed.

"Come on, Dad, my date's curfew."

The kid never appreciates my humor. "Who's the girl?"

"Melissa Phelps."

"Where are you going?"

"What's this, the third degree? I'm not a suspect," LJ said, moving food around his plate.

"No, you're not a suspect. You're my son—my underage son, who wants to borrow my car. I'd like to know where you're going. You're sixteen, remember that."

"I thought we'd go to the movies and get something to eat after," he replied, looking down at his food.

"LJ's got a girlfriend, LJ's got—" Marisa taunted.

"Stop it, Marisa. Leave your brother alone. You can have the car, LJ, and your mother and I agreed you'll take her cell phone with you, in case of an emergency."

"I wouldn't have to take her phone if you allowed me to have one."

"We've been over all this before."

"It's so unfair. Everyone in my class has a phone but me." LJ hunched over his plate.

"Do you not want to go out on Saturday?"

"No. I'll take it."

Louie looked at his younger son, who remained silent through the whole meal. "What's up, Carmen?"

"Nothing, Dad," he said as he sulked.

What is wrong with all of them tonight, Louie wondered. "Got a problem?"

"Do I have to go to school every day?"

"It's the law," Louie said.

"Well, it sucks." Carmen tapped his fork on the table.

"What happened?" Louie lay his hand over Carmen's to stop the noise.

"Greg took my lunch again. If I were two feet taller, I would've smashed him right in his face."

Louie hid his feelings. There would always be bullies in the world. Carmen, the runt of the litter, would have to fight his way through life. "Carmen, you have to tell the teacher, or I will. This has been going on way too long now."

"Dad, it would make it worse."

"I'll swing by the school tomorrow and walk Carmen home," LJ offered.

"You're too old to get involved, LJ," Louie said.

"I'm only going to talk to Greg. I promise, nothing more."

Louie left it there. He knew LJ would use discretion when he spoke with the kid. After dinner, he helped Sophia clean up then settled in the living room where they sat to enjoy their coffee and quiet as all the kids raced to their rooms to call friends under the pretense of doing homework.

"It's been a tough couple of weeks, Louie," Sophia said.

"Yeah, it has. Sorry for missing so many dinners." He smiled at her as he took her hand in his.

"It's part of the package. But I missed you, as did the children."

"Since when did Marisa become such a wise guy?"

"Since always, but you used to think it was cute."

"Well, someday someone's going to take exception to her comments."

"She's joking. What's bothering you?"

"I guess I'm frustrated with the cases. Jake's frustrated with the cases. Plus, there's a chance Spaulding might get out. So much evidence came in this week on the Wagner murder, but it still doesn't point to any one person. This case is ripping Jake apart. Last week, I walked into his office... Lord, he had tears running down his face..."

"What did he say?" Sophia asked.

"He said to leave it be. He wouldn't talk about it."

"You're not his guardian angel, Louie. This is his baggage, not yours. He's the one who has to deal with it."

"It's a good thing the other guys didn't see it."

"Yeah, God forbid he showed any emotions. Like it would kill his authority," she said sarcastically.

"I feel helpless. It's like sitting on pins and needles waiting for the prison system to submit George Spaulding's DNA results. I'm afraid what it will do to Jake if they don't match the ones from Eva's scene. On an up-note, it looks like things are going good with Mia. He went to dinner at her place on Saturday and didn't get home until this morning," Louie said.

"You told me this earlier, remember? It's still awesome."

"Yeah, it is."

"I see you have your file folders out. Working tonight?"

"If you don't mind, I want to spend an hour or two on it." He knew his wife, so he asked instead of telling her—and got the results he hoped for.

"It's not a problem." She picked up a book and started reading.

He opened the file on his lap and began reviewing everything in it for the hundredth time.

Chapter 26

Jake's neck ached. He'd been buried in the Wagner file for hours. Standing, he stretched, reached for the ceiling, and then walked from the kitchen to the living room and back again. He was a little restless and a lot lonely. It amazed him that in such a short time how his feelings for Mia had grown. Him—a "love 'em and leave 'em" kind of guy. The thought brought a smile to his face. Normally, he cherished his time alone when in a relationship. A loner, he hated to have his privacy invaded. That was before Mia came into his life. He used to be able to spend hours on his files, dissecting them without interruptions or complaints. Now all he wanted was Mia to be there, to talk to her, joke with her, and most of all, make love to her. Shaking his head, he laughed. He decided to dig into his files to keep his mind occupied.

* * * *

Tuesday morning proved to be busier than Monday. Another trip to Judge Eisenberg's chambers had them waiting over forty-five minutes before he called them in.

"What's up now, Jake?" Eisenberg asked.

"I need some search warrants on the Wagner case."

"What are you searching for?"

"The diary we told you about yesterday."

"Where are you going to look for it?" Eisenberg asked.

"I need warrants for the Wagner's house, Meryl Drake's house, Mark Cavilla's house, and their cars," Jake said.

"What's your probable cause?"

"I read her old diaries last night. They explain her relationships with Chloe, Meryl Drake, and Mark Cavilla. They weren't always flattering. Chloe Wagner called me last night."

Eisenberg interrupted. "I thought you had a restraining order on her? Doesn't it also include contact on your personal phones?"

"Yes, it does. She called because Cavilla called her last night, after months of no contact and asked about her arrest and if there was any new evidence. He also asked if she knew the reason for the new interviews."

"That's it?"

"Chloe Wagner, when asked, had no qualms about telling us about the diaries, and where they were kept. She even offered the old ones, stored at her parents' house. She gave them up without a warrant."

"If that's the case, why get a warrant for her house?"

Jake talked himself down. He needed to remain calm, lay out his logic. "Maybe she held back on the last one. We need to be sure. Your Honor, the violence in this crime suggests a crime of passion. Both Drake and Cavilla were Shanna Wagner's lovers. We feel the recent evidence, and new information, warrants a second look."

"Relax, Jake. I want to make sure it's not another goose chase. You have your probable cause, get it done." Eisenberg issued the warrants.

Outside the courthouse, Louie asked, "Are we taking a team with us?"

"Yes, but I want a few minutes to explain to the Wagners, including Chloe, why we got a warrant this time." Jake looked at Louie, noting his frown. "She turned the other diaries over without a warrant."

Louie nodded.

"Are you leaning toward her for this?"

"What if she's the guilty one?" Louie asked.

"Louie, we'll be talking to her at the house. I'm not giving her advance warning. Besides my gut tells me she's not the one."

"Well, Jake, didn't your gut tell you last week she was the one?"

"No." With Louie he could be honest.

"No? Then why'd we detain her?"

"Last week she crossed a line when she went after Mia. What would you have done if she'd gone after Sophia?" Jake asked, staring at Louie.

"The same thing." Louie patted Jake's shoulder.

"Let's go set up our teams for Drake and Cavilla's houses. I want to take the Wagners first to eliminate them."

"I'll review today's roster, see who's on," Louie said.

"I'll update the captain while you're at it. Meet me in my office in twenty minutes."

Louie nodded as they parted ways.

Jake chose his team, consisting of three uniformed officers—Burrows, Sherman, and Jones. He briefed them and showed them the diaries he confiscated yesterday to give them an idea of what they were looking for. Officer Jones hid a smile as she coughed into her hand.

"Is something amusing, Officer Jones?" Jake asked.

"No, sir," she replied, coming to attention.

"It's going to be a long day. We're not going to stop until we find the diary. Pick up lunch on your way to your first assignment. We'll eat on the road on our way to the second house. Sergeant Romanelli or I will give you a call when we're on our way. Questions?" Jake looked around.

In unison he got, "No, sir."

"Great, we'll see you in an hour or so."

Officer Jones hung back. "Sorry, sir, for the smirk."

"What's so funny?"

"The diary, sir, and you having to explain what it was." She flashed him a big, toothy grin.

"Most men, Officer Jones, don't have a clue a woman keeps them."

"I know." She continued to grin as she turned, and left his office. He laughed at her back.

Jake had called the Wagners, and was surprised to find Chloe home from work. He told them he needed to speak with them about the diaries, offering no other explanation.

"Lieutenant?" Mr. Wagner opened the door before Jake had the chance to knock.

"Can we come in?"

"Yes. Anna's at a doctor's appointment. I dropped her off before your call."

"Good, we don't want to upset her." Jake looked up as Chloe walked into the room.

"What's this about, Jake?" Chloe asked.

"Chloe, you gave us the diaries with no warrant. I wanted to return the courtesy. We have a search warrant here to see if Shanna's missing diary is still hidden somewhere within the house…"

"You mean if I hid it, after I killed her," Chloe said bitterly.

"Yes." He couldn't offer her more. "In order to lock down the killer we need to be thorough. We have warrants for all the suspects in the case and we can't show favoritism." He stressed the word suspects.

"Do you understand? It'll be me and Louie. I'm not bringing in a team." He decided that on the way over.

"You have to do this to eliminate Chloe?" Mr. Wagner understood what Jake wasn't saying.

"Yes."

"Get it done, Lieutenant. We'll be in the kitchen having coffee. Do either one of you want coffee?"

"No, thanks." Jake and Louie walked down the hallway to Shanna's room and began their search.

They rummaged through the drawers and the closet. They tested the floor boards and found the loose one where Shanna had kept her diaries.

Jake walked back into the kitchen and spoke to Chloe. "Your room's next. Do you want to be there?"

"What, and watch you rifle through my underwear? No, thank you." She turned away and poured another cup of coffee.

A few minutes into the search of Chloe's room, a thought hit him and Jake headed to the kitchen. He stopped outside the kitchen door when he heard Joe talking.

"I'm sorry I ever doubted you, honey. Please forgive me," Mr. Wagner said.

"Dad, I wish there was nothing to forgive. I understand Jake planted the seed in your head, but you should have had more faith in me."

Guilt tugged at him when the pain in Chloe's voice cut through his thoughts as he eavesdropped. Unfortunately, in a murder investigation the innocent sometimes got burned while the police dug for their answers and the killer. Sometimes it ripped their lives apart and it could never be mended. He was always sorry for his part in it, but it was the victims he worked for, not the survivors.

"I understand your grief. Nobody realizes how much I miss Shanna. You should never have doubted how much I loved her."

"I have no explanation, Chloe. I do love you as much as I loved Shanna. Finding the ring in her room—it threw me. I forgot Meryl was here... I rushed to hock it just to get it out of the house. I knew they'd look at you first. I didn't want you involved. I can't lose you. Please forgive me?"

"Yes."

"Honey, these last few months almost destroyed us. Maybe the three of us can go away for a couple of weeks when this is settled. We'll try to heal."

"Will we ever heal, Dad?"

"We'll always miss her, Chloe. We'll never be whole again without her, but we'll heal somehow and go on with our lives."

"I love you, Daddy."

"I love you too, honey."

Jake decided he would ask his question later. He went back down the hall to help Louie.

* * * *

They searched the whole house, from the attic to the basement. They found nothing. Jake called the team as they headed to Drake's apartment complex.

On the way, they stopped off at Nardelli's and picked up grinders for lunch. It was already eleven o'clock, and he didn't want anything to hold him up from leaving on time tonight. Nothing less than a bomb would keep him from seeing Mia.

Chapter 27

Jake gave Meryl Drake a call. She wanted to be present for the search. As they waited outside her building for her to arrive, Louie turned to Jake.

"I'm glad it wasn't at Chloe's," Louie said.

"I am too."

Meryl pulled up to the curb.

Jake explained the scope of the warrant when she walked up to them and explained what they were looking for. He also introduced her to the team. Though not happy, Meryl cooperated.

"If I took the diary, Lieutenant, I wouldn't be stupid enough to leave it here."

"People leave incriminating stuff lying around all the time," Jake stated.

"I do have a request though." She looked away. "If you do find it, can I have it after the case is tried?"

"Meryl, her parents are her heirs. You'd have to ask them."

"Oh."

Jake, along with Louie, searched the bedroom. Officer Jones searched in the kitchen, Officer Burrows searched in the second bedroom, which was being used as an office. Officer Sherman searched the basement storage bin assigned to Meryl Drake.

Meryl stayed in the bedroom while they foraged through her most intimate things. Jake understood the anger he saw in her eyes.

He noticed the pictures lined up on Meryl's dresser of Shanna and her at different stages in their lives.

Jake asked, "You don't keep a diary?"

"No, it's too much work."

"Why did Shanna?"

"Her mother gave us each one for our sixth birthdays. Shanna had nice things to write in hers, I didn't. My parents are alcoholics—abusive. I didn't want it to get out. I thought if someone read it, they'd take me away from Shanna. My mother always threatened if I told anyone, I'd be worse off."

It was the most she'd ever said about herself and he found himself feeling sorry for her. It explained a lot about Meryl's personality. He'd seen it often on the job—the abused child—and it still generated sympathy for the adult the child became.

"I'm sorry, Meryl. Is that why you always hung out at the Wagners?"

"Yes. They even called social services once. SS thought the Wagners exaggerated the situation. So they recommended no action be taken—left me with my parents to fend for myself. I could've sued when I reached legal age. Turns out the SS agent was a friend of my mother."

"Sometimes the system doesn't work, Meryl. Why didn't you sue the state?"

"Because by failing to do her job, the woman gave me the one thing I wanted—to be near Shanna. Nothing else mattered to me." She wiped the tears from her eyes. Jake watched her eyes become unfocused and wondered where her mind took her. When she came back to the present, she abruptly turned away and walked out of the room.

He and Louie spoke with the other officers when they finished their search. They also found nothing. Jake thanked Meryl for her time and apologized for the mess they left behind. There wasn't a neat way to search an entire apartment. He asked her to tell no one.

"Who am I going to tell, Lieutenant?"

"I don't know, Meryl. For now, keep it to yourself. We have others we need to search today, so I repeat, please don't talk to anyone."

Chapter 28

Cavilla wanted to be there. Jake and Louie waited in front of Cavilla's house for twenty minutes. Annoyed, Jake put a call into Mark's cell phone. When his voicemail picked up he left his message.

"We have a runner. Let's get the search started. If we find anything then we'll put out an APB on him."

Louie nodded. Jake knocked on the door.

A petite woman in a loose-fitting dress and fuzzy slippers opened the door. Her gray hair stuck up in all directions. Jake figured he was speaking with Mark's mother.

Jake spoke up, explained their warrant and how it would be executed. He asked her to stay in the living room while they conducted the search of her home.

"You can't do this. Where's my son? He didn't do anything. He's a good boy. Get out of my house."

"He was asked to join us here, but he hasn't arrived yet. Where is he, Mrs. Cavilla?"

"He's at work, naturally. He's a good boy." Mrs. Cavilla folded her arms across her sagging chest.

Jake looked over at Louie. Louie shook his head no. He already checked in with the accounting firm where Mark worked.

"He's not at work. Where would he go, Mrs. Cavilla?"

"He has to be! He'll lose his job if he takes time off." Tears started to fall down her cheeks. "What's this about?"

"It's about Shanna Wagner. Mark's a person of interest."

"I'm going to call my husband." She stood, started to walk to the phone.

"Mrs. Cavilla, while the search is in progress, you're not allowed to make any calls or have any visitors. Your son had the opportunity to be here while we searched. He chose to stay away. If he calls you, tell him it's in his best interest to contact me." Jake handed her his card. She took it and tossed it on the table by an old brown and white flowered chair. He didn't move until she sat back down. Looking around the room full of aged furniture it spoke volumes to him. Jake picked up the portable phone and took it with him to start the search.

In most of their searches, Louie held the video recorder, while Jake did the actual searching. Mark's extremely organized closet gave Jake a glimpse into Mark's personality. In Mark's closet Jake found the diary and Shanna's purse hidden behind two stacks of shoe boxes.

I got you, you son of a bitch!

Jake turned toward Louie. "Call in the APB, Louie. I want Cavilla's ass in interview before this day is over."

Bagging the diary, Jake forced himself to continue the search instead of stopping and reading it on the spot.

The team of officers in the rest of the house followed the same routine. Officer Burrows held the video recorder, while Sherman and Jones searched the different rooms. "Where's Mark's car?"

"He drove it to work."

After they finished up, Jake let Mrs. Cavilla call her husband and explain the situation. After she spoke to him, Jake took the phone and explained to her husband if Mark called either one of them they needed to contact him for Mark's safety.

He stationed a plainclothes detective outside the house in case Mark came home. Satisfied, he and Louie went back to the station house.

What they didn't find at the house was the murder weapon.

* * * *

Jake closed his office door, settled into his chair and placed his feet on top of his desk as he grabbed Shanna's diary and started to read. It broke his heart as he got inside Shanna's head. She hated Mark and regretted her lapse in judgment at accepting a date with him. Shanna broke it off quickly but Mark wouldn't go away. He followed her wherever she went. A smart girl, she outlined every instance where he had confronted her. Her feelings for Meryl were mixed. She resented how she tried to control her. And on other days when Meryl was acting like the friend she needed, she loved her. In the diary, she listed all the cities where she wanted to work. Shanna had made up her mind to move far away from both Meryl and Mark. She wanted to be in control of her life. An asterisk next to Chloe's name caught his attention. Shanna had planned on asking her sister if she was game to relocate with her and start over. As he read the diary to the end, it was clear Shanna was under a tremendous amount of pressure and she resented it. She even listed the campus police number in the diary as well as Wilkesbury's for when she was home. Ironic, the morning of her disappearance she'd written she had planned to place a restraining order against Cavilla the next day, after she finished taking her exams.

He scribbled in his notepad questions he would toss out at Cavilla once he caught up to him. Meryl, he couldn't do anything about. She was a mean, obsessive woman who had pushed Shanna away. Rubbing his eyes, he dialed Shamus's extension. Once McGuire answered, Jake brought him up to date. Shamus agreed with him, both Chloe and Meryl should be notified and be on the lookout for Mark. Jake didn't believe Cavilla would harm either one of them but he didn't want to take a chance. A cornered man struck out at anything in his path.

Sightings trickled in on Cavilla but nothing solid on his actual whereabouts. Louie combed the streets for a couple of hours toward the end of shift. Jake sent him home around eight.

"I have the Adams file with me. If anything pops I'll give you a call," Louie said.

"Okay. I'm going to hit a few bars around town. Maybe Cavilla's holed up in one of them. His father gave me his list of relatives in and out of town. So far no one's seen him. Or so they say. Tomorrow if he doesn't turn up, we'll split the list and see for ourselves." Jake hoped something popped soon.

"Okay, good night."

Jake hung up. After he finished scouting out the bars there'd be nothing left for them to do today.

Chapter 29

Jake spent three hours going from bar to bar, showing Mark Cavilla's picture around. No one saw him or recognized him except the bartender from the night Shanna died.

"He didn't stop in here today," the bartender said as he poured beer for a customer.

"You sure?"

"Yep, he's a cheap son of a bitch. This one never tips." The bartender flicked his finger on the picture.

Jake left the bar. In the car, he put a call in to Mia. "I'm finishing up now with my interviews. Is it too late to come over?" He was exhausted but needed to see her.

"No, did you eat?"

"I can't remember. Don't put yourself out."

"I made extra, there's a plate in the microwave for you."

"Thanks, give me a half hour and I'll be there." He was weary, but after talking to Mia he felt recharged.

* * * *

Jake knocked on Mia's door. She answered it barefooted, wearing a pair of white shorts with a black halter top, her face bare of makeup. He'd never seen a more beautiful sight. As he leaned in for a kiss, she reached and pushed the door closed and locked it and kissed him back. He spun her around, pinning her back to the door, dragging her hands over her head as he explored her mouth. He ran his hands down the length of her, stopping at the small of her back, and crushed her to his body. He loved the smooth, soft feel of her skin. Mia lowered her arms and wrapped them around his neck. After a few minutes, they broke away.

"I've wanted to do that since yesterday morning," he said.

"Was it worth the wait?" she asked, still holding on to him.

"Yep."

They walked to the back of the condo. Jake noticed the one place-setting, a reminder that he'd missed dinner tonight. The pile of papers by the plate perked his curiosity.

"What's this?"

"If you're too tired don't feel obligated...it's my manuscript."

"I get to read it? I thought I couldn't..."

"It's finished."

"Wow, I'll read it while you're gone."

"I...thought...you could read it tonight," she said nervously.

"Tonight? Mia, you're killing me. I want every minute I can with you." He couldn't believe she wanted him to read it tonight. It had to be three hundred and fifty freakin' pages.

"No, not the whole thing, Jake, only the first fifty pages I sent out to the agent. I want your honest opinion on it."

"Do you mind if I read while I eat?"

"I do. I want you to enjoy the meal. You need to relax. I'll set you up in the living room after dinner while I do the dishes."

"I'd relax better in your arms." He noticed her anxiety and then nodded his agreement.

Damn, I had other plans for tonight. I'm a fast reader, but how long will fifty pages take?

After dinner, he went into the living room with his coffee, careful not to spill anything on her white furniture. An hour later, his coffee untouched, he finished reading the first fifty pages and wanted to continue.

As he walked into the kitchen Mia turned from the counter with an anxious look on her face. He gave her his best cop stare and blanked his expression.

"Well?"

"It's great, Mia. From page one it grabbed my attention. Your main character's funny, smart, and serious all at the same time. I like the storyline too."

"You're not just saying you like it so I'll be nice?" she said.

"No, it's good. This grabbed me right away. Can I take it with me, so I can read the whole story while you're gone?"

"Yes, if you promise to lock it up."

"I will."

He took the fresh cup of coffee she handed him and walked out to the deck to enjoy the mild spring night awhile longer. Conversation flowed between them. Around ten, Mia took his hand and led him inside and up to her bedroom.

They spent the rest of the night making love, and fell asleep in each other's arms. Jake woke with a start around one o'clock. He climbed out of bed and tried not to wake Mia.

"What time is it?" she asked in a voice laced with sleep.

"It's after one, go back to sleep. I'm going home, so I don't throw off your schedule tomorrow." He reached over for her. "Good luck." He leaned over and kissed her.

"I'll give you a call tomorrow night?" Mia mumbled and turned on her side away from him.

"Reset the alarm," he said and quietly, he let himself out.

* * * *

As he stepped outside, a man ran from the front of Mia's unit and hopped into a dark four-door car, maybe a late model Ford. Jake had to jump over something on the doorstep as he ran after him. The guy had too much of a head start. Jake was able to get a partial on the license plate—*356*—but he was unable to get the letters as the man sped away. He walked back to Mia's front steps and examined the package. Cursing, he dialed his friend Dave's cell, hoping he'd pulled the late shift again. He hadn't. Dave came out in his personal car. Together they opened the package. Inside was a dead squirrel. First a skunk, now a squirrel—why and who was doing this to her?

"I'll run the plate for you, Jake, while the lab processes the package. Any ideas on who is doing this?" Dave asked.

"Mia couldn't come up with anyone she's had a fight or disagreement with. The car's either black or blue. I can run the plate, if you like. I'll start with Woodbury, Middlebury, Watertown, and Wilkesbury. Okay?"

"Are you going to tell her about this package?"

"No, she's heading into New York for the next couple of days on important business. I don't want to upset her. I'll tell her when she gets back. Could you give her condo a few extra passes this week?" Jake asked, concerned.

"I will. Relax, Jake, we country bumpkins know how to handle ourselves." Laughing, Dave drove away before Jake could say another word.

* * * *

Louie looked up, surprised to see Jake there so early on a Wednesday morning. He followed Jake as he made his way to his office. "What, she threw you out?"

"No. She had to leave early this morning, so I left around one."

"You look mad. What's wrong?"

"Last night, as I left her place, I saw a man running from her steps." He filled Louie in as he started the run on the partial plates. "What did you find?"

"Nothing yet, the search is still running."

"How'd Mia react when you told her?"

"I didn't tell her about this one. I asked Dave not to tell her. Don't look at me like I did something wrong. I'll tell her when she gets back." He stared at Louie, added, "I didn't want to worry her while she's away."

"You're being overprotective. She might be able to shed some light on it. It could be a disgruntled lover."

"When she gets back I'll tell her. Some work here." He tilted his head. "Did anything turn up overnight on Cavilla?"

"No. I'm assuming you got nothing at the bars except a hangover."

"Nothing, not even a hangover. How'd you do last night on the Adams case?"

"I thought of something last night. I called the lab, told them when the Jeff Adams sample comes in I want them to compare the DNA sample from Jeff to his kids, see if there's any match in relationship there."

"Great idea, run with it."

Jake put a call in to Neptune, Florida, and spoke with Chief Beau Taylor. "How'd it go yesterday?" Jake asked.

"As expected—Lola Adams is not a forthcoming woman. She refused to supply her DNA and called her lawyer. Her husband gave his sample immediately and then left her to fend for herself when he went back to work."

"He didn't hang around?"

"Nope, the man's reached the end of his rope with his new improved model. Imagine." Beau laughed. "Me, I would've tossed her back after a week. She's as mean as a catfish on your arm."

Jake laughed. "Well, if my hunch is right, she'll need it to survive in her new home."

"You feel that strongly about her?"

"I do, but no solid evidence yet. And I'm not sure if the husband was in on it."

"Gotcha, I'll keep a guard on her. She was antsy, and I wouldn't put it past her to run."

"I appreciate it, Beau. I got one who ran this week. I don't want another. The results are being rushed. I should have them before the end of the week."

"Take care, Jake."

* * * *

The week dragged for him with Mia gone. The Wagner case was in limbo with Mark Cavilla on the run. The kid had disappeared. They'd checked with each of his friends and relatives and had turned up zilch. The Adams case had become a watch-and-wait game. They reviewed all the statements and facts again. Dissected individual statements and alibis but turned up nothing new. He needed the lab work if he was going to nail a suspect.

"This case...it had to be someone close to her, someone who studied her habits. Everyone but the ex-husband and his new wife were fans of hers," Louie said, frustrated.

"Yep."

"Sophia wants you to come to dinner tonight. I have to warn you, she plans on picking your brain about Mia."

"Did she make gravy?" He called it sauce. His Italian friends called it gravy. No one made it better than Sophia, except for Louie's mom.

"Yes."

"She can ask whatever she likes. Did she make bread too?"

"Naturally."

"I'll be there. I haven't seen the kids since the party."

"No, you've been too busy with your new girlfriend," Louie said.

"So, I have a good excuse."

"You bet."

* * * *

Dinner at the Romanellis' killed one night for Jake. On Thursday night he stayed home, read Mia's manuscript from cover to cover. It was a rare thing for a crime drama to hold his attention, but hers did. Around eleven she called.

"I didn't wake you, did I?"

"No, how's it going?"

"It's…good. The agent is giving good feedback," Mia said, though he picked up a hint of disappointment.

"Mia, I finished reading the book a little while ago, it's great. It's real and it's entertaining. You tell them a reader loved it."

"You loved it?" He could hear in her voice how much it meant to her.

"I did. When will you be coming home?"

"At this point it looks like Saturday."

"Oh."

"Something came up with the family." *Curious,* Jake thought when she gave no details. Why did she always stop short when speaking of her family?

"If I can, I'll give you a call tomorrow night. If not, I'll call when I'm on my way Saturday."

He told her the name of the restaurant, in case she got back sooner than expected.

They talked for another half hour. He didn't want to hang up but he heard the exhaustion in her voice. After the call ended, he wondered again what the deal was with her father. And once again, she'd reminded him how little he knew about her.

* * * *

All week tips poured in on Cavilla but nothing panned out. The seven-thirty reservation Jake made on Saturday night was a bit late for Louie and Sophia, but he hedged his bets—hoping Mia would get back in town by then to join them.

He didn't fool the Romanellis. They knew why he'd picked Woodbury, and the time, and they went along with it.

The waiter had arrived with their dinners when Jake's cell phone vibrated in his pocket. He checked the caller ID and then excused himself. Once out of the main dining room, he answered his phone.

"Hey."

"Is it too late to join you?"

"No. Did you eat?"

"No, I didn't have time. I'll have dessert with you, don't fuss."

Jake walked back to the table with a huge grin on his face. Sophia elbowed Louie.

"Yeah, yeah, I see it."

"Oh, Louie, you're such a romantic." Jake sat back down.

Sophia said, "So how is she?"

"Great. She'll be here in about fifteen minutes to join us." He motioned for the waiter.

"Can I help you, sir?"

* * * *

Mia walked in fifteen minutes later and caused all eyes to turn her way. She wore a royal-blue silk blouse and matching pants. The outfit set off her eyes and hair. Jake couldn't wait to get her home.

Under his breath, Louie said, "Wow." Sophia elbowed him again. "What, don't you agree? Wow," he said again.

"Yes, I do," Sophia said.

Jake stood, greeted her with a kiss. He held out her chair. As soon as she was seated, the waiter appeared at her arm.

"May I get you a drink?"

"Yes, Three Olives Cherry Vodka, with some seltzer," she answered, looking back at Jake. She took his hand, smiled, and turned to greet Louie and Sophia. "I haven't seen the two of you since the party. How are you?"

"Great. How'd it go in New York?" Sophia asked.

"They want me," she said with a smile.

"There isn't a man alive who wouldn't want you. What?" Louie said when Sophia elbowed him again.

"It's a good thing I love you, Louie, or you'd be mincemeat right now." Sophia laughed.

After dinner, Mia suggested they take the dessert to go and have coffee at her house.

In the car Louie turned to his wife. "We're not going right home? We have the house to ourselves until noon tomorrow. Remember? No kids. We don't need dessert," Louie complained.

"Don't worry, Louie, we're still going to celebrate when we get home. I'm not going to pass up a chance to see Mia's house."

Jake had decided earlier to ride with Louie and Sophia to the restaurant, hoping Mia showed up.

At Mia's condo, he climbed out of the passenger seat while Mia unlocked the door leading in from the garage. She walked to the back of the car, opened the trunk, and reached for her suitcases.

"I'll get those for you," Jake said.

"Thanks, you can put them up in the bedroom while I start the coffee." Mia walked to the kitchen at the back of the condo. Jake headed upstairs.

He heard Louie and Sophia come in as he started down the stairs. Sophia complimented Mia's decorating. Louie accepted the offer of coffee.

"This place is great, Mia," Sophia said, poking her head in every room while she followed Mia down the hallway.

"Thanks, I love it."

"You're not afraid out here by yourself?"

"No one bothers me," Mia said.

"Louie told me about the packages you received. It doesn't bother you that someone's stalking you?"

"There's only been one package." She looked from Louie to Jake, as Jake flashed Louie the evil eye.

Jake saw Sophia's embarrassment, her eyes begging for forgiveness. At the moment, he had none in him.

"Sophia's referring to the second package. The one I found when I left here on Tuesday night, Mia," Jake said quietly.

"When were you going to tell me about it?" She put a hand on her hip and raised her brow. It floored him how fast her mood had changed.

"I planned on telling you when you got back from New York. I thought I'd save you the stress until you got home. I'd already closed the door—I didn't see the need to wake you."

"I've spoken to you every night since. Still didn't see the need to inform me?" Her eyes narrowed.

"No. I gave everything to Dave Guerrera, the officer who took the first package. He's been doing extra passes by the condo while you were gone. I planned on telling you when you got back tonight. My mistake," Jake said, defensively.

Her anger hung thickly in the air. She didn't take her eyes off Jake. Mia didn't speak. Her silence said it all. He recognized the look on her face. Not only had Sophia blown it, so had he.

"Well, let me tell you, Lieutenant Carrington, I'm a big girl. One who's quite capable of taking care of herself. I don't need you or anyone else making decisions for me. Also, don't assume you're spending the night. Got it?" Mia said.

"Clearly," he replied, hurt. He turned, headed for the door. It would have been a dramatic exit if he hadn't had to turn and ask Louie and Sophia to join him.

"Are you ready?"

"Yes," Louie replied, his shoulders hunched. His hands in his pocket.

"I'm sorry, Mia. I didn't mean to start anything," Sophia said.

"You didn't. I'm sorry I'm cutting this evening short. Good night." She walked them to the door and slammed it closed once they passed through it.

He stood by the car, waiting for Louie to unlock the door. It was a stressful ride home. Jake cut Sophia off every time she tried to apologize. He also cut Louie off when he tried to smooth out things between them.

When they drove up in front of his house, Jake climbed out of Louie's car. He walked away without a single word to either Sophia or Louie.

Chapter 30

Upset, his reflexes slow, it took a moment too long for Jake to realize he wasn't alone when he walked into his house. The under-counter light in the kitchen put the intruder in the shadows. He assessed the height and voice of the visitor.

"Right there is far enough. Drop your weapon on the floor." The burglar stepped from the shadows.

"I'm going to reach into my holster to get the gun. I'll place it on the floor so it won't go off." He hoped it brought him enough time to grab the gun in his ankle holster. "What do you want?"

"Keep your movement slow and easy. What I want is enough money to get out of this crummy town and for you to leave me the hell alone."

"It's not going to happen, Mark. You took a life."

"Damn you, she wasn't worth all this trouble. How'd you figure it out?"

"Mark, put down your weapon and we'll talk." It looked like a gun he was waving around, but Jake couldn't make out the type or caliber in the darkened room. "Why don't you turn on a light?"

"Shut up. No one tells me what to do. Understand?" Cavilla had him in a sticky position. He was wide open with nothing to hide behind. If he could maneuver into the living without getting shot...

"Yes." Cavilla's voice grated on his nerves. *The whiney brat.* "Mark, I'm going to bend down and put my gun on the floor now."

"For Christ's sake, do it."

Jake leaned down and carefully took the safety off and placed it on the floor. "How'd you get in here?" He hoped Mark followed his left hand while he lifted his pant leg with the right one.

"Fool, you didn't turn on your alarm. Some cop you are." Cavilla snickered. "Nice and easy, stand up."

"Give me a minute, my knee locked up."

"I don't care. Stand now or I shoot."

Jake didn't doubt Cavilla would, either. On the count of three, Jake moved an inch to his right, then grabbed his gun and fired low. Cavilla's screams filled the room. Jake rolled as Cavilla started shooting wildly. A bullet flew over his head as he moved to the left, then right. Jake heard a crash of glass as the mirror by the door shattered. A foot away from Mark, Jake charged him. He took Cavilla down as he wildly emptied his gun into the ceiling. He flipped Cavilla onto his stomach and kept his knee in his back. Damn, his handcuffs were in the bedroom.

Sirens blasted in the distance. Jake hoped a neighbor had called the police when the gun had gone off. A few seconds later the sirens grew louder, their sound blasting away as the patrol cars approached his house. He didn't even have his radio to warn the cops everything was under control. Jake hoped they didn't come in shooting and finish Cavilla's job.

He dragged Mark up by his shirt collar and then put him in a head lock. "Don't make a move. I'll choke you if you fight—you need to understand I won't hesitate," he whispered, tightening his grip on Mark. "Where's your car?"

"Find it yourself," Mark said gasping for breath.

As he made his way over to the front door it flew open. Louie rushed in with his gun leading. "Glad you could make it. I got everything under control."

"If that's the case, why didn't you answer your freakin' phone?" Louie asked.

"I was a little busy. You got your handcuffs on you?"

"Yeah." Louie tossed them to Jake. He caught them with his free hand and placed them on Cavilla.

"They're a little tight," Mark complained.

"No shit," Jake said and walked away from him. "Put him in a patrol car. I'll meet you at the station."

Louie handed Mark off to a patrolman and walked back to Jake. "Are you all right?" he whispered in Jake's ear.

"I feel like a fool. I didn't even turn on my alarm. For Pete's sake, I'll never live this down."

"It's the least of your worries. Hey, I heard on the radio a uniform found Cavilla's car a block over."

Without another word, Louie turned, and walked out. Jake didn't move until he was alone. He walked to the kitchen cabinet over the refrigerator and pulled out the whiskey, then placed it back on the shelf. It wouldn't do to go into the station smelling of alcohol.

* * * *

Jake took his time going into the station to give the CSIs time to work over Mark's car. He let Cavilla sit and stew as he skimmed through Shanna's diary again. He wanted her pain and fear in his head when he questioned Cavilla. In one passage, she described the fear she felt when she had come upon him in her parking lot at school. How he had begged her to get back together. When she had talked to him she'd thought she'd made it clear they were through. At the end of the diary, in what he thought might be Cavilla's handwriting, Mark had scribbled across the page in bold childish lettering, *It was all Shanna's fault.*

Behind the observation glass at Interview Room One Jake and Louie watched as Cavilla and his attorney settled into their seats. The room was not designed for comfort. Four hard, wooden chairs were pulled up to the matching table that had graffiti scratched into it over the years, circa 1936. The stark walls painted in light, putrid, institutional green offered no forgiveness. Imbedded in one wall was a two-way mirror—a suspect would have to have been from Mars not to know of its existence.

Jake's cell vibrated in his pocket.

"Jake, it's Minski from the crime scene investigations. The Cavilla car was a treasure trove of evidence. We have the Wagner girl's blood and the weapon that killed her."

"Thanks, Minski, for rushing it. What kind of weapon?"

"A silk scarf and the billy club that assaulted her. Nail the bastard, Jake."

* * * *

As Cavilla and his attorney sat in silence, Jake and Louie entered the room.

"Do I need to reread you your rights, Mr. Cavilla?" Jake said.

"Lieutenant, we'll stipulate to the reading," Attorney Calvin said. "I also want it on record the police brutality Mark said was perpetrated on him."

"Is that a fact, counselor? You don't want to play that card. Mr. Cavilla broke into my home and held me at gunpoint. I got the advantage and took him down. Isn't that right, Mark?"

"You didn't have to put the cuffs on so tight."

Sniveling bastard, Jake thought. He shrugged his shoulders and looked at the lawyer, who turned away with, if he wasn't mistaken, a grin on his face.

"Okay, let me make a note of who's present and get the housekeeping chores out of the way," Jake said, taking a seat at the table. He had Louie take up a position behind Cavilla.

"Mr. Cavilla, are you aware we found Shanna Wagner's purse and diary in your closet?"

"Yes."

"Would you like to tell us how it got there?"

"How did you find it?"

Attorney Calvin interrupted Mark's reply. "Lieutenant, you haven't stated the charges or what deals are on the table."

"Deals, Calvin? You're kidding, right?"

"No, I'm not."

"Mr. Calvin, your client had in his possession the victim's purse and diary, which places him at the crime scene, as well as the billy club used to violate and beat her, and a bunch of bloody rags, now at the lab for testing and DNA profiling. That's right, Mark," Jake said as he watched Mark's face morph from an expression of arrogance to one of shock. "We got the evidence from your car as well as your house." Jake turned back to the attorney. "There are no deals on the table at this time, though a confession now will work in your client's favor. It'll be up to the district attorney to deal with the both of you." Jake wanted to get the action going so he added, "I heard you killed her because you couldn't get it up. Isn't that right, Mark?"

"You bastard." Cavilla jumped up from his seat. Chains attached to Mark's ankles and fastened to the floor held him in place. Jake nodded to Louie, who walked over to Cavilla and pushed him back in his seat.

"Lieutenant, this interview is over."

"Nice try, counselor. Sit down. Mark, answer my question," Jake said.

"I'd like to end this interview. I need time to speak with the D.A. personally."

"I'm sure you would, but it's not going to happen, John. I'll have Sergeant Romanelli contact him and inform him of your request." Turning to Cavilla, Jake played a hunch. "What kind of drug did you give her, Mark, something to make her horny?"

"Lieutenant, my client is not going to—"

"I could get it up. The bitch was frigid. She made me a laughingstock at work. Why did she even accept a date from me in the first place?" Mark asked. "I can't believe she wanted a dyke over me. Besides, who said I gave her anything?"

"Did you?" Jake asked.

"Mark, don't say another word." Calvin put his hand on Mark's arm.

Inside Jake smiled when Cavilla pushed his attorney's hand away. "Am I going to be executed?"

"It's not up to me, Mark. Did you drug her?" Jake didn't bother to tell Mark that the State of Connecticut had abolished the death penalty in 2015. He didn't see it as his responsibility. Apparently, neither did his attorney.

"I gave her a little something to cooperate. She was so freakin' nasty."

I got you, you bastard. "The charge is murder in the first degree."

"If I confess, do I still have to stand trial?"

"You should field this question, John," Jake told the attorney.

"Mark, we need to talk before you confess," Calvin stressed.

"Counselor, you and your client were given two hours to consult before this interview. What did you do with the time?"

"I want it noted my client is going against his attorney's advice if he confesses."

"Mr. Cavilla, do you understand you're under arrest for the murder and rape of Shanna Wagner?"

"Yes."

"And are you going against your attorney's advice of your own free will?" Jake asked, staring into Cavilla's eyes.

"Yes. I want it to be over with, but I don't want to die."

"I'm sure Shanna Wagner didn't want to die either."

"She wasn't the sweet innocent girl everyone thought she was. She was a total witch and a lesbian."

"Her sexual preference was a valid reason to kill her?" Jake quirked his brow and made a mental note to add hate crime to his list of charges.

"No, no. I want to tell you what happened in my own words. No one's going to put any in my mouth," Mark said.

"Mr. Cavilla, I'm going to tell you again not to speak until we are able to confer," Attorney Calvin said.

"Confer?" Cavilla laughed. "We are conferring. You're fired."

Jake smiled inwardly. He had counted on Cavilla's ego, and it was coming through loud and clear. "Mr. Cavilla, are you asking for a different lawyer at this time?" Jake asked.

"No, I don't need a lawyer."

He'd been waiting for those words. *All righty then, I should have this wrapped before the night is through.*

"Mr. Cavilla, I'm stressing this is not in your best interest," Attorney Calvin said, trying to warn him.

"I'm not stupid. I understand what I'm doing. You're fired." Calvin stood abruptly and left the room.

"Let the record note Attorney Calvin has left the interview," Jake said, looking up at Louie. Louie coughed into his hand to hide his smile behind Cavilla's back. "Mark, when did you first decide to kill Shanna Wagner?"

"I'm going to tell this in my own way. It started with a conversation with Chloe after her arrest. She taunted me and wouldn't answer any of my questions. She more or less said you were coming after me. Why now? Three months have passed, I don't get it." He stared at Jake.

"Evidence is why now."

"I covered myself good. You guys should have found her damn ring in your first search of the Wagner's house. What took you so long?"

Jake stared Cavilla down. Silence filled the room.

Shaking his head, Cavilla continued. "Never mind, it's not important. I read her diary every night. And every night it made me madder. I'd kill her again if I could. I'm sure you'll read all about it after we're done here, but the bitch said some nasty things about me."

Jake interrupted him. "Who?"

"Shanna Wagner, who else?" Jake nodded for Cavilla to continue. "I called her at school and asked her if we could meet and talk. All I wanted to do was talk. But Shanna said no and didn't bother to give me an explanation." Cavilla stopped and took a drink of water from the plastic cup Louie had put on the table before the interview.

"It was Friday night, so I went out for some drinks. The more I drank the angrier I got. Why wouldn't she agree to talk? I left the bar and sat in my car for about a half hour, toking on a joint. The higher I got, the more determined I was to talk to her. I drove up to Storrs."

"Did she agree to talk to you, Mark?" Jake asked.

"No, she was leaving her dorm with some other girls, including her pet dyke, Meryl. They didn't see me. So after they piled into a car, I followed them. They went to a pizza joint and met some guys. I'm sure she was doing them too."

"So she was only a lesbian with you?" Jake gave Cavilla a lopsided smirk.

"Don't put words in my mouth, man. She was bisexual and who cares anyway. I didn't want to be caught outside the pizza joint so I headed back to her dorm and waited for her."

"How long did you wait?"

"Until they got back," Cavilla said.

"An hour, two?"

"It was about an hour and a half."

"I bet you were getting pissed by then?" Jake said. *Ah, premeditation.* Jake almost jumped with joy.

"I was, so I smoked another joint to calm my nerves."

"Okay, go on."

"See, I wanted her to give me another chance. The one time we made love was a disaster. She left crying. When she left, I thought it was my fault and she let me believe it. If she'd talked to me, everything would've been fine. We could've fixed it," Cavilla said. Cavilla looked at the mirrored wall, his eyes unfocused. Jake didn't care where Mark's mind wandered, he wanted the whole story now. He had not one ounce of sympathy for Cavilla. The kid had killed a woman because she had rejected him. *Pull back, Jake. This isn't the time to think about Eva.*

"Mark, what happened the night Shanna died," Jake said, not able to hide his impatience.

"Don't push me, I'm getting to it. It's all related." Cavilla waved his hand in the air in a gesture that had Jake grinding his teeth. *The little bastard assumes he's in control here.* He bit down on his anger. Jake needed Cavilla to detail everything to lock him in.

Mark's eyes lost focus as he continued.

"When she got back to the dorm, Meryl kissed her good-bye and drove off. The other girls went inside. Shanna must have needed something from her car because she headed over to the parking lot. As she leaned into her car, I grabbed her from behind—"

"You planned on raping her?" Jake asked.

"No. No, I told you, I wanted to talk to her. I pushed her into my car because she wouldn't get in it. Then she started yelling at me. Lord, you should've heard her. I panicked. She asked if I was nuts. I told her to shut up because we were going to talk. She screamed that she wasn't going to talk to me today, tomorrow, or ever. I hate her. I told her she humiliated me at work and she owed me this conversation. I told her she made a joke of me and broke my heart as well as screwing with my career. I'd have to find another job to make the jokes go away. She said she didn't understand. We had a couple dates and she'd said nothing to anyone. Shanna didn't understand how anyone at work knew," Mark said.

"Mark, how did they find out at work?"

Mark ignored the question

"You didn't tell a buddy over drinks or say something at lunch like she was frigid?" Louie asked from behind Cavilla.

Cavilla turned to address Louie. "One of the guys at lunch said how she was hot and I might've mentioned it."

Jake pulled Cavilla's attention back to him. "Did you tell him she was frigid, or gay?"

"I might've mentioned bisexual."

"So it was you who made a joke of you and not Shanna?"

"No...yes...no, I didn't mean to. I was mad at her. God." He put his head in his hands. "She was beautiful and smart. Everything I wanted in a wife. But she didn't want me."

"After you got her in the car, what happened?" He wanted to push Mark but didn't dare in case Cavilla shut down.

"I had her by the wrist so she couldn't leave the car and she tried prying my fingers off her arm. Yelling how I was bruising her. Shanna told me if I let her out of the car she wouldn't report me. I didn't trust her, not for one damn second. Lord, my head was pounding and I couldn't think—I reached for the water bottles. I uncapped one and gave it to her. She pushed it back at me. Damn it, she made me madder."

"You gave her the one with the GHB in it?" Jake asked.

"Yeah."

"You understand Gamma-Hydroxybutyrate is an illegal substance?" Jake wanted the full name of the drug on the record.

"Yes."

"What happened when she pushed the bottle away?"

"I jumped on top of her and forced her to drink. She spit it in my face. Before I knew it, I slammed my fist into her face. It took one punch to knock her out. When she started to come to, I forced the bottle to her mouth and poured it in. She started to choke, but she drank enough to feel the effects..." Cavilla stared into space, his eyes narrowed on a spot on the wall. "I tied her hands together."

"How did it affect her, Mark?" Cavilla either didn't hear his question or was ignoring it. Jake asked a second time and waited him out.

"Shanna didn't react like she was supposed to. I drove her to Wilkesbury to a dead-end street I knew. Instead of getting horny, she fought me. The drug made her aggressive. It was easy to control her. She didn't weigh much. I stripped her down and then took the billy club from my trunk. The bitch wanted a stick. I was going to give her a stick."

Heat burned his face as Jake tried to control his anger. He pushed down his temper as he listened to Cavilla's account of the night Shanna died. *Bastard*, if they weren't on video he'd smash the kid's face into the concrete wall and violate him with a hard-wooden stick to teach him a lesson. The

M.E.'s report flashed back into his head, recounting each trauma Shanna had endured with the club.

Yes, the bastard deserves his turn at the end of the stick. He could only hope he got it in prison.

"What happened next?" Jake struggled for control, his temper on a thin leash.

"Even stoned she kept pushing me away, fighting me—I lost it. Minutes later, I think, it was like I came back to myself and realized what I'd done. She was dead. I keep water and soap in my trunk to wash the car, so I pulled it out, along with a tarp and a mini vac, and I dragged her to one of the houses being built and washed her down to get rid of any evidence. I cleaned under her nails and combed and vacuumed the body for any stray hairs. I wasn't going to leave my DNA. I watch those shows." Cavilla stopped and took another sip of his water.

"What did you do next?"

"I dragged her to the woods and rolled her down the hill. After that I went to the bar to establish my alibi because I was there earlier and wanted the bartender to remember me."

"So instead of calling the police and an ambulance, in case she wasn't dead, you cleaned her and dumped her in the woods like trash?" Jake said.

"Yes."

Jake saw the anger he felt mirrored on Louie's face. The room filled with a heavy silence as he let the interview run through his mind. He had a few more things he needed to get on the record.

"When did you write in her diary it was her fault?"

"Last night after I spoke with Chloe, all she had to do was talk to me, but no, she was too good for me. It pissed me off."

Good, he's showing no remorse. It will help hang him. "Louie, do you have any questions for Mark?"

"Why did you keep the ring, her purse, and her diary?"

"I loved her. I wanted something of her with me always," Cavilla whispered.

"You don't comprehend the word love or what it is, Mark," Louie said as he unlocked the leg chains and yanked Cavilla to a standing position then ushered Cavilla to the door to the uniforms waiting outside the room.

Drained, Jake watched as they left the room—a predator stopped. But he knew full well another would follow right behind this one.

One more victory, Eva, though hollow. God, I wish I could stop them before they take more innocent lives.

* * * *

When Louie came back from booking he came into Jake's office. Jake opened his bottom drawer and took out his bottle of Johnny Walker Blue. He poured two glasses, handed one to Louie.

"To closure." Jake raised his glass in a toast.

"To closure." Glasses clinked before each began downing their drinks.

"I better give the Wagners a call," Jake said.

"Okay. I'll start the report while you do that."

Jake filled Joe Wagner in on the arrest though he withheld some details. He gave them nothing more than what he planned on giving in his press release. "Cavilla's lawyer stated he's going to order a psych exam for him. But the thing is, he fired his lawyer. I'm sure this will still happen. Either way, Mr. Wagner, it should still come to trial within months."

"Thank you, Lieutenant. I understand we came to blows a lot. I'm sorry. You weren't working for us, but for Shanna," Joe Wagner said.

"I'm sorry, too. Sometimes a murder investigation steps on the survivors. Do you want to tell Chloe or do you want me to?"

"No, I'll do it. She needs to stay away from you."

"Thanks." Jake hung up and then walked to the captain's office to update him.

While Shamus finished a phone conversation, Jake stood by McGuire's window and looked out over the downtown area. The captain hung up and turned his attention to Jake.

"The samples have been collected from Spaulding. The commissioner put a rush on the results. We hope to have them back within a month or two."

"You said either today or tomorrow. Why wasn't I notified?"

"For the same reason, you can't touch the case. It's a conflict of interest."

It doesn't matter. One way or another Spaulding will pay for killing Eva. It was his duty and his promise to her.

Chapter 31

Around one on Sunday morning, Jake stepped back into his house after working Cavilla most the night. Wired, unable to sleep, he fidgeted around all night and day. He needed to go into the station and finish his reports but he had no energy to do so. He wanted to call Mia and apologize, but every time he reached for the phone, he got angry. She was the one being unreasonable, not him. Run her life, his ass. For crying out loud, all he'd done was try to make things easier for her. Last night Louie had tried to speak to him about it, but he pushed him away. He'd already called three times this morning, and it wasn't even noon.

* * * *

Mia woke at ten o'clock, feeling groggy. She hadn't slept well last night. Her anger at Jake hadn't abated. How dare he assume he could make decisions for her. She didn't need another interfering man in her life. Her father was one too many.

She was sorry she had embarrassed him in front of his friends, but Friday's dinner with her parents hadn't turned out well, thanks to her father's ambush. She still couldn't understand why he had invited her former, low-life, fiancé to join them. From there things deteriorated to the point of no return. Her blood boiled even now at the audacity of it.

She and Logan Andrews had gone back and forth over her responsibilities as defined by him. He had taunted her about her meager job and her book— her tolerance level had peaked. She had pushed away from the table, said her good-byes, gave her mother a peck on the cheek, and started to walk out. She refused to put up with her father's criticism any longer. Over her shoulder she had asked, "Father, did you send me a dead animal as a way of scaring me home?" She hadn't waited for his answer.

* * * *

Wrapped in his reports on Monday morning, Jake heard a noise at his door. He looked up to see Louie standing there. "What's up, Louie?"

"You okay? I called yesterday."

"I didn't feel like talking to anyone. I still don't."

"I'm here if you change your mind."

An awkward moment of silence fell over the room. Jake was grateful when the phone rang, saving him from having to come up with a reply. "Lieutenant Carrington, this is Joanne Gale from the UConn Medical Center. I have the results on the samples you wanted rushed."

"What are they?"

"I'm sending you an email now," Joanne said.

You're driving me nuts. Get to the freakin' point. "Thanks, Joanne, what are they?"

"Both samples match the samples taken from the car," she said.

"Both?" Jake asked, surprised.

"Yes, both."

"What sample matched who?"

"The hair fibers matched Jeff Adams. The skin cells, saliva, and sweat matched Lola Adams."

"Thanks again, Joanne. When should I see the email?"

"It should be there now. I already sent it."

The email popped into his inbox. He printed out two copies of the report, one of which he handed to Louie. He kept the other for the murder book.

"What do you think? According to Beau Taylor, he verified Jeff Adams's schedule with his boss for said weekend. He couldn't be in two places at once."

"Do you think Lola planted it there to incriminate him?" Louie asked.

"I don't know what to think except that we're going to be heading down to Florida within the next couple of hours to see for ourselves. I'm going in to talk to the captain." Jake got up from his chair and started out of the office.

"I'll start the paperwork on the request for flights." Louie grabbed Jake's arm before he could leave the office. "Jake, please give Mia a call and straighten things out."

"Let it be, Louie."

Jake explained everything to the captain. McGuire asked, "Are you going to call Chief Taylor and tell him the results?"

"No, he said he interviewed the manager at the restaurant where Adams worked. He verified his work schedule for the weekend of the sixteenth. I'm inclined to trust him, but I want to verify his alibi for myself."

"I'll get the paperwork ready for extradition. Have Katrina take care of the flight and hotel scheduling."

"Louie's already on it."

* * * *

Jacksonville, Florida, temperatures were in the mid-nineties when they landed. Back in Connecticut they were still in the low seventies, even this late in June. After Jake signed for the rental car, Louie took the keys from the clerk and loaded their bags into the truck. It was a short drive to Neptune, without any stops until they reached the police station. The receptionist/dispatcher seemed surprised to see them when he slipped his badge on the counter.

"Hi, Lieutenant," she said in her southern drawl as she studied it. "You look like you sound."

"Good or bad?" he joked. The room was filled with Florida sunshine, some from the windows, the rest from Sammy.

She laughed. "Good." Shifting back to work mode, she said, "Do you want to see the chief? He didn't say you were expected."

"Things came down fast. We booked our flights and hoped we'd catch the chief before the end of his day. Is he here?" Jake said.

"Yes, he's in his office. I'll go get him." Before walking down the hall, he noticed she had switched off her computer screen.

Jake thought she too looked like she sounded—a cute, petite blonde, standing no taller than five-three, with a voluptuous figure. If a person didn't look directly into her eyes they'd miss the cop, the worldly knowledge of the underbelly of what coexisted alongside decent law abiding citizens.

Beau Taylor followed Sammy back down the hall to greet them. At six-two with sun-bleached blond hair and pale blue eyes, Taylor's swagger reminded Jake of John Wayne. A thin and lanky frame didn't fool Jake.

He saw the biceps peeking out from under his shirt sleeves and figured he could handle himself in a fight.

Grinning, Taylor walked toward Jake with his hand out. "You must be Lieutenant Jake Carrington," Beau said.

"How'd you tell me from the sergeant here?"

"I'll use the dreaded word in law enforcement now. I profiled you. Carrington, Irish. The sergeant, he looks Italian." He pronounced it Eye-Talian. "Am I right or wrong?"

"You're right. Chief Beau Taylor, Sergeant Louie Romanelli, my partner." They took Beau's hand in turn.

"It's nice to meet you, Louie. What do I owe this unexpected pleasure to, Connecticut?"

"Things came down fast today. A couple of hours ago we got the DNA samples back. They match both Mr. and Mrs. Adams—hair fibers from him—skin cells, saliva, and sweat from her. We'd like you to interview them again with us, since you have such a great rapport with Lola. We'd also like to interview the restaurant manager, and recheck Adams's alibi," Jake said.

"Why didn't you call? I could have checked it all out for you and saved you a trip," Beau asked, watching Jake with a trained eye.

"To be honest, I wanted to get here and interview them myself. I always like the element of surprise. If you went to speak with them again, they might have taken off. I didn't want to chance it, Beau."

"You don't trust me, Connecticut?" Beau asked, still not breaking eye contact.

"I do, Beau. I can't put my finger on it, but something's not adding up. How would you have handled it?"

"Probably the same way." He smiled at Jake. "Let me contact my officers. I have one watching the house and another one watching the restaurant."

"Can we surprise them too?" Jake asked.

"We can, if you tell me why."

"Jeff Adams is good with electronics. He might have a police scanner in his home and could be monitoring your broadcasts. I don't want to take any chances."

"Leave your rental here. We'll take my car. The house is about six miles away, the restaurant four miles. We'll hit the house first. I want you to have the pleasure of meeting Mrs. Adams—"

"She left quite an impression on you?" Jake interrupted.

"She did. In Desert Storm, I didn't take as much fire as I did from her. She's the queen of mean."

"Do we need our cups?" Louie joked.

Beau started laughing. "I don't think it would hurt to wear one around her. I can tell you her husband has no balls left. She runs the show there."

Chapter 32

The three of them pulled up alongside an unmarked car. Beau got out of the car, and walked over to speak with his officer. He came back and sat in the driver's seat.

"Officer Hatcher said Mrs. Adams never left her home this morning. Are you ready?"

"Yes, are you ready to arrest her if it warrants it?" Jake asked.

"Yes, you have your paperwork in order, correct?"

"Correct," Jake said, handing it to Beau to review.

After reading it Taylor said, "Let's get it done."

As a unit, the three of them approached the front door. Taylor rang the bell. Mrs. Lola Adams answered. She couldn't have been more than twenty-eight. Her hair was streaked with blond over black, heavy makeup caked on her eyes. She wore short-shorts and a tube top which barely contained her breasts, along with her ornate sandals. *Cheap with a capital C*, Jake thought.

"What do you want?" She spoke to Beau, ignoring him and Louie.

"Mrs. Adams, may we come in?" Beau said.

"Why?"

"These officers have some questions for you."

"Who are they?" He and Louie didn't say a word, happy to let Beau run the show.

Beau ignored her question and asked again, "Can we come in, Mrs. Adams?"

"And if I say no, what will you do?"

"I'll handcuff you right here in the street for all your neighbors to see. Then I'll call for a patrol car. I'll make sure he has his lights and sirens on too. We wouldn't want anyone to miss the show. Any neighbor who missed the handcuffing will get to see you placed in the patrol car. Am I clear?" Beau towered over Lola. Jake thought it a great stare. It even put the fear of God in him.

"Oh, come in." Lola played with her necklace as she waved them in. "This is ridiculous. I'm going to call the lawyer again. Sit down and don't touch anything." She started walking toward the kitchen in the back of the house, muttering, "I had an easier life when she was alive."

"Excuse me, Mrs. Adams, did you say something?" Beau smiled at Jake. She yelled from the kitchen, "No."

"I didn't think so," Beau said, turning toward Jake again. "Didn't I tell you? Delicate creature."

Jake stifled a laugh because Lola Adams had returned to the room.

Louie said to her, "Mrs. Adams, is your lawyer coming?"

"He'll be here in ten minutes. In the meantime, don't touch anything while I continue my chores."

"Excellent, I'm glad he's available on such short notice," Louie said.

"He's always available to me," she said.

All three exchanged a look, not bothering to acknowledge her comment. They sat around and no one spoke while they waited on the lawyer. Lola left the room and didn't offer them anything, not even a glass of water.

Jake called out, "Is your husband home?"

"No, he's working. Does he need to be here?"

"No, we want to speak with you first," Jake said.

She walked back into the room with a dishrag dangling in her hand. "And you are?"

"When your lawyer gets here, we'll tell you." *Two can play this game.*

It took the lawyer thirty minutes to get there, not ten. Jake could tell Lola wasn't happy with him. She showed him no mercy as she dragged him into the kitchen when he arrived. In the living room, the three of them heard her giving the lawyer a piece of her mind.

Lola and her attorney re-entered the living room after five minutes of yelling at each other. The introductions began.

Beau greeted the lawyer by his first name. After all, it was a small town. "Hey, Wayne."

"Beau." A small man, Wayne Ford stood five-four, weighing in at a hundred sixty pounds. Fortyish, he wore his salt-and-pepper hair cut close to his scalp.

"Jake, Louie, this is Wayne Ford, attorney at law. Wayne, this is Lieutenant Jake Carrington and Sergeant Louie Romanelli of the Wilkesbury,

Connecticut, Police Department." Beau finished the introductions as they watched Lola's reaction. She didn't disappoint.

"Why are you here in Florida?" she demanded, springing from the couch.

"We have a warrant for your arrest in the murder of Chelsea Adams," Jake said.

"What are you, assholes? I didn't kill anyone," she said. "Wayne, can they do this to me?"

"Sit down, Lola. Lieutenant, can I have the warrant?" Jake handed Ford a copy. Wayne took his time reviewing it. "It's in order, Lola," he said after ten minutes.

Lola and Wayne seemed quite intimate with each other.

"Florida doesn't have to give me up. Right, Wayne?" Lola asked.

"We have reciprocal agreements with Connecticut, Mrs. Adams. They did their homework. All their paperwork is in order for your transfer into their custody. We're going to take you to the station. There they'll process you and question you further." Chief Taylor answered instead of Wayne. "You can fight extradition, but I don't recommend it."

"Why not?"

"Because Connecticut repealed the death penalty, Florida hasn't."

Daggers flew from her eyes as Lola stared her attorney down. "I need a glass of water." Lola got up and walked into the kitchen.

The four of them sat there waiting for her to come back into the room. After a few minutes Beau answered a knock at the front door. He invited his female officer into the house. The patrolwoman had a tight grip on a barefooted Lola, who was screaming at the top of her lungs.

"A stupid move, Mrs. Adams, you've added an extra charge to the list the lieutenant has."

Chief Taylor gave his officer her instructions, explaining she needed to stay with the prisoner until their return. "I'm suing you all for treating me like this," Lola kept yelling as the officer cuffed her and dragged her away.

Taylor informed the attorney that he had about an hour to talk with his client before they got back to the station. First, they wanted to search the premises.

After completing the search, the three of them headed to the restaurant where Jeff Adams worked and took him in for questioning. Evidence on him was thin, a single hair. The evidence against Lola was solid. In their discovery process, they had unearthed her plane tickets, her hotel bill for the weekend in April, the statement from her friend, her DNA from the sweat and saliva she had left behind in the car. They sent Jeff Adams to the station in a patrol car, while they questioned his manager again.

Under questioning, he didn't change his story. Jeff Adams had worked the whole weekend. The manager saw him there. No one had punched him in and no one punched him out. His time card proved he got paid for the whole weekend.

"I'd offer you our security tapes, but we reuse them every thirty days. If you'd asked sooner…" The restaurant manager shrugged his shoulders. "It wouldn't have been a problem. I've been the manager here for six years, Beau. I wouldn't lie for an employee. They come and they go, as you know. Jeff Adams is one of the more reliable ones. Can you keep me in the loop? Please call me as soon as possible if I have to replace him," the manager said.

"Thanks, Brian, will do. He's only being questioned at this time," Taylor said.

They interviewed Jeff Adams. He didn't want a lawyer. He stressed he had worked all weekend. Louie took a seat across from Jeff. Taylor and Jake stood on either side of the door.

"Jeff, can you tell me how your hair fibers were discovered in a car in Connecticut? The car we found Chelsea's body in?" Louie asked.

"You're lying. I was here in Florida and was at work most of the time. I haven't seen Chelsea since I moved here. When we would talk on the phone it was about the kids." Sweat poured down Adams's face. When they handed him the receipts to review, Adams had to wipe his face and eyes to read them.

"Do you always sweat this much, Jeff?" Jake asked.

Jake loved working with Louie. Their natural rhythm complemented each other. Jake felt Beau's stare. He turned his head and exchanged a look with him.

"I do down here. The humidity kills me," Adams said, wiping his hands across his face again.

"We're indoors, Jeff, and the air-conditioning is on," Louie said.

The room filled with silence. Jake pushed off the wall where he stood next to Beau and asked, "What information do you have on Chelsea's death, Jeff?"

"I don't have any. I'm not involved. How could I? I'll tell you again, I worked here all weekend."

"You keep repeating yourself, Jeff. You sent Lola to Connecticut to do the deed, while you stayed here to cover yourself?" Jake said as he took a seat next to Louie.

Adams jumped out of his seat. "What, are you crazy? I'd never hurt Chelsea. She's great. I mean—"

Taylor walked behind Jeff, pushed him into the chair.

"If she was great, why'd you divorce her?" Jake asked.

"I'm an ass, that's why," Adams whispered.

"Excuse me?" Jake said.

"I said, I'm an ass," Adams said, louder. "Life got too comfortable, boredom set in. This young thing came on to me at work. Well, it got out of hand. Before I could blink, I'm getting a divorce, and Chelsea and I are in the fight of our lives. It was a helluva time for her to get mean. She gave it to me good. Chelsea took everything."

Changing tactics, Louie asked, "Do you think one of the kids killed her for the money?"

He jumped up again, going after Louie. "Don't you dare say anything about my kids—they love their mother. They'd never hurt her." He was breathing hard when he finished, face bright red, his sweating increased. Jake and Beau grabbed Jeff by the arms and shoved him back in his seat.

"Do you have a heart condition, Jeff?" Jake asked, ignoring Jeff's outburst.

"No."

"You stated Lola visited her friend in Miami on April sixteenth for the whole weekend." Jake looked at Adams, figuring they'd have to call in the paramedics soon.

"She said she went to Miami to visit her friend."

"And you believed her?" Louie asked.

"Yes, why wouldn't I?" Jeff said.

Jake dropped the airline tickets, the hotel bill, and the charge slips on the table.

Adams picked them up and started reading them. He looked up at Jake then back down at the receipts a couple of times before he focused on Jake's face.

"What are you saying?"

"I think it's obvious, Jeff. Lola went to Connecticut on the weekend of the sixteenth. She lied to you. You're going to sit there and tell me you didn't have a clue? Come on, no one's that stupid," Jake finished.

"I guess I am," Jeff stated before he started hyperventilating.

Beau called for the medics.

* * * *

At the soda machine in the hallway they each got a drink while they waited for the medics to transport Adams.

"Well, fun, fun, fun. What do you think Lola will do when we tell her Jeff's been rushed to the hospital?" Beau asked.

"Let's go find out," Jake tossed a smirk over his shoulder.

"I have a feeling she's not going to be too concerned," Louie said.

"Oh, Louie, you have such a negative outlook on people," Jake said, poking him in the side.

"Yeah, years of dealing with the earth's scum," he replied, shrugging his shoulders.

"I hear ya," Beau said.

With their best cop faces in place, the three of them walked into the interview room holding Lola and her attorney. Wayne Ford jumped up as soon as they entered. "Why have you made us wait this long? What's going on?"

Beau nodded to the officer at the door and dismissed her. He turned back to the lawyer.

"Wayne, we had a medical emergency and took care of it first." He addressed Lola Adams. Jake noted Lola's casual demeanor. She lounged in her chair, as if it were a bar stool. *Takes all kinds*, he thought.

"Mrs. Adams, your husband had some kind of an attack while being interviewed. We had to call the paramedics. Jeff's on his way to the hospital," Chief Taylor said.

"What's wrong with him?" She leaned forward.

"Not known at this time."

"Is that why you kept me waiting?" She patted her hair.

"Yes."

"I see. You interviewed him first?" she asked, annoyed. All thoughts of her husband were gone.

"Yes," Beau said.

"What did he tell you?" She leaned forward again.

"This is not how it works, Mrs. Adams," Jake interrupted. "We'll ask the questions, you answer them."

"And if I don't want to?" Lola sat back, draped an arm over the chair next to her.

"We return you to lockup, where you will stay until we transport you to Connecticut," Jake said, staring her down.

"Ask your questions." Her scrunched up forehead reminded Jake of her mother.

"You were in Connecticut the weekend of April sixteenth. Did you kill Chelsea Adams?" Jake asked.

"No."

"No, you were not in Connecticut or no, you didn't kill Chelsea Adams?" Louie asked.

"No to both questions."

Gotcha! Jake handed her the receipts for the airline ticket, her charge cards, and the hotel bill. He watched shock register on her face.

"Where'd you get these?" Lola slapped her hands on the table.

"Mrs. Adams, we're not playing games here. A woman lost her life because someone thought they had the right to take it. Now, I'll ask again, were you in Connecticut on the sixteenth of April and did you kill Chelsea Adams?" Jake asked again.

"Yes, I visited a friend in Connecticut. Why would I kill Jeff's ex?"

"You tell me."

"No reason."

"What did you do in Connecticut?" Louie asked, waiting for the lie.

"I visited a friend," she said, acting bored. Jake watched her take control of her emotions.

"What's her name?"

"Who said it's a woman?" She played him, or tried. Jake didn't buy it.

"Who's your friend, Lola?" Jake asked.

"Katy Bonita."

"You spent the whole weekend with her?"

"Yes, I did."

Jake handed her the hotel bill. She and her attorney looked at it. Putting their heads together, they whispered to each other before Lola answered.

"I stayed in the hotel on Friday night, because I got in late. On Saturday, I stayed at Katy's."

"What did you do on Friday night?" Jake asked.

"What do you mean?"

"Did you go out?" Louie asked, taking over the questioning.

"I went down to the hotel bar for a little while." Lola looked between them, not sure who to address.

"No, you didn't. We questioned the bartenders, showed your picture around. No one remembers seeing you," Louie said.

"I can't help it if I'm not memorable." She shrugged her left shoulder.

"Come on, Lola, I expected better from you. I'm disappointed," Jake said.

"You think you know me?"

"We run into your type all the time," Louie jumped in, baiting her.

"Yeah, what type is that?"

"'The world owes me' type," Louie said.

"What do you know, you bastard? My father drank to shut out my hard-ass mother, and ignored me. Don't act like you understand me."

They didn't get much more from her. They decided not to spend the night in Florida. Beau sent for a female officer to accompany them to Connecticut. They arranged transportation to the airport and thanked Beau for his hospitality. Taylor would question Jeff Adams again, and pinpoint his movements on April sixteenth as soon as the doctors released him from the hospital.

Touching down in Hartford at eleven PM, exhausted after twelve hours on the road, Jake saw no rest in their near future. They still needed to deliver the prisoner to the station and process the paperwork. He picked up his car up from the short-term lot, then drove to the station and turned custody of Lola Adams over to the duty officer. Before he headed to his office, he had a uniform take the Florida officer to the Marriot for the night. After thanking her, he made plans to take her to the airport in the morning. After another hour of paperwork, he told Louie to call it quits for the night.

On their way out, Jake asked, "Do you think it'll stick?"

"I hope so. Our evidence is solid. She's no Cavilla. She won't confess," Louie said.

"No, she won't. Do you think her husband knew?"

"It was hard to read him."

"It was." Jake had never gotten a vibe from him.

Chapter 33

When Jake got home, he fell on his bed fully clothed and passed out. He never listened to his messages until morning. Around six, he got up and showered before he went into the kitchen to start the coffee. With it brewing, he cracked a couple eggs into a pan. As they started to cook, he turned from the stove to reach for the pepper and noticed the flashing light on his answering machine. He hit play.

"Mr. Carrington, it's Doctor Glass. Tomorrow I have to turn the dog over to the humane society and wanted to check in with you before I did, since you showed an interest in her. Please give me a call."

Jake wrote down the vet's number. The next message started playing as he turned back to the stove to flip the eggs. His body went rigid as Mia's voice filled the kitchen.

"Hi, Jake, it's Mia. I wanted to call to apologize for my rudeness on Saturday. I could have handled my anger better. I'm sorry. I understand you thought you were protecting me and doing something nice, but I'm not helpless—" Her voice cut off. The machine moved to the third message, and Mia's voice continued.

"I don't want to end this on a bad note. I need my independence. I can't be with someone who wants to control me or protect me. When it comes to me I make the decisions. No one else. It was a rough visit with my parents. Though it isn't an excuse, it affected my mood more than I thought. I'd like the opportunity to discuss this with you in person, because I'm not a coward. You do deserve an explanation—" The machine cut off the message again.

On the fourth message, Mia finished up her speech. "When you get this, Jake, please give me a call. I'd like to schedule a time for us to discuss this issue."

The machine went dead.

He poured another cup of coffee. As he sipped it, he debated. Should he call her back? The smoke alarm started blasting as smoke filled the air. Turning to the stove, grabbed the pan, and burnt his hand and dropped it back on the stove. Eggs ruined, he threw them away. He picked up a towel and waved it under the smoke alarm until it stopped blaring. He picked up his cup and took a sip. What was wrong with him? How could one woman make him react this way? Days ago, he'd realized he loved her. It seemed like years now. Although he understood where Mia was coming from, he still believed he'd done what was best for her.

And he couldn't let the dog die. Brigh deserved a chance after all she'd been through. Jake left a message for the vet.

"Doctor Glass, I'll take Brigh, but I'll need to meet with you to understand her needs and treatment. It's been a while since I had a dog. Please give me a call tomorrow at the station. I'd like to schedule some time with you and Brigh." He left his number. Lord, he had to be crazy, adopting a dog now.

Unaware of the time, he dialed Mia's number. He contemplated hanging up, but she answered on the third ring, in a sleepy voice, before he got the chance. "Mia, I'm sorry. I woke you?"

"What time is it? Jake?"

He looked over at the clock on the stove and winced. "It's around six. Louie and I went to Florida yesterday to pick up a suspect. We didn't get back until midnight. I got your message a few moments ago." *Why am I apologizing?*

There was an awkward silence. Where did they go from there?

"Jake, I'm sorry about Saturday night—the way I handled it. I'd like the opportunity to explain in person."

"I'd like an explanation. I never meant to hurt you, Mia," he said.

"When's a good time for you to meet with me?"

"I can do it after work today."

"Around seven?"

"Fine."

"I'll meet you at the Four Seasons for a drink."

"No. Come to my house. I don't want to do this in public, Mia." He didn't want to be embarrassed by her again.

She seemed to understand. "All right, I'll be at your house at seven then."

* * * *

At seven on the dot, Mia rang the bell. Jake opened the door and let her in. No kiss or hug this time. Tension showed in her face and shoulders. He asked if she'd be more comfortable in the kitchen or the living room. She picked the kitchen. He got her a cup of coffee, and placed pastries on the table.

She smiled down at the pastry. "I guess I'll start. First I'll give you some background." She looked over at him. He hadn't moved since they had sat down. He locked his gazed on hers.

Unnerved, she continued, "Jake, I come from a powerful family, one who owns a lot of things, including a big publishing house. I could have published my book years ago, but I didn't want any favors from my father. When I get published it will be because I've earned it, and the book is good. It won't be based on my surname.

"Needless to say, when a man is as powerful as my father, he sometimes forgets his children are not subsidiaries of his business empire. He likes to wield his control over everyone and everything." She recapped the dinner, the ambush, and how she hoped she'd put an end to the ten-year war with her father. She even explained her suspicion that her father was behind the dead animals.

"I wanted to be alone, to rethink my choices. I still came up with the same answer—with one variation. I want you in my life, because I care for you. When I saw you Saturday, my whole body lit up. I've never felt like this toward anyone else.

"When Sophia said you withheld something from me, something I had a right to know, well, I felt hurt and betrayed again. You acted like my father, like you had the right to take control. I can't—no, I won't, give anyone control over me, Jake. I want you to understand, though I care for you, I can't commit to anything more permanent." Wiping the tears from her face, she waited him out.

* * * *

Jake sat there, processing what Mia had said, formulating his own answer.

"You want it both ways, but you can't have it," he said.

"No, I don't."

"Yes, you do. You called me first instead of the local police when the package with the dead animal first appeared. You wanted me to take care of it. You also called me when Chloe stalked you. You're sending me mixed signals."

"Chloe was a different situation," Mia said, trying to defend her position.

"I don't want control over you, Mia. Life isn't fun, if it's not equal. I tried to help, nothing more. You humiliated me in front of my friends, because you were angry. You gave no thought to anyone else. You acted like a spoiled brat—no, don't interrupt me. I almost didn't call you back...I shouldn't tell you this—hell—I love you. I came to the realization while you were away. But I don't see how it can work out either." They sat there in silence for awhile. With nothing left to say, Mia got up, and walked around the table to Jake. Bending down, she kissed him on the cheek.

"I'm sorry, Jake." She left the kitchen, heading toward the front door, tears rolling down her face.

Jake followed her. He took her in his arms, kissed her with all his pent-up frustration.

"I'm sorry too." He wiped her tears with his thumb then released her. His eyes burned as she walked out the door—out of his life.

Deep in his heart, he knew they'd be together someday. Mia needed to come to the same conclusion. He'd bide his time before he went after her.

She'd better not take too long to decide.

All the Hidden Sins

Don't miss the next gripping Jake Carrington thriller by Marian Lanouette.

Coming soon from Lyrical Underground,
an imprint of Kensington Publishing Corp.

Keep reading to enjoy an intriguing excerpt . . .

Chapter 1

"What am I going to do with you, Brigh?"

Jake Carrington stared down the brown-eyed beauty, then bent over to wipe the floor with the cleaner and paper towels. What a way to spend his much-needed day off. The dog had a nervous bladder, which let loose every time the doorbell rang. *What was I thinking adopting a dog now?* Oh, he knew what he was doing. *We each understand cruelty.* They made quite the pair. Brigh learning to trust again, and him, trying to keep his mind occupied while dealing with the possible release of George Spaulding, the man convicted of killing his sister. Then there was Mia, the love of his life who had dumped him. He missed her though she wasn't an easy woman to get along with. It had taken only one look into Brigh's big, chocolate eyes, for the dog to own him lock, stock, and barrel.

The bell rang again. Jake pointed to Brigh before he started toward the door. "Go lie down." Trembling, she inched her way to her bed. With one last look at the dog, Jake turned and opened the door.

"Why didn't you answer the door?" his partner, Sergeant Louie Romanelli, asked.

"Me and Brigh were having a conversation on protocol."

Louie scratched his chin, staring first at Jake then at Brigh.

This is all Louie's fault anyway. He pushed Brigh on me. Jake studied his friend and partner as he walked in the house. With his olive complexion and brown hair and eyes, Louie was his opposite in every way except for height and weight. He was the one man Jake would go through a door with and never give it a second thought.

Brigh turned her big doe eyes up at him as if she knew what he was thinking. Not for one minute did he regret his decision to adopt her, but, it was going to take some big-time adjustments for the both of them before they got used to each other. At least the dog occupied his thoughts and pushed Mia out. And what was he going to do about her? Jake bent and gave Brigh a rub between the ears.

The two men went into Jake's comfortably furnished living room.

"I thought Brigh and I should get acquainted with each other," Louie said. "LJ will be over later to play with her. This way they'll get used to each other for her walks."

Louie's teenage son bit at the chance to make some money. Jake hired him to walk the dog after school to keep Brigh from getting lonely. It was also insurance he'd have no surprises waiting for him when he got home from work.

"I'm glad he's agreed to walk her every day after school. Brigh's one skittish dog, she hates to be alone."

"It's been quiet, don't you think?"

"After dealing with the last two cases, I don't mind the quiet. I'm enjoying the down time. It's giving me time to adjust to the addition of the Missing Persons Department."

"Yeah, anything interesting there?"

The missing person's case he was looking into intrigued him. He'd bet the house the guy was dead.

"A few cases I'm reviewing there." Jake sat on the couch. Brigh inched over and laid her head upon his lap. He stroked a hand over her coat.

As Louie approached, Brigh's body shook like a tree in a storm. "Shush, it's all right. Louie, sit for a few minutes here but don't touch her."

"Have you heard from Mia?" Louie asked.

"No, and I told you, the subject's off limits."

Louie shrugged.

"Now start to pet Brigh while I'm holding her. Once she gets used to you, I'm going to head to the pet store."

"You want me to babysit your dog?" Louie tossed him a pained look.

"Yes, until LJ shows up."

"Jake, it's a dog. She'll be fine on her own. Besides, I need to run some errands for Sophia."

"Then I'll take her with me."

Louie cocked his head to the side, studied him, and then left without another word. Alone, Jake and Brigh gauged each other.

"I'm not going to baby you." Brigh licked his face. *Crap, the dog already has me wrapped around her paws.*

On the ride to the store, Brigh stuck her nose out the window. After he parked, he lowered the window for Brigh and then poured some water into the dish he'd brought along for her. Inside the pet store, he picked up a few chew toys and more dog food. If he didn't gain control, he'd buy out the whole damn store for the dog. Deciding he had enough stuff, he got in line to check out.

A riot of red curls greeted him. He wasn't one for redheads, but he wanted to see the face all that hair belonged to. A small boy darted between him and the woman.

"Mom, can I get this for Zelly?"

He got his first look of the woman's face when she turned to speak to the child. Deep green eyes stared down at the boy. Her bowed mouth firmed as she spoke. "Trevor, we have enough stuff for the cat. Put it back. And apologize to the man for pushing by him."

"He's fine," Jake said.

"Sorry, mister."

The kid pushed past him. Jake smiled at the woman before she turned back to the clerk to continue checking out.

He paid the kid at the counter, headed to his car, and put his all purchases, except for the chew toy, in the trunk. He unwrapped the rubbery toy and placed it in front of Brigh. Once he was sure Brigh was okay, he walked across the lot to the grocery store. He had to eat too.

* * * *

Kyra Russell brought Trevor back to his father's place. A depressing action—it ripped at her heart as she left him there.

"You're welcome to come in," Tom Russell said.

"Trevor, give Mommy a kiss. And I'll see you on Wednesday." She wrapped her arms around her son.

"We could be a family again if you'd get help."

She swallowed the barb that jumped to her lips. Instead she said, "We've been over this, Tommy. Leave it be." She released Trevor and left with a broken heart.

She didn't remember when she'd given her soul to the devil. But she had. Leaving Trevor behind proved it. Her life, her son, her marriage had been destroyed by no one but her. She pulled the car from the curb. Thoughts of her cold, empty condo pulled her mood lower. Without her son, the place always reminded her of the morgue. Noise and people were what she needed. Turning the car around, she headed to the casino.

Stepping into the lobby from the garage elevator, the cheap glitz, the noise, the smoke seeped into her bones, and relaxed her. Ah, she was home and better yet, her favorite machine stood empty. *Slot machine therapy is better than any shrink*, she thought.

* * * *

"Son of a mother," Kyra whispered, two hours later.

Life's not fair. Since she'd been here she'd dumped over three thousand dollars into the freakin' machine. *I can't believe this bitch sat right down and hit the jackpot on the first spin. I'll never get Trevor back this way.*

Kyra Russell pushed her long hair back over her shoulder. Why couldn't she hit the jackpot? Ten grand would pay for the lawyer to fight Tom for custody. Taking another hundred-dollar bill out of her purse, she stuffed it into the machine and banged the maximum-credit button. Her stomach jumped with excitement as the wheels spun. Each time, her mind cheered, *This is it!*

As the wheels rolled into place, a cold chill raced through her veins. One by one, they landed. By the time the second symbol stilled, she realized she'd lost again. Her heart hammered in her ears like a jackhammer on concrete, spiked her anger. *It's the next one*, she told herself, banging the maximum-credit button again. She needed to take a pee break, but didn't dare leave her machine for fear someone else would hit the jackpot after she'd primed the machine.

Kyra counted along with the attendant as he paid the woman next to her, seventy-five big ones. The attendant turned to leave. Kyra waved him down.

"Excuse me," she called.

"Yes, ma'am?"

"I need to use the restroom. Can you watch my machine or lock it down?"

"I need to call a supervisor over. It'll be a few minutes."

He pressed the button in his earpiece, whispered into it. After ten minutes, the supervisor came over and locked down the machine for her, and informed her she had to be back within the hour or they'd release it.

"Thank you."

"Not a problem, Kyra," the supervisor said.

He read her name off her reward card, addressing her as if he knew her. *Well, screw him.*

She pushed off her seat and rushed to the ladies' room. Kyra didn't want to stay away too long, giving them a chance to reprogram the machine against her or reset it. She hated the new system with the tickets. Since they'd installed it, she hadn't won like she used to. Why else would she lose all the time?

Winning used to be the norm when she had started. One night she'd won eight thousand dollars, and the next night there she'd won twenty-five thousand dollars on one spin. The feeling was indescribable when those wheels rolled into place and the bells went off. The noise the machine made when it hit a jackpot had crowds surrounding her. On the night of her big win, she'd gone home with twenty thousand dollars—she'd blown five grand trying to win more. Greed always took over. Winning excited her but not as much as the rush, the euphoria she got waiting for the wheels to fall into place.

The casino had treated her like royalty and had given her a host. He got her into the popular shows or restaurants anytime she wanted. Nothing was too good for Kyra, as long as she showed up and put her money into the machine. She became a regular at the players' lounge—eat and drink for free. *Yeah, free, her ass. The cost was extreme.* Somewhere along the line, she'd lost her self-respect—along with her marriage, her son, and her savings.

As time went by, she put more money into the machines, hoping for bigger payouts. How it got out of control was anyone's guess. But soon everything she loved would be gone. *The bastard doesn't want custody of Trevor—he wants to bring me to my knees.*

Losing Trevor would kill her. He needed her. She needed him. A big win would solve everything. Tears rolled down her face as she sat on the toilet. Not caring who heard her cry, she whispered, "Please, God, give me one big win and I promise I'll never gamble again."

She listened, but He didn't answer. She washed up and hurried back to her machine. Three hundred dollars left, her Visa card maxed out. Worse, the payment on her loan was due soon. Tommy—the asshole—had drained their bank account. Her debit card no longer worked.

Kyra tried to stay away, honestly, she did. But after a day she'd get antsy. Her fingers itched. More than anything, she needed to get to the casino. She couldn't explain it to anyone. Hell—she couldn't explain it to herself. No wonder the nuns at school always preached against the evils of gambling.

Head down, she sat at her machine, waiting on the supervisor to come back—to unlock the machine. Her fingers itched, she wanted to play again. She needed the win. A hand landed on her shoulder, startling her. Jerking away, Kyra turned to see mean muddy eyes looking at her. Joe Dillon's dark eyes matched his greased back hair. Small in stature, he lorded over his people. *Crap, not the supervisor. Joe Dillon, not the person I want to see right now.*

"Kyra."

"Joe."

"How's it going?" Her host sat down next to her.

"Not good," she whined.

"I'm sorry to hear it. Your payment is due this week."

Double crapola. "Yes, I know."

"Why don't you leave the machine for a while? Come have something to eat with me?"

"Why?" What did he want, besides money?

"Let's discuss your loan payment over dinner, explore your options."

What options? There weren't any. All week she'd racked her brain trying to find a solution. Though a quiet guy, Joe scared her. He wasn't a person she'd want to cross. He worked for both the casino and the loan company. When she got in trouble and owed the casino the money, he had gotten her the loan when her bank wouldn't give her one. Deep inside, she understood he could destroy her.

He might be the final nail in her coffin.

* * * *

Well, we got what we wished for, Jake thought as he pulled to the curb. He noted Louie hadn't arrived yet. As he climbed out of the car, he spotted the uniform. Kudos to Russo, he'd cordoned off the scene and had the bystanders pushed back. Russo, a twenty-year veteran, understood his job. At five-eight, the guy packed a solid punch, Jake knew. A few times he and Frankie had sparred in the gym.

"How many people trampled my scene, Frankie?" Jake asked, studying the body and surrounding area.

"No one, I got here before the EMTs, Lieutenant. When I arrived I found the body, not the caller. Nothing's been touched. It was obvious he was dead a while. I didn't let the EMTs near him." Jake nodded for Russo to continue. "At first, with all his track marks, it looked like an overdose, but..."

"Give me a minute," Jake said. He liked to form his own impressions before the uniform gave his. He walked over to the body, leaned down, and studied it. Russo was right. The wound on the head hadn't been created by his fall. Someone had whacked the poor kid hard on the noggin.

Louie walked up to him with a coffee in his hand.

"You got one for me?" Jake asked.

"No, but I'll share. What have we got?" Louie asked as he sipped his drink.

Damn, that coffee smells good, Jake thought.

The medical examiner pulled up behind Louie's car. The crime scene boys were scouring the area outside the scene until the M.E. got a chance to examine the body.

"How'd we get the top dog on an O.D. victim?" Jake asked.

A tall, lanky man, Lang always looked in need of a meal. The doctor carried his one hundred and eighty pounds on a six-foot-four frame. His skin gave off a translucent glow, the same color as the corpses. Lang worked ridiculously long hours, not seeming to care if he saw daylight or not.

"Been a wild night, Jake. The team's spread all over the state," Doc Lang said.

Jake stepped away from the body to stand beside Louie. "After Doc Lang finishes up, I'll look for cash, needles, or his stash. But I'm betting it's gone," Louie said.

"Hopefully, they left his I.D."

"You smell like alcohol. Where are you coming from?" Louie asked.

"I was at a party. Is it that bad?" Jake wasn't on call tonight but dispatch had notified him when the lieutenant on duty had been tied up on another homicide.

"Yeah, I better take the lead on this one. We don't want to compromise the case," Louie said.

Jake nodded.

The department was a political landmine at the moment. He stepped away from the scene. At his car, he wrote down his impressions. Diagramed the angle of the body, and proceeded to make notes about the wound and needle marks on the body. He'd compare them to Louie's and the crime scene team tomorrow.

Acknowledgments

Thanks to Ralph Russo, Ret. Officer WPD, for his patience in answering all my questions. And to Candace Majewski who always knew what word I had in my mind but couldn't pull out. And the last-minute help from Spencer Gebhardt for his data processing skills and Lee Theroux for proofreading.

Thanks also to my beta readers Joanne Ryan, Esq., Brenda Piel, Gail Latka, and Nancy Peterson.

To all the members of SinC and CTRWA, especially Kristan Higgins, who gave her time and advice freely. I have learned a great deal from each of you, thank you.

And a special thank you to my editor, Michaela Hamilton, for taking a chance on me, and to my literary agent, Doug Grad.

Meet the Author

Photo by Brenda Piel, Apieling Pictures LLC

A self-described tough blonde from Brooklyn, **Marian Lanouette** grew up as one of 10 children. As far back as she can remember Marian loved to read. She was especially intrigued by the *Daily News* crime reports. Tragically, someone she knew was murdered. The killer was never found. Her Jake Carrington thrillers are inspired by her admiration for police work, her experience in working a crematorium, and her desire to write books where good prevails, even in the darkest times. Marian lives in New England with her husband. Visit her on Facebook or at www.marianl.com.

CPSIA information can be obtained
at www.ICGtesting.com
Printed in the USA
BVHW03s1952050418
512617BV00001B/55/P